# Re-Write

Attachment theory-based treatments including depth psychology, somatic psychology, holistic therapy, and Eye Movement Desensitization and Reprocessing (EMDR) are becoming even more popular and desired by clinicians, health systems, and the patients they care for. Up until recently, cognitive behavioral therapy and medication management were the mainstays for trauma-informed care, although we are witnessing a demand for a more somatic, holistic, and, therefore, deeper level of treatment to target attachment injury and change/re-write the trauma narrative. This book provides the response and tools to meet this current need.

Due to the pandemic, lockdowns, and significant changes in our stability, the economy, sense of belonging, and community, there is a heightened level of triggering which has resulted in multifactorial trauma responses. The devastating traumatic impact spans nations, ages, and socio-economic statuses. Unfortunately, domestic violence, child abuse, substance use, medical trauma, self-injury, suicide, and violence turned outwards have all increased significantly in the past two years.

This workbook focuses on the healing journey of the trauma survivor, utilizing easy-to-use methodologies for long-lasting effects. It includes various exercises, writing prompts, coping mechanisms, and soothing techniques with the intention of allowing the person to create an individualized experience. This empowers the person to go in the order they choose, experiment with different techniques from different modalities, and find the ones that meet their needs the best. The authors also address generational trauma, societal trauma, and trauma at the family and individual levels, and their work can be used in conjunction with a clinical treatment plan or by the end user.

*Re-Write: A Trauma Workbook of Creative Writing and Recovery in Our New Normal* employs practical strategies using evidence-based methodologies, with psychological theory within a human-centered design framework.

# Re-Write

## A Trauma Workbook of Creative Writing and Recovery in Our New Normal

Duygu Balan, LPCC
Yener Balan, MD, DFAPA

Illustrated by Nadir Balan

Routledge
Taylor & Francis Group

A PRODUCTIVITY PRESS BOOK

First published 2023
by Routledge
605 Third Avenue, New York, NY 10158

and by Routledge
4 Park Square, Milton Park, Abingdon, Oxon, OX14 4RN

*Routledge is an imprint of the Taylor & Francis Group, an informa business*

ISBN: 978-1-032-34780-6 (hbk)
ISBN: 978-1-032-34680-9 (pbk)
ISBN: 978-1-003-32381-5 (ebk)

DOI: 10.4324/9781003323815

Typeset in Garamond
by codeMantra

Dedicated to Jim Kelleher:

Your wisdom and kindness changed our lives.

We are eternally grateful for you.

-Duygu and Yener Balan

August 2022

# Contents

Testimonials .................................................................................. xiii
Acknowledgments .......................................................................... xix
Foreword........................................................................................ xxi
Authors ....................................................................................... xxiii
Illustrator ................................................................................... xxvii
Introduction ............................................................................... xxix

## PART 1   OUR HEALING JOURNEY BEGINS

1   Intro and Current State........................................................3
   Current State ........................................................................ 3
   What to Expect..................................................................... 4

2   Identifying and Treating Trauma..........................................7
   Introduction .......................................................................... 7
   Trauma as a Diagnosis .......................................................... 7
      Adjustment Disorder ........................................................ 8
      Acute Stress Disorder ....................................................... 8
      Posttraumatic Stress Disorder........................................... 8
      Prior Risk Factors...........................................................10
      Biopsychosocial Determinants and Risk ...........................11
      Continued Consequences................................................ 12
   Treatment ............................................................................13
      Non-Pharmacological Therapies ......................................15
      Pharmacological Options .................................................18
      Pharmacological Options: Antidepressants........................21
      Pharmacological Options: Other...................................... 22
   Conclusion........................................................................... 23

## PART 2   TOOLS FOR OUR SUCCESS

3   Value of Treatment .............................................................27
   Introduction ........................................................................ 27
   Prevalence........................................................................... 28
   Economic Burden ................................................................ 28
   Expressive Writing Therapy ................................................. 28
   Benefits: Physical and Physiological ..................................... 29

Benefits: Mental and Emotional ........................................................ 30
Benefits: Personal Reasons ............................................................ 32
Benefits: Financial........................................................................33
Posttraumatic Growth ................................................................. 37
Preparing: To Heal ...................................................................... 37
Preparing: Support Network.......................................................... 38
Preparing: Community.................................................................. 40
Preparing: Healing Environment.................................................... 40
Preparing: Sea Analogy.................................................................41
Conclusion.................................................................................. 42

**4   Balan 3-2-1 Method............................................................43**
Introduction ............................................................................... 43
Balan: Three-2-1 ........................................................................ 44
Balan: Three-2-1: The Body .......................................................... 44
Balan: Three-2-1: The Setting ........................................................45
Balan: Three-2-1: The Breath ........................................................ 49
Breathing Technique 1..................................................................49
Breathing Technique 2.................................................................. 50
Breathing Technique 3...................................................................51
Breathing Technique 4...................................................................52
Breathing Technique 5...................................................................52
Breathing Technique 6...................................................................53
Breathing Technique 7.................................................................. 54
Balan: 3-Two-1 ...........................................................................55
Balan: 3-2-One ...........................................................................56
Balan 3-2-1: Summary ................................................................. 58
Analysis ..................................................................................... 58

## PART 3   DOOR TO OUR MIND

**5   Language of Mind and Body................................................65**
Language and Culture ...................................................................65
Connecting................................................................................. 68
Messaging................................................................................... 68
A New Mental Model ................................................................... 69
Making Sense and Moving On ........................................................ 70
Mind and Body ........................................................................... 70
How Do You Feel?........................................................................ 71
Interpreting................................................................................. 72
Synthesizing................................................................................ 79
Centering and Mindfulness ............................................................81
Mindfulness Exercise ....................................................................81
Gratitude ................................................................................... 82
Writing Example: Gratitude .......................................................... 83
Gratitude, One Step at a Time........................................................ 83

**6   Brain–Body Connection** ......................................................................**89**
  Introduction ........................................................................ 89
  Limbic System ..................................................................... 89
  Thalamus ...........................................................................91
  Thalamus: Function ..............................................................91
  Thalamus: Impact of Trauma....................................................91
  Amygdala............................................................................91
  Amygdala: Function ..............................................................91
  Amygdala: Impact of Trauma ................................................. 92
  Hypothalamic Pituitary Adrenal (HPA) Axis .............................. 92
  Hypothalamus ................................................................... 92
  Adrenal Glands.................................................................. 93
  Hippocampus .................................................................... 93
  Hippocampus: Impact of Trauma ............................................ 94
  Prefrontal Cortex ............................................................... 94
  Prefrontal Cortex: Function ................................................... 94
  Prefrontal Cortex: Impact of Trauma........................................ 94
  Autonomic Nervous System ................................................... 94
  ANS: Sympathetic Nervous System .......................................... 96
  ANS: Parasympathetic Nervous System ..................................... 96
  Serotonin ......................................................................... 97
  Acute Physical Trauma ......................................................... 97
  Medical Consequences.......................................................... 98

**PART 4   WINDOW TO OUR SOUL**

**7   Family, Children, and Resilience** ..........................................................**103**
  Introduction .....................................................................103
  Creating Connections: Attachment Theory ................................104
  Volatility Early On: Adverse Childhood Experiences (ACEs) ...........105
  ACEs: Impact on the Individual and Society...............................106
  ACEs: Emotional Abuse .......................................................107
  Case Example: The Other Daughter ........................................107
  ACEs: Neglect ...................................................................109
  Case Example: Neglected Boy................................................110
  ACEs: Isolation and Stigma ..................................................110
  ACEs: Issues at School and Work............................................111
  ACEs: Care and Management.................................................112
  Protective Factors in the Family System ...................................113
  Case Example: Young Couple ............................................... 114
  Protective Factors: Parenting Style .........................................118
  Protective Factors: Family Dynamics.......................................121
  Creative Prompt: Family Crest............................................... 124
  Example: Balan Family Crest................................................. 127
  Protective Factors: Culture and Community ..............................129

Stressors ........................................................................................................131
Youth: Post Trauma ....................................................................................131
Youth: Traumatic Stress .............................................................................132
Schools..........................................................................................................133
Schools: Pandemic ......................................................................................134
Post Trauma: Caregiving ............................................................................134
Post Trauma: Goals .....................................................................................135
Conclusion....................................................................................................137

**8  Culture, Identity, and Society ............................................................139**
Introduction .................................................................................................139
Culturally Sensitive Approach....................................................................139
Identity Trauma ...........................................................................................140
Roles ..............................................................................................................144
Case Example: Contracts ............................................................................146
Trauma: LGBTQIA+ ...................................................................................148
Racial Discrimination .................................................................................148
Occupation Specific Hazards......................................................................149
    Healthcare Providers ..............................................................................149
Military .........................................................................................................152
Military: Moral Injury .................................................................................152
Risk Groups..................................................................................................152
Risk Group: Cyber Victimization ..............................................................153
Risk Group: Displaced Populations ...........................................................153
Risk Group: Pregnancy...............................................................................154
Case Example: Boundary Setting................................................................156
Risk Group: Sexual Assault ........................................................................157
Risk Group: Substance Use .........................................................................157

**9  Gaslighting and Other Betrayal Traumas .........................................161**
Introduction .................................................................................................161
Gaslighting ...................................................................................................161
Betrayal Traumas .........................................................................................162
Clinical Gaslighting.....................................................................................162
Violence Turned Inward and Outward ......................................................163
Case Study: Executive Gaslighting.............................................................164
Discussion.....................................................................................................166
Empowering Yourself at Work ...................................................................167
Results of Gaslighting..................................................................................168

**10  COVID, Disasters, and Loss .............................................................173**
Introduction .................................................................................................173
Fear................................................................................................................174
Repercussions...............................................................................................175
Long Term ....................................................................................................182
Grief ..............................................................................................................185

## PART 5   RESOURCES FOR OUR FUTURE

**11   Safety Planning** ....................................................................................**193**
Introduction ...........................................................................................193
Section 1: Warning Signs...........................................................................194
Case Example: Self-Medicating .................................................................196
Triggers....................................................................................................197
Section 2: Coping Strategies .....................................................................199
Section 3: Family, Social, and Professional Contacts...................................201
Section 4: Keeping Me Safe ..................................................................... 202
Section 5: Signature Section .................................................................... 203

**12   Long Haul to a New Normal, Our Path Forward**................................**207**
Our Path So Far........................................................................................ 207
Equitable Access ..................................................................................... 208
Reducing Harmful Effects ........................................................................ 208
Going Forward ........................................................................................210

**Appendix** ....................................................................................................**215**

**Bibliography**...............................................................................................**219**

**Index** ..........................................................................................................**229**

# Testimonials

"The Balans have created an especially useful workbook on recovering from trauma in our post-pandemic world. It is comprehensive, eclectic, interactive and highly educational."

**Bruce J. Schwartz, MD**
*Deputy Chairman and Professor of Psychiatry*
*Montefiore Medical Center and Albert Einstein College of Medicine*

"This timely, interactive book on trauma addresses our current mental health realities in the context of the pandemic and provides hope in the healing journey. *Re-Write* explores adverse childhood experiences, intergenerational trauma, and gaslighting in a culturally sensitive framework that will resonate with readers. Inspirational and accessible, the Balans have produced another must-read book."

**Arpan Waghray, MD**
*Chief Executive Officer, Well Being Trust*
*Chair, Behavioral Health Committee, American Hospital Association*

"This book brings the perspective and skills of two mental health professionals with expertise in the science and treatment of trauma and adversity. Their approach blends mindfulness, thoughtful reflection, narrative writing and creativity supported by clear explanations, easy to follow steps, and interactive exercises. This book is a practical guide for anyone on a healing journey."

**Brigid McCaw MD, MPH, MS, FACP**
*Clinical Advisor, California ACES Aware Initiative*

"Duygu and Yener Balan have written a must-read primer for clinicians and comprehensive self-directed treatment manual for individuals who have experienced trauma all in one. Please read this book – and learn practical approaches you can take to support yourself or others on the path to recovery."

**Anton Nigusse Bland, M.D.**
*Associate Professor of Psychiatry*
*University of California, San Francisco*

"Balan and Balan, as therapist and psychiatrist, bring their diverse experiences and wealth of knowledge to an expertly put together and easy-to-understand book on trauma. *Re-Write* provides a timely, evidence-based view on healing and recovery, in the context of empathy and mindfulness. The creative prompts and interactive exercises are designed for individuals and clinicians alike."

**Neil Leibowitz, MD, JD**
*Chief Medical Officer, Beacon Health Options*
*Former Chief Medical Officer, Talkspace*

"With so many treatments available to address trauma, it is understandable to be confused as to which treatments are the most effective and where to go to get them. *Re-Write* helps the reader become an informed consumer of mental health treatments which is key in supporting shared decision making. We know that individuals who are knowledgeable about treatment options and engage in a shared decision-making dialogue with their clinician show improved adherence and satisfaction with treatment."

**Andrew Bertagnolli, PhD**
*Assistant Professor, Alliant International University*

"*Re-Write*, by Balan and Balan, is a comprehensive book on trauma related stress, and offers expert case examples and writing prompts that invite the reader to reflect and rewrite their own trauma narrative. A must have in every clinician's library, this workbook written with compassion and humor, will bring new insights to many in need."

**Carlos Rueda, MD, MBA**
*Chairman of Department of Psychiatry, St. Joseph's Healthcare System*

"*Re-Write* comes at a time when expectations of ourselves, healthcare, and the economy, are rapidly shifting. Trauma is ubiquitous and trauma-inducing shocks (from climate change, political instability, economic disruptions) are projected to increase in frequency. We need to prioritize our minds and brains. This book intertwines evidence-based medicine with self-guided writing prompts and creative exercises. It is a novel approach, and we desperately need new strategies for mental health. Cultural sensitivity and the relevance of trauma-informed care are highlights of this must-read book. Let us hope that it's therapeutic value can achieve impact far and wide. Humanity needs it now and into the future."

**Harris A. Eyre, MD, PhD**
*Lead, Brain Capital Alliance*

"This a great book! Balan and Balan harness the power of narrative to help patients and their caregivers access the healing process. A must read for families, clinicians and anyone who has struggled with trauma."

**Noam Fast, MD**

"Surprisingly innovative: I remember experiences I was forced to forget, I forgot trauma I kept remembering and I chose to re-write the memories of who I am."

**Yannis Angouras**
*International Healthcare Executive*

"A practical blend of evidence-based insights, personal and professional experience, and helpful guidance and exercises, *Re-Write* is an important and innovative addition to the toolset for those recovering from trauma."

**Patrick Courneya, MD**
*Chief Medical Officer, HealthPartners*

"*Re-Write* is an excellent workbook by Duygu Balan and Yener Balan that is timely, practical, and informative - the years of experience, passion and research culled into one power-packed book. A must read for practitioners as well as individuals affected by trauma."

**Uli K. Chettipally, MD, MPH**
*Founder & President, InnovatorMD*

"*Re-Write* balances clinical case examples with theory, and grounds it on experiential and thought-provoking healing techniques. The writing prompts and resources can be used at the individual level, to support loved ones, and clinically as a teaching tool. I recommend this book to anyone interested in gaining an introspective view on self-growth and healing past traumatic pain."

**Jennifer Christian-Herman, PhD**
*Vice President, Mind Body Medicine/Behavioral Health,*
*Blue Shield California*

"Dr. Balan has written an exceptionally well-researched, timely, and practical text on dealing with one of the harder to manage issues in Behavioral Health. It is a must read for anyone struggling with trauma themselves or managing it in their practice."

**Andy Rink, MD**
*Partner, Healthcare Foundry*

## Other Books by the Authors

*Big Book of Emergency Department Psychiatry: A Guide to Patient Centered Operational Improvement.* CRC Press, 2017.

## Praise for *Big Book of Emergency Department Psychiatry: A Guide to Patient Centered Operational Improvement*

by Yener Balan, MD, DFAPA, Karen Murrell, MD, MBA, FACEP, and Chris Lentz, MS, MFT

"All clinicians in emergency departments espouse to provide care for the whole person, yet those individuals with psychiatric and mental health conditions in EDs all too often find timely and competent care woefully lacking.

"Similar to the recent trends of integrating mental health services into primary care, this book provides expertise and practical guidance for ED physicians and nurses to increase competencies for diagnosing and treating common mental health conditions.

"This innovative model of care in EDs proactively and reliably addresses the majority of patients' psychiatric and mental health needs and reserves psychiatric consultation services and transfers to psychiatric treatment facilities for those patients who cannot be adequately treated by ED clinicians."

**– Patricia Rutherford, RN, MS**
*Vice President*
*Institute for Healthcare Improvement (IHI)*

"The authors not only have a deep understanding of emergency psychiatry but also of operational improvement. The mix makes this book a needed reference for anyone focused on a patient centered approach for this vulnerable population."

**– Kevin Nolan, Statistician, Improvement Advisor, and Senior Fellow**
*Institute for Healthcare Improvement (IHI)*

"The authors have organized and written a timely and necessary book on the care of the acute psychiatric patient in the emergency department.

"Over 2 million people a year seek care for behavioral health care problems in hospital EDs at a cost of over $4 billion. Behavioral health patients seeking care in the emergency department have the same hopes, needs, and fears as the rest of the patients who present to our EDs for evaluation and treatment.

"The ED is often an intense and stressful work environment where staff must perform rapid assessments and make swift treatment decisions. ED staff and team members, dedicated, focused, and highly trained, too often feel overwhelmed, burdened and at times even threatened by the need to provide care for behavioral health patients.

"There is a great deal of variation in ED expertise, training, and resource allocation for emergency mental health problems, which can lead to sub-optimal care and negative patient and staff experiences.

"The management of acute behavioral emergencies and crisis intervention are simply and clearly described in this book. The tactics, tools, and techniques outlined here can elevate our approach to emergency department psychiatry and allow our emergency medicine colleagues to rise above our current challenges and frustrations.

"Balan et al. apply approaches, lessons, and insights from both evidence-based medicine and Lean service operations to behavioral health patients, defining best practices and demonstrating the benefits and positive impact on patient care, flow, and safety.

"*Big Book of Emergency Department Psychiatry* is a practical playbook for the challenges at hand. The authors explain simply and clearly how to get it done."

**– Kirk Jensen, MD, MBA, FACEP**
*Chief Innovation Officer, EmCare, Inc.*
*Chief Medical Officer, BestPractices, Inc.*
*Studer Faculty Member and National Speaker*
*Institute for Healthcare Improvement (IHI) Faculty Member*

"The management of psychiatric patients seeking care in the emergency department is one of the most complex and important issues in modern emergency medicine. The patients are frequently disenfranchised and do not receive high-quality or timely medical care. As a result, these patients impose a tremendous impact on ED resources and flow.

"This book provides comprehensive insights into psychiatric care in the ED and operational improvement using Lean healthcare concepts. It will help you and your leadership team create a patient-centric culture where a community of scientists continuously improve value for psychiatric patients, hospital, and society."

**– Jody Crane, MD, MBA**
*Principal, X32 Healthcare*
*Author of The Definitive Guide to Emergency Department Operational*
*Improvement: Employing Lean Principles with Current ED*
*Best Practices to Create the 'No Wait' Department*

"Innovative, informative, and inspiring book, with captivating stories that display the ins and outs of psychiatric emergency services. A must read, especially the chapters on correctional emergency psychiatry and the concept of Lean in healthcare."

**– Mardoche Sidor, MD**
*Assistant Professor of Psychiatry, Columbia University*
*Medical Director*
*The Center for Alternative Sentencing and Employment Services (CASES)*

"*Big Book of Emergency Department Psychiatry* is big as it should be; it is the most comprehensive text on emergency psychiatry in print. Not only does it guide one to the diagnosis and management of emergency room patients, but it also addresses operational issues in various settings.

"The emergency room is a team effort and *Big Book of Emergency Department Psychiatry* includes the perspectives of its members: psychiatrist, nurse, social worker, and non-psychiatric emergency doctor.

"Make room for it on your bookshelf."

**– David W Preven, MD**
*Clinical Professor*
*Department of Psychiatry and Human Behavior*
*Albert Einstein College of Medicine*

"Complete, accurate, and especially timely. A must read for any emergency department leader engaged in improving care for this vulnerable population."

**– Seth Thomas, MD, FACEP**
*Director of Quality & Performance*
*CEP America*

"*Big Book of Emergency Department Psychiatry* is empathically written and valuable to anyone that has ever experienced or cared for someone dealing with a psychiatric emergency. It has a dose of rigor, evidence, and science, and it conveys the personal experience of some of our peers and it keeps you wanting to read more. It is a tremendous compendium of the state of knowledge of the specialty and art of emergency psychiatry.

"Very soon, this book will become the must read for this specialty for trainees and experienced mental health professionals alike.

"I congratulate the authors on an excellent, disciplined, rigorous work that retains the human perspective while educating the reader."

**– Carlos Rueda MD, MBA**
*Chairman, Department of Psychiatry*
*St. Joseph's Healthcare System*
*Trinitas Regional Medical Center*

# Acknowledgments

First and foremost, we would like to acknowledge and express our sincerest appreciation to our darling son, Evrim Kai. He is our love, our reason, our passion, and our source of joy. He is the reason why we continue to work so diligently to maintain our focus on our own mental health and wellbeing, as well as to model and teach resilience in the face of adversity and trauma.

We would then like to acknowledge our families. The only way we have made it this far in any aspect of our lives is because of you. Any time we have faced a struggle, or needed help or guidance, our parents have been there for us. Thanks to Aysun, Yıldız, Enin, and Ahmet. Thanks to our siblings, Öykü, Nadir, and Nilüfer, and their spouses, Jared, Jen, and Gökberk. Their infinite support and genuine love continue to nourish our bonds and allow us all to move forward healthily.

Next, we want to recognize and thank our mentors, colleagues, and teachers who have taught us antifragility. They guided us with their experience and instilled us with strength to go on. Thanks to Dr. David Preven, Dr. Neil Leibowitz, Joanne Pearl, Diana Spechler, and Neslihan Pınar.

Lastly, we would like to acknowledge Kristine Mednansky. Thanks for your visionary support and opportunities Taylor and Francis and your team continue to provide us.

**Duygu and Yener Balan**
*August 2022*

# Foreword

Trauma has become a new normal for Americans. Adverse childhood experiences, COVID-19, societal divisiveness, and social media have all contributed to the pain people feel.

Clinicians recognize the impact trauma has on individuals not just in the moment they are happening, but for decades and even generations into the future. Professional assistance including therapy and medication can help us recognize and manage the trauma in our lives and from our past, but there is more we can do to help ourselves.

In *Re-Write*, the Balans provide opportunities and exercises that we can use to contribute to our psychological health. Through this creative writing workbook and techniques to increase mindfulness, the authors offer powerful, risk-free approaches that can benefit us in our personal lives.

You'll find the creative writing recommendations the book offers helpful in overcoming the past and present traumas that stand in the way of personal health and fulfillment. Trauma with its psychological impact is inevitable, but we can act to free ourselves from its continued harm. Confronting the pain and creating a plan to diminish it are vital first steps.

This book will help you begin that journey.

**– Dr. Robert Pearl**
*Author of Uncaring, How the Culture of Medicine Kills Doctors & Patients*

# Authors

**Duygu Balan, LPCC,** is a licensed professional clinical counselor, and she provides psychotherapy for individuals and couples addressing trauma, attachment injury, depression, anxiety, relational issues, shame, and self-esteem. Duygu is a PACT (Psychobiological Approach to Couples Therapy) Level II trained couples therapist and a certified clinical trauma professional. She additionally holds a master's degree in school- and college-level counseling. Duygu has worked as a therapist at one of New York State's most prominent Employee Assistance Programs (EAP).

Duygu has an extensive background in writing and authored the chapter on personality disorders for the best-selling medical textbook *Big Book of Emergency Department Psychiatry*, and she provides seminars and workshops internationally.

Duygu incorporates an existential, relational, humanistic, and client centered trauma informed approach. She draws from Gestalt Psychology and utilizes mindfulness and somatic techniques. Duygu brings creativity to the therapeutic process by drawing from her background in dance, yoga, writing, and poetry.

**Yener Balan, MD, DFAPA,** is a board-certified psychiatrist, best-selling author, and speaker, and he is currently the vice president of behavioral health and medical specialty services for a major health care organization. He is also a distinguished fellow of the American Psychiatric Association.

Yener currently provides health plan oversight and direction to the behavioral health programs as well as the medical specialty services as they develop integrated models for the future of health care. His accountabilities include investing in technology, people, and research to drive market leading performance; engaging patients and families in quality improvement efforts; implementing processes that focus on proactive interventions and preventions; and engaging with organizations within the community to help shape the growth, education, and training of the workforce.

Yener has extensive years of experience working in high-volume community emergency departments; he is an expert in hospital operations, health care business, and management; and he has given lectures and workshops worldwide.

Both Duygu and Yener have dedicated many years assisting their communities with outreach and counseling of the homeless, mentally ill, and substance using populations on the margins of society.

They believe in the connection of the mind, body, and spirit and use a holistic treatment approach that combines Western therapeutic techniques with ancient healing practices.

# Illustrator

**Nadir Balan** is an award-winning illustrator who has been working in the field for two decades. He learned the ropes at Marvel in 2002 and has since worked on a large variety of projects in many genres.

He worked with Ray Harryhausen to relaunch the movie franchise *Clash of the Titans* and *Wrath of the Titans*.

With Stan Lee and William Shatner, he won "Outstanding Book of The Year" for his work on *God Woke*.

In addition to his art being featured in galleries, his paintings are in the permanent collection of the New Haven Museum where, as an avid history buff, he gave lectures on painting techniques and World War I.

His work has graced the covers of scientific and academic books ranging from medical to philosophical to theatrical. He recently worked on all three volumes of Dan Fogler's *Moon Lake* and his comic book work is featured in *Heavy Metal Magazine*.

A true renaissance man, in his spare time Nadir moonlights as the Operations Director at an Ivy League university theater. Whatever time he finds left he spends helping animals.

# Introduction

Congratulations!

To you, the reader!

By picking up this book and beginning to read it, you are taking an important step in the direction of your healing journey.

Whether you are an individual looking to understand and better yourself, or a clinician planning to advance the care of your clients, you will find valuable evidence-based information throughout this book. If you are a loved one or a concerned relative or friend and are looking to help guide someone in your life, you have found the appropriate book.

> One does not become enlightened by imagining figures of light, but by making the darkness conscious.
>
> *– Carl Jung*

In a time where our eyes have been opened to the power of information and the dominance it has over our day-to-day lives, we chose to publish this book to counter all the negativity and reinforce the positive.

After the success of our first medical textbook, *Big Book of Emergency Department Psychiatry: A Guide to Patient Centered Operational Improvement*, we were completing a follow-up textbook on hospital operations from a broader lens, although the advent of the pandemic changed everything.

Previously established operational norms and expectations shifted extremely rapidly. The world's collective traumatization and each individual's plight to survive and make meaning of the new world we found ourselves in drove us to pivot to writing about trauma.

*Re-Write: A Trauma Workbook of Creative Writing and Recovery in Our New Normal* is more relevant and timelier than ever. We share evidence-based medicine, lessons learned, insights, interactive writing prompts, and coping skills throughout the book.

From the bottom of our hearts, thank you and congratulations once again for embarking on your healing journey.

# OUR HEALING
# JOURNEY BEGINS

**1**

# Chapter 1

# Intro and Current State

## Current State

This book is designed to help you re-write your own narrative. This is an evidence-based medical textbook developed to be interactive and informative while reinforcing hope and the ability to heal.

Trauma is ubiquitous.

To be able to understand our bodies and minds, we must allow ourselves to be in touch with the multiple angles that trauma impacts.

Over the past several years, the effect of previous and current trauma has been magnified. During the writing of this book, there is a global pandemic, and numerous wars waging in various countries. The political climate and polarization of the public has widened and deepened.

Our identities have changed. How we view ourselves and our relationships have been altered. During this new normal, we are working to understand our realities.

Since the beginning of the pandemic in 2020, there has been a significant increase in mental health and related physical symptoms and diagnoses. There has been a dramatic increase in demand for mental health and substance use treatment. Upwards of 90% of all visits to medical doctor offices are now in some way related to stress!

It is painfully evident that there is a mismatch between the supply of safety-net organizations and available expert clinicians to address this tsunami of demand. Researchers, health care organizations, politicians, advocates, and anyone interacting with other humans in the last several years are able to see these increases.

There has been a significant increase in depression, other affective disorders, anxieties, obsessive disorders, phobias, acute and posttraumatic stress disorders. Substance use disorders, including alcohol use, as well as opioid, and stimulant use have increased. The increase in consumption of substances has brought with it an increase of accidental overdoses. There has been an increase in existential angst, resulting in a rise in violence turned inwards including self-injury and suicide attempts.

There has also been a surge in the prevalence of violence turned outwards. There has been an increase in intimate partner violence, formerly known as domestic violence. We unfortunately witness daily violence, anger, and aggressivity with or without the involvement of firearms.

DOI: 10.4324/9781003323815-2

Impulsivity as well as rage has captured the population's attention, and as we transition to the next phase of the pandemic and work toward healing, it's imperative that we begin with ourselves.

As clinicians, we see these existential and manifested biological concerns that are exacerbated by the significant prevalence of trauma. This workbook with its interactive nature is designed to allow the user to focus and wake up from all of these disrupted processes.

During the pandemic and the associated media messaging, our attention span and ability to concentrate on one thing at a time has been disrupted. As humans, we have significant reservoirs of resilience to stress both mentally and physically. In the context of the heightened fear, uncertainty, and a global infectious disease, our ability to think about the meaning of our lives and our family stories took a back seat.

When the body and mind is in fight-or-flight mode and works to shut down all non-immediately vital functioning in an effort for basic survival, we are unable to thrive. The stress incurred on the body in the long term becomes deleterious and defeats the purpose.

Just as we know that a healthy immune system is foundationally important to be able to ward off physical ailments, people are becoming increasingly aware that having a healthy mindset is also critical.

As we come out on the other end of the pandemic, matters such as environmental concerns, economic inequality, food insecurity, the need for sustainable development, structural racism, inequity as well as the general economic instability and potential incoming financial recession are all weighing heavily on our minds.

These are not separate from the political polarization as well as generated biosecurity and digital enforcements that many countries are having to deal with. The context of an international war, with the implications of sanctions, as well as the impact on our supply chains in general, has influenced our safety, security, and ability to plan for the future.

Most nations are reporting significant inflation as well as unprecedented shortages in various supplies including, and most importantly, food products. For the past several years, we have normalized social distancing and we are experiencing the sequelae of social isolation in context of this new cognitive framing.

The narrative bias that all of these aforementioned calamities have instilled on us wields significant power.

In an effort to disrupt this, toward an ability to care for oneself on the path to resilience, we applaud you for picking up this book.

## What to Expect

This book is written by two expert clinicians, with dozens of collective years of experience in private and public clinical care. The authors have designed this book so that it is user friendly and is written in a manner that they will use and recommend for their colleagues and clients.

This book sets itself apart from other medical textbooks on trauma that include interactive elements such as creative and narrative writing, in that it is based on real-world experience and written in the context of the pandemic.

Up until recently, cognitive behavioral therapy and medication management were the mainstays for trauma informed care. We are now witnessing a demand for a more somatic, holistic, and therefore deeper level of treatment to target attachment injury and to change and re-write the trauma narrative. Our medical textbook provides the response and tools to meet this current need.

There have been several articles written about the global pandemic and the trauma response that we reference in this book. Due to the pandemic, lockdowns, and significant changes in our stability, the economy, sense of belonging, and community, there is a heightened level of triggering which has resulted in multifactorial trauma responses. The devastating traumatic impact spans nations, ages, and socio-economic statuses.

Unfortunately, intimate partner violence, child abuse, substance use, medical trauma, self-injury, suicide, and violence turned outwards have all increased significantly since the pandemic began in 2020. The proliferation of scientific journal articles that identify these issues demands a solution for treatment that this book provides.

While the contents of the book are serious and difficult to process at times, the authors employ humor as a defense mechanism as well as artistic drawings to illustrate various concepts.

The book is separated into five parts.

The first part, titled "Our Healing Journey Begins," is comprised of the first two chapters, and it offers an introduction and detailed analysis of identifying and treating trauma.

- The breadth and scope of this book spans individuals as well as families, and it can be used as a self-guided textbook, as well as in the context of individual or couples or group counseling with a clinician.
- The authors use trauma informed psychoeducation, written in a manner that is relatable and easy to understand.

The second part, titled "Tools for Our Success," dives deep into the value of treating trauma and related disorders, and it introduces the Balan 3-2-1 Method.

- The book reviews the types of treatment that are evidence based and available for people with traumas.
- In addition to the target audiences of individuals as well as clinicians, this book is recommended to be used by healthcare administrators as there is significant evidence included as to the value of expressive writing and the return on investment of such therapies.
- The authors introduce the Balan 3-2-1 Method, a creative writing experience, and use clinical case examples as well as review of literature to prompt and guide the user during the writing exercises.
- The authors draw from somatic exercises including mindfulness, bibliotherapy, self-compassion, meditation, writing prompts drawn from narrative psychology, as well as psychodrama drawn from Gestalt psychology.
- This interactive workbook includes various exercises, writing prompts, coping mechanisms, as well as soothing techniques with the intention of allowing the person to create an individualized experience. This empowers the person to go in the order they choose, experiment with different techniques from different modalities, and find the ones that best meet their needs.

Part three is titled "Door to Our Mind," and it includes Chapters 5 and 6 that examine the language of the mind and body, as well as the biology of the brain and how the nervous system impacts our emotions and behaviors.

- The reader will learn psychobiology and information without it being overwhelmingly jargon heavy.

- There are sections in this book that describe specific medical aspects of the brain and the impact of trauma and other experiences on the physical body and how that interacts with our mental health and wellness.
- This gives the individual a sense that their experiences and symptoms are shared by others, and that they are not alone. It provides a sense of control and notion that they can be healed.

Part four encompasses Chapters 7–10, and it is titled "Window to Our Soul."

- This part includes numerous case examples discussing family systems, adverse childhood experiences, culture, gaslighting, identity, and the current pandemic.
- The focus on families as a subunit within society and the impact of trauma on children is discussed in great detail.
- This book can be used in sessions for clients who need more guided treatment or prompts. It can be used in conjunction with therapy to keep the client in a more continuous therapeutic process, specifically for those that benefit from homework outside the sessions.
- As clinically appropriate, this can also serve as a touch point between sessions for continued contact with the clinician.
- This book can additionally be used in group therapy sessions while treating specific trauma symptoms, as well as for self-guided healing. This can initiate awareness and coping mechanisms that can later be evaluated and expanded upon in session.
- Elements of the client's responses can also be documented in the medical record and used to track outcomes of care.
- There is a chapter dedicated to gaslighting within interpersonal relationships as well as in professional settings.
- The authors discuss the impact of the global pandemic and impact on the biopsychosocial norms of individuals and societies.

The final part is titled "Resources for Our Future," and it includes the final two chapters that discuss safety planning, coping skills, and helpful websites and phone numbers for future reference.

- The authors also use their extensive clinical background and expertise to provide an interactive chapter on safety planning that can be completed alone, as well as with a clinical team.
- The workbook is rounded out with lengthy references to articles and books, as well as phone numbers and websites for societies and organizations as further resources.

# Chapter 2

# Identifying and Treating Trauma

Shadows on the wall
  Noises down the hall
  Life doesn't frighten me at all

*– Maya Angelou*

## Introduction

Thankfully, in recent years, the stigma of mental illness has decreased, and comfort with which folks are feeling about obtaining psychological treatment has increased.

While people may have a general understanding of what basic emotions are and what the concept of trauma is, in clinical practice there are set definitions and guidelines with which a diagnosis is made.

## Trauma as a Diagnosis

The American Psychiatric Association updated the fifth edition of the Diagnostic and Statistical Manual of Mental Disorders (DSM) in the first quarter of 2022. Trauma- and stress-related disorders continue to be listed under and in close relationship with anxiety disorders.

The main criterion of being exposed to a traumatic or stressful event is the hallmark of trauma disorders. These disorders include posttraumatic stress disorder, acute stress disorder, adjustment disorder, reactive attachment disorder, disinhibited social engagement disorder as well as prolonged grief disorder.

This workbook focuses specifically on trauma and its aftereffects later in life, and therefore, it will predominantly discuss aspects of acute stress disorder and posttraumatic stress disorder.

DOI: 10.4324/9781003323815-3

The authors weave in other clinical diagnoses and elaborate with case examples as applicable to the specific chapter.

To conceptualize severity and the family of trauma- and stress-related disorders, adjustment disorder could be considered less severe. In terms of timing of the onset of symptoms relating to a traumatic event, acute stress disorder would be considered more severe. Potentially chronic, longer-term consequences could then manifest as a posttraumatic stress disorder.

## Adjustment Disorder

The DSM criteria for an adjustment disorder are that they begin within three months after exposure to a stressor. Similar to all other psychiatric diagnosis, the symptoms experienced must impact the person's day-to-day functioning.

For these trauma- and stress-related disorders, there's always a specifier indicating that the symptoms experienced must be separate from normal bereavement or prolonged with grief.

The framework of an adjustment disorder is that it is limited to not much more than six months after the three-month window after being exposed to the stressor.

## Acute Stress Disorder

There are a significant number of overlapping diagnostic criteria listed in the DSM for both acute and posttraumatic stress disorder. The lengthier description is below. The main thing to understand about the difference between acute and posttraumatic stress disorder is the time of onset of symptoms and duration of pathology.

Acute stress disorder, according to the DSM, persists typically three days to one month after exposure to the traumatic event. Posttraumatic stress disorder, on the other hand, involves symptoms that last for four weeks or longer.

For an academic distinction between the two, we refer you to the DSM.

## Posttraumatic Stress Disorder

Posttraumatic stress disorder, like every other list of criteria for a specific diagnosis in the DSM, includes descriptors of required criteria and then followed by several specifiers. The important aspect of psychological pathology is that it interferes with the individual's day-to-day life. This one criterion is in every single diagnosis throughout the DSM.

For any specific psychiatric diagnosis, it must also be able to be identified separate from a medical issue that may be affecting the brain or any substances ingested that might alter the brain and behavior.

As mentioned above, there must be an exposure to the threat of serious injury or death, or sexual violence. The individual must have experienced this either directly, have witnessed it, or learned of the traumatic event from a close family member.

Traumatic experiences could be things like fighting in a war, being attacked physically either as an adult or abused as a child. Natural disasters such as experiencing an earthquake or a fire where the individual feared for their lives may also be the cause of the problems.

Man-made traumatic events such as attacks, robberies, or accidents may also be the cause. The individual may also be someone like a first responder or a police officer that goes to the scene of crimes or accidents and may be affected by repeated exposure to extreme stimuli.

Due to their experiences, veterans have a very high incidence of posttraumatic stress disorder, as do firefighters.

The consequences of experiencing such a life-threatening traumatic event often occur shortly after the event, although clinically we have seen the symptoms of posttraumatic stress disorder develop months or years after the exposure. The immediate reaction after a traumatic event may sometimes develop into the diagnosis of an adjustment disorder or an acute stress disorder, which then after time may progress into a posttraumatic stress disorder diagnosis.

The individual must be experiencing the physical and psychological consequences described below for more than a month, and as mentioned earlier, must cause clinically significant impairment in the daily functioning of the person.

Once this baseline is established, the individual must experience symptoms that are associated with the traumatic event. Intrusive, recurrent thoughts and memories of the event, dreams, and nightmares that are bothersome and distressing that began after exposure to the trauma are common.

Flashbacks, where the person feels as if they are experiencing the traumatic event, as well as intense distress when exposed to things that remind the person are some classic and quite common aspects of the diagnosis. The reactions that include re-experiencing the event can include perceptual distortions as well as the intrusive thoughts. These may also heighten the triggering response experienced, especially in context of a flooding of emotions that may make rational thinking challenging.

Reactions that then may develop include things like avoiding aspects that are associated with the trauma. The individual may try to avoid external stimuli such as a place or a person, or they might try to avoid thoughts and memories about the traumatic event. Clinically, there may be cognitive changes such as decreased ability to remember aspects of the traumatic event, as well as elements of denial.

Dissociation from self and others is another symptom seen as a coping mechanism that typically does more harm than benefit the individual. It is a compensatory mechanism born from a place of extreme fear. The brain and body, specifically the parasympathetic nervous system kicks in, and the individual who is dissociating goes into a shut-down mode to protect itself. See Chapter 6, Brain–Body Connection, for detailed explanation of the biological and psychological processes including information on the parasympathetic nervous system.

Thoughts that one may not have a future or anything to look forward to are certainly concerning when they occur as a response to the stressor. In an attempt to avoid or numb the feelings, some resort to alcohol or other substances, that may be linked with or exacerbate other psychological processes such as depression and/or anxiety.

In posttraumatic stress disorder, self-care can also suffer, as activities of daily living are neglected or substituted, such as new onset of poor eating habits, poor sleeping habits, poor grooming, and hygiene habits.

Emotional, physical, and psychological consequences of the traumatic event include worsening mood, decreased desire to spend time with others, worsening negative beliefs about themselves, feeling detached from others as well as the inability to feel positive emotions. The feeling of deriving decreased pleasure from things that at one time used to give the person pleasure is called anhedonia and it can be observed as part of the clinical symptomatology.

In addition to the consequences described above, there may be behaviors such as hyperreactivity, increased emotional lability, irritability, anger, aggression, and reckless behavior that develop after the traumatic event.

An exaggerated startle response, hypervigilance, and problems concentrating are also commonly associated. People with posttraumatic stress disorder may have these heightened reactions to unexpected things such as loud noises and display an increased arousal state.

Problems with prolonged hyper-reactivity, as one may expect, include exhaustion as well as physical health consequences. These may range from feeling tired to exacerbations of chronic medical conditions. A pattern of decreased stress tolerance develops, and a body exposed to continuous fight or flight hormones (see Chapter 6, Brain–Body Connection for more information) is at risk of heart and other immunological diseases.

When the individual experiences difficulty monitoring themselves and their internal emotional states, they may develop skewed perceptions of their own vulnerability in context of a traumatic stress or any day-to-day stressor.

Regarding social interactions and relationships, there are often repercussions on the quality and interest in socializing. Isolating self, increased mistrust as well as impact on boundaries in interactions may be observed. In addition to anhedonia, there may be an accompanied decreased interest in sexual encounters, as well as a generally poor self-image.

Paradoxically, the individual with hyper-reactivity is also at increased likelihood of risk-taking behaviors, such as unhealthy substance use, driving under the influence, gambling, and risky sexual encounters.

Sleep disturbances such as difficulty falling asleep or staying asleep or waking up early may all be part of the clinical symptomatic picture as well. Insomnia is seen within the hyper-reactivity states described above. Upwards of 90% of people suffering from posttraumatic stress disorder experience nightmares. Self-destructive behaviors sometimes manifest. Examples include things like risky sexual behaviors and drunk driving.

As mentioned earlier, trauma is ubiquitous, is a part of life, and sometimes may be experienced multiple times throughout one's life. Different people that go through the same traumatic event may have different reactions to the experience. Similarly, not everyone that witnesses a traumatic event or is physically or sexually abused develops posttraumatic stress disorder.

The literature suggests that between a third and one half of those that experience a traumatic event as outlined above go on to then develop clinical posttraumatic stress disorder.

## Prior Risk Factors

In addition to the life-threatening traumatic event, there are several known research based prior risk factors that are correlated with an increased incidence of posttraumatic stress disorder.

If the individual has other psychiatric issues, that is associated with an increased risk. Examples include a history of other anxiety disorders such as panic disorder, as well as mood disorders such as depressive disorder. Comorbid medical issues that may interfere with the person's foundational resilience also are associated with an increased risk.

Temperamental vulnerabilities such as the person's disposition and outlook on life are also correlated with risk. Victims of childhood events that were traumatizing, also known as adverse childhood experiences, described later in this book, are also at an increased risk.

The severity of the trauma itself and the length of exposure to the trauma are also factors that contribute to an increased risk of developing the disorder.

A fascinating study that looks at the regulation of the heart rate at the time of traumatic event describes the correlation. The study by Blanchard et al. (2002) reveals that patients who had a traumatic event, sought treatment in the emergency department, and then discharged with a heart rate that went back to their baseline were unlikely to develop posttraumatic stress disorder. Conversely, those that left the emergency department with a continued elevated heart rate compared to their baseline were at higher risk of developing the disorder.

## Biopsychosocial Determinants and Risk

There are a number of biopsychosocial factors that are associated with increased risk of developing posttraumatic stress disorder.

- **Age:** Typically, younger children have a decreased incidence of posttraumatic stress disorder, while older individuals have an increased risk.
- **Culture:** Depending on the response and cultural understanding and the meaning given to a traumatic event, the individual and society within a specific culture may have increased risk factors. Think, for example, of the culture that provides acceptance, versus a culture that reinforces shame, hiding, and repressing of experiences or symptoms.
- **Education:** Lower levels of education are associated with increased risk factors.
- **Employment:** Unemployment and the associated lack of income are associated with increased risk.
- **Environment:** Research suggests that in addition to the type of employment, the neighborhood where one grows up as well as being exposed to bullying and racism are increased factors. Repetitive exposures to trauma, either by nature of one's occupation or where one lives, are associated with increased risk. We know that our zip code essentially determines the trajectory of our lives, from the quality of our physical and mental health as well as our longevity!
- **Ethnicity:** Studies indicate that exposure to structural racism and cumulative trauma has a significant impact on the development of trauma- and stress-related disorders, as well as the passing on down through intergenerational lines of trauma. Studies suggest that folks exposed to repetitive racism have a higher incidence of posttraumatic stress disorder as well as an increased chronicity of the illness.
- **Gender:** Research as well as clinical evidence suggests that women have a higher prevalence of posttraumatic stress disorder. Associated risks may be things like increased prevalence of exposure to trauma such as physical and sexual abuse.
- **Genetic factors:** Studies indicate that there may be a link within families, as seen in studies that look at twins. There is an increased incidence of developing posttraumatic stress disorder within family clusters, indicating that there may be an intergenerational, genetic component as well.
- **Place of birth:** In addition to the cultural factors briefly described above, studies indicate that a family's origin, as well as factors such as where someone is born, is associated with risk factors.
- **Occupation:** There are certain occupations known to have an increased risk of being exposed to traumatic events, developing trauma- and stress-related disorders such as adjustment and acute as well as posttraumatic stress disorders. Examples of professions that have increased risk include military personnel, first responders, police officers, and firefighters. See Chapter 8, Culture, Identity, and Society, for an in-depth discussion on these and other risks.
- **Socioeconomic status:** As per the indicators above, a lower socioeconomic status is associated with an increased risk of developing posttraumatic stress disorder.
  - Research indicates that children from lower socioeconomic statuses are more likely to be medicated for their mental health conditions, as compared to others who are provided psychotherapy and alternatives to medicating as an initial option.
  - The relevance in this is twofold: one is decreased energy spent to course correct with more time and resource intensive options; the other is the reality that people from high-stress and high-trauma environments likely show up to treatment at a more progressed stage in their traumatic symptomatology and pathology.

While this chapter focuses specifically on the identification of trauma disorders and associated risk factors, see Chapter 7, Family, Children, and Resilience, for detailed descriptions of protective factors that provide resilience and a buffer to mitigate the development of clinical pathology.

## Continued Consequences

Those that are then diagnosed with posttraumatic stress disorder have a host of associated continued consequences in addition to the symptoms of the disease itself.

A study by Bozzatello et al. (2021) discusses the role of childhood trauma and the association with development of borderline personality disorder. The article discusses the role of adverse childhood experiences and the impact on various systems in the body, such as change in gray matter volume, white matter connectivity, and disruption in neurotransmitters, which likely contributes to personality pathology in addition to other comorbidities later in life.

The cycle of trauma, suppression, expression of emotions, the overwhelming negative emotions, and what appears to be an inability to control them likely contribute to traits in personality pathology, particularly borderline personality disorder.

Studies indicate that posttraumatic stress disorder can lead to poor day-to-day functioning, a decrease in marital satisfaction and perceptions of other relationships. It can lead to a lower quality of life, such as the sleep disturbances described above.

Fundamental psychological experiences and symptoms include things like feeling numbness, fear, helplessness, hopelessness, feeling trapped, and feeling shut down as well as extreme anger.

Self-identity and the view of the self are altered. The individual may start to feel that they are not deserving, inept, or damaged, and that they do not deserve a regular life like everyone else. Relationships are also impacted by mistrust, which is exacerbated by isolation, and the belief that loneliness is the only way to exist safely.

Myths, negative self-talk, and thinking errors occur in the setting of a traumatic stress disorder. Concepts such as all or nothing thinking, overgeneralization, catastrophizing, and discounting the positive are seen in depressive disorders as well as trauma-related ones. This workbook will allow the reader to explore their beliefs and narratives through coping skills, interactive exercises, and writing prompts.

The psychological diagnosis of posttraumatic stress disorder can also contribute to the worsening or development of chronic physical conditions. Literature suggests that people suffering from posttraumatic stress disorder have an increased utilization of medical resources. There is an increased incidence of ailments such as back pain, headaches, asthma, blood pressure disturbances, heart disease, and stroke.

## Writing Prompt

Consider using the space below to reflect on the following:

**What are your myths and thinking errors? What can you do to challenge them?**

_____

_____

_____

_____

_____

_____

_____

_____

_____

_____

_____

_____

## Treatment

By definition, pathology directly affects the person's day-to-day ability to function in society, relationships at work, and relationships with their loved ones.

The primary function of treatment is alleviation of and potentially remission of symptoms. Based on the understanding of the self and in context of clinical assessment by a mental health professional, the clinical treatment plan and goals should be constructed specific to the individual.

Depending on the symptoms, many of them delineated above, the goals may include things such as identifying triggers as well as how to stay safe. These are in the context of the trigger as well as thoughts of self-harm.

We encourage everyone to begin to understand the potential connection between psychological symptoms, thoughts, and feelings, as well as their impact on bodily sensations and reactions.

Throughout the course of treatment, the individual may desire to explore aspects of self-control, over their anxiety and fear states, and how their body and mind responds to them. It may be beneficial to address associated thoughts of shame or grief. Learning coping skills as the person uncouples traumatic memories from responses also allows for future growth and resilience.

If the individual is interested in doing so and is at a point in their treatment to address physical health symptoms, such as sleep and exercise routines, as well as potential substance use and misuse patterns, this can also be done in a clinical setting.

From a social and behavioral perspective, the ability to connect with others may also be an aspect of treatment focus. Improving the integration of self, how the person understands themselves in relation to others, while improving boundaries is important. Learning and relearning how to listen to one's body and mind further aids in improved communication and relationships with others. Aspects of self-esteem and self-acceptance are also critical in appreciating how the past trauma impacts current relationships.

In attachment trauma, we hear the client say they feel that their experience is not important, and they feel they have been told that they are exaggerating. The person may have been told that their pain is not for everyone to see and to "get over it." The person with trauma learns that they are alone in the experience, and their feelings and emotions do not matter. This especially occurs when the feelings with stigma are associated with them, such as sadness, jealousy, or envy. The person compares themselves to others, and they may have feelings of disappointment or sadness.

Oftentimes in relationships when there is attachment injury, the person may hear "don't be sad" or "don't be jealous" from others and think that they should not be having these emotions. A key aspect of trauma therapy and treatment is learning that these feelings are indeed necessary.

In therapy, your feelings are validated, and the client learns that every sensation they have in the moment is acceptable. This serves as a different experience for the client, fostering a paradigm shift of having a restorative, healthy experience in a relationship.

The more the person has these experiences, the more they feel and learn that these feelings are like the weather and clouds, that they are part of being human, and that they will pass. When we don't resist the feelings and realize there are teachings in them, we can get in touch with them and learn they are pieces of ourselves that need to be heard.

The person learns that if they have the most difficult experience of deep sadness or deep jealousy, they are able to survive them and come out of them intact. As in everything in life, things have their natural balance, and there are also the feelings of joy and curiosity and excitement that counter the other emotions.

As we experience life, if we dim or put a strain on ourselves to not have the strong negative emotions, for example, if we dim the anxiety or worry, we also dim all the other emotions. To have the ability to feel and experience the full spectrum of emotions, we must have all of them. We must have them in a safe environment, such as therapy, where we can say that while it was difficult, we came out of the emotional experience alive and unbroken.

This book is intended for the individual or clinician, although as mentioned earlier, can be used as a guideline for hospital administrators as there are significant returns on investment in terms of the values of investing in treatments for this disorder.

In addition to the improvement in quality and satisfaction, mindfulness will also be discussed. Subsequent chapters will discuss how the method described in this book can be incorporated into one's life.

Clinically, we know the following aspects that improve outcomes in treatment:

■ Treatment engagement
■ Therapeutic relationship and alliance
■ Establishing trust
■ Interpersonal connectedness

Certainly, one size does not fit all, and we have reviewed available options in this section. We know that people with more severe symptoms of posttraumatic stress disorder and with different types of traumas will require lengthier treatment and may take longer to respond.

As we are healing, like anything else in life, we must realize the results are not linear. Healing does not occur one point after the other. It almost always happens in a rotating, windy way. There will be moments where we will resort to our old coping mechanisms.

The defense mechanisms that have evolved for the person to survive for so long may kick back in. We don't want to consider that experience as regressing or losing progress in therapy treatment. That does not mean you are going backward or failing. When these moments of old defense mechanisms kick in, like reactivity while working in an anger management session, one should congratulate the moment and the response. That was the response that kicked in over and over again in the past that allowed the person to survive dangerous environments.

Reframing this and congratulating yourself to recognize that this is how you were able to survive is tremendously beneficial. The same goes for aspects of shame as a defense mechanism or freezing. By making oneself small in the past, the person made it so that they did not get the attention from their aggressor or surroundings. It helped them survive before. Of course, now it may get in the way of healthier progression, but it is important to congratulate and understand why they were formed rather than to get critical and berate oneself up.

At times when one is vulnerable, they may resort back to these moments, and as they are working on them, they might find that they are reacting in a way that resembles their old ways.

It is important to give yourself permission. Frame it as a visitation, that you are feeling the emotions, although aren't staying in that state. Remember that it typically stems from what was lacking, which was compassion. When there is compassion, there is room for growth. When you give yourself compassion, you are allowing yourself to grow.

We grow in compassion and wither in criticism.

*– Duygu Balan, LPCC*

Below we have outlined an alphabetical list of therapies, therapeutics, and modalities available that are evidence based and currently in use for the treatment of posttraumatic stress disorder. We include brief descriptors of the more commonly available therapies.

## *Non-Pharmacological Therapies*

- Breathing Techniques
  - Deep breathing, specifically exhaling, triggers the parasympathetic nervous system. See Chapter 4, Balan 3-2-1 Method, that includes detailed information regarding breathing techniques.
- Cognitive Behavioral Therapy (CBT)
  - CBT addresses maladaptive thinking patterns, thoughts, and behaviors that may be dysfunctional.
  - The client works with the therapist to address automatic thoughts and beliefs that influence the way they act and feel.
- Cognitive Processing Therapy (CPT)
  - CPT is a series of twelve weekly sessions that address distorted beliefs, issues of blame surrounding the trauma. The client receives writing assignments such as essays about their trauma and its impact
  - The work with the therapist is reflecting on the thoughts and working toward modifying them. The client also receives assignments to be completed at home between sessions.
- Cognitive Behavioral Writing Therapy
  - There is evidence supporting the efficacy in reducing posttraumatic stress disorder symptoms with the use of cognitive behavioral writing therapy. Meta-analyses done by Kuester et al. (2016) and Lewis et al. (2019) support the use of internet-based cognitive behavioral writing therapy.

- The study by Gawlytta et al. (2022) was the first to look at treatment to reduce posttraumatic stress disorder after intensive care in patients and their spouses.
■ Eye Movement Desensitization and Reprocessing (EMDR)
  - EMDR is a model that works on the emotions and physical sensations of the client and stimulates the person's processing of information to help incorporate the traumatic event into a memory that is adaptive.
  - The person is asked to recall the traumatic event in their mind, while the clinician moves their finger slowly back and forth in front of the client's face. The client is asked to introspect and notice what they are feeling.
  - EMDR facilitates the retelling of the event, without the re-traumatization. It is successful, safe, and significantly more effective than medications alone in reducing posttraumatic stress disorder symptoms and has a long-lasting effect.
■ Expressive Writing Therapy
  - In Expressive Writing Therapy, the client writes about their traumatic experiences for around twenty minutes, three days in a row.
  - The emphasis is on regulating the self, while writing about their thoughts and feelings.
  - Studies indicate Expressive Writing Therapy is effective in the treatment of symptoms of posttraumatic stress disorder.
■ Group Therapy
  - Being able to be with and hear from others with similar experiences and reactions to their traumatic events is therapeutic and beneficial.
  - Depending on the needs of the individual, there are different modalities of group therapies, including CBT and supportive groups.
  - Group therapy decreases one's sense of being alone with the experience, can assist with coping mechanisms as well as prevent relapse of symptoms.
■ Imagery Rehearsal Training (IRT)
  - IRT is a cognitive behavioral therapy-based treatment for nightmares.
  - Individuals write their nightmares and are instructed to change them, thereby adding layers of protective elements, which helps process the nightmare.
  - IRT reduces the intensity and frequency of nightmares, improves sleep quality, and helps with the negative beliefs and impact nightmares have on the person.
■ Imaginal Exposure Therapy
  - The goal is to have the person think about and try to remember the event as much as possible, with the intent to relive the memory and work through processing them in a safe environment.
■ Logotherapy
  - In logotherapy, the client is instructed to write their own epitaph, with the goal to describe and introspect on the meaning of things in their life.
  - First described by Victor Frankl, it was designed to bring out existential concerns, anxieties, as well as to work on goals.
■ MDMA-assisted therapy
  - 3,4-Methylenedioxy methamphetamine, aka MDMA or ecstasy, at the time of writing this book, was federally illegal in the United States.
  - As of December 2022, MDMA is not currently approved for the treatment of anything.
  - MDMA is, however, in phase 3 in the Food and Drug Administration (FDA) development process and has received "breakthrough" description, indicating it may have potential to provide improved outcomes over current treatments.

- MDMA is a psychedelic compound used predominantly for recreational purposes.
- It has serotonergic properties and is under clinical investigation for use in various psychiatric diagnoses.
- MDMA is known to increase pro-social behaviors, improve self-awareness, reduce fear and response to fear, as well as trauma-related fears.
- The research article by Mitchell et al. (2021) discusses their significant findings of the effects of MDMA on significantly reducing posttraumatic stress disorder symptoms.

■ Mindfulness Meditation
- Recent research has shown that practicing mindfulness meditation has improved insular functioning and connectivity in the brain.
- Links to improved understanding and connection to the sensations from inside one's body, called interoception, have also been made.

■ Narrative Exposure Therapy
- In this form of treatment, the client writes a lifeline of their experiences, with stones that represent the negative and flowers that express positive experiences. This technique works through exposure to develop healthy coping mechanisms.

■ Positive Memory Processing (PMP)
- PMP employs recalling, writing, or narrating positive memories, and then processing the feelings and thoughts associated with the memories. This focus then results in decreased severity of symptoms of posttraumatic stress disorder, and improved affect and cognitions.
- The study by Contractor et al. (2020) reviews the effects of focusing on positive memories for individuals with posttraumatic stress disorder. The authors discuss that focusing on positive memories improves mood regulation and increases attention on the positive, thereby reducing the negative thoughts.

■ Positive Psychology
- In this method, the client expresses thoughts in a positive framework using gratitude, hope, forgiveness through writing exercises and letters.
- The goals include improving symptoms of trauma-related stress and regulating emotions from a positive perspective.

■ Prolonged Exposure
- During prolonged exposure, psychoeducation regarding posttraumatic stress disorder and breathing techniques to help cope and relax are provided. This is followed by repeated exposure to thoughts and images of the traumatic event.
- The client goes through their thoughts from least to most stressful, fearful aspects that remind them of the trauma, and the exposure therapy progresses.
- The goal is to reduce the symptoms of stress and fear in a safe environment.

■ Relaxation Techniques
- These include breathing techniques, physical activity, and yoga.
- Nature therapy and animal-based therapies are parts of this modality.

■ Somatic Experiencing (SE)
- SE is a form of trauma therapy that focuses on the autonomic nervous system by using bottom-up processing, inner attention, and directs the user's awareness to their internal sensations.
- Payne et al. (2015) present a detailed look into SE and demonstrate how interoception, the visceral, and proprioception and kinesthesis, the musculoskeletal, are effectively used.

- As compared to exposure therapy, SE is more similar to the way mindfulness and meditation works.
■ Therapeutic Yoga
  - Studies have shown that yoga can improve mental health and wellbeing including:
    • Balances the mind, body, and spirit
    • Decreases depression
    • Decreases stress
    • Improves concentration, focus, memory, attention
    • Improves academic and work performance
    • Decreases anxiety, worry, fear
    • Decreases sleep disturbances
  - Research suggests therapeutic yoga promotes physical health including:
    • Metabolism
      ■ Decreases inflammation
      ■ Improves weight control
    • Cardiovascular system
      ■ Improves blood pressure
      ■ Positive impact on circulation
    • Respiratory system
      ■ Regulates breathing
    • Digestive system
      ■ Regulates the gut microbiome
    • Immune system
      ■ Decreases stress-related hormones and associated inflammation
    • Musculoskeletal system
      ■ Positive and protective impact on the muscles and joints
■ Written Exposure Therapy (WET)
  - WET is the repeated exposure of the trauma by writing over a course of five sessions. The clinician instructs the client to write alone, then they review the responses together in session. Based on the review by the clinician, the client continues to write at the subsequent session.
  - WET recommends a significantly lower number of sessions and requires less intensive training of the clinician.
  - According to studies, WET has similar effectiveness at reducing symptoms of posttraumatic stress disorder as exposure and cognitive processing therapies.

## Pharmacological Options

Any time when there is a consideration of starting a medication, the main issues discussed with the prescriber, described below, can be summarized with two words: Informed consent.

Informed consent is not a luxury.

*— Yener Balan, MD*

We cannot stress enough the value and power of knowing what one is putting in their body and for what reason. The individual, especially someone with a history of trauma and who is under treatment for posttraumatic stress disorder, has already a cluster of issues including a loss of sense of control or an inability to make sense of bodily sensations or expectations and hope.

Informed consent in the medical setting is not a luxury, it is not a waste of time, it is not something that the prescriber or client should gloss over. If you have a question, ask it.

If you don't understand something, ask again. And again. If it's overwhelming or you need time, take the time.

It is your body, and the prescriber has to ensure the person they are recommending medications to know the positives as well as the potential not-so-positives about taking that medication.

The choice of starting and continuing to take a medication is exactly that: a choice. It is not a mandate; it is to help you and your ability to do the things that you want to do.

Thankfully, the most commonly used medications for posttraumatic stress disorder are easy to prescribe, easy to take, very well tolerated with minimal side effects, and work well. That being said, medications typically aren't prescribed in a vacuum.

Multimodal treatment, including medications and some other forms of therapy, is almost always more beneficial in reducing symptoms of posttraumatic stress disorder than medications alone.

Below are a list of empowering questions we suggest you ask your prescriber:

- What is the reason the prescriber is recommending it?
- What is the diagnosis or set of symptoms the medication targets?
- How is the medication taken, such as once a day or more often?
- Is there a titration schedule, is the starting dose the maintenance dose? If not, how will the person taking the medications know when or how often to return to the prescriber for adjustments?
- Some medications take a while before significant clinical effects are felt, what is that time for the suggested medication? What will the person taking the medication do while waiting for the medication to start taking effect?
- What are the side effects of the medication?
    - Inquire about side effects that are most relevant to the person's life, occupation, and responsibilities. Things to look out for are drowsiness, how it affects driving a car, appetite, weight gain or loss, stomach aches, nausea, diarrhea, sexual side effects like problems with arousal, erections, ejaculation, and orgasm.
    - Also ask about other things one puts in their body – for example, interaction of the medication with alcohol or other drugs the person is taking. Ask about interactions with any over the counter vitamins or other supplements the person takes.
    - Ask about potential interaction with diet. Some medications are affected by seemingly innocuous things like grapefruit juice that can decrease the effectiveness of medications.
- Do the benefits of taking the medication outweigh the risks of not taking the medication?
- Does the medication interact with other medications the person is on?
    - Make a list of all prescribed medications and go through them one by one with the prescriber.
- Do you need to get blood tests or other physical checkups while on the medication?
    - Some medications can be measured by a simple blood test. This could be to detect the amount of medications in the blood stream, to verify that the person is taking the meds, to mitigate or reduce side effects.
    - If there are side effects that the prescriber discloses, and the person taking the medication and the prescriber agree that the benefits indeed do outweigh the risks, what physical signs and symptoms should be monitored? For example, some medications may affect blood pressure. How often should blood pressure be checked?
- If the person is currently or may one day want to try to become pregnant, does it affect any aspect of sexual function?
- If the person taking the medication becomes pregnant, does it affect the unborn baby? Will it cause harm to the unborn baby?
- If the person is breastfeeding, does the medication pass through the milk to the baby? Will it cause harm this way to the baby?
- What happens if the person forgets to take a dose?
- Do you have to slowly reduce the dose (taper) in order to stop taking it?
- What happens if the person abruptly stops taking it, are there serious withdrawal effects?
- Is it a controlled substance? Meaning, are there any restrictions about how many pills the person can get, or any concerns about traveling with the medication?
- Can one get addicted to the medication?
- How long do you have to take the medication? Three months? Three years? Forever?

- What if the person doesn't want that specific medication and wants to try something they heard of on TV or that a family member responded to?
  - There is a genetic element to a number of the psychiatric diagnoses, as studies have shown the increased prevalence of certain issues such as major depression are linked within families. This is why the clinician asks about family history (see above for associated genetic and other risk factors). Interestingly, although when one thinks about it, it makes sense that if a certain medication worked for a family member with the same condition, it is worth bringing up to the prescriber, as it may also have a similar beneficial effect on the individual as well.
- What if the person doesn't want to take medications at all? What are the alternate options?
- If the person has health insurance, does the insurance cover the cost of the treatment? If not, are there options that are covered to reduce cost? If none are available, can the prescriber choose a medication that costs less at the pharmacy?
- Regarding cost, does the prescriber or insurance company have a preferred pharmacy? Do they have a recommendation for a source such as an online site to order the medications from?

## *Pharmacological Options: Antidepressants*

Medications cannot undo the trauma, they cannot erase the memories associated with the intense affect linked to the event. They cannot provide insight or judgment. They cannot provide hope or better relationships.

What medications can do, however, is ease the symptoms of anxiety and depression, allowing the individual to tolerate the other modalities of therapy, exposure, narration, introspection, mindfulness and ensuring the course of treatment as effective as possible. This work that the person puts in, over time, will allow for better integration of the understanding of memories, an ability to appreciate themselves, and to connect healthily with others.

We are acutely aware of the umbrella review by Moncrieff et al. (2022) that concludes that there is no support for the hypothesis of a link between low serotonin levels and depression. We are listing the currently available and approved treatments for posttraumatic stress disorder and will leave the current media sensationalization of the findings out of this book. See Chapter 6, Brain–Body Connection, for further discussion of our current understanding of serotonin and its interaction with mental health and our behaviors.

- Selective Serotonin Reuptake Inhibitors (SSRIs)
  - SSRIs are first line medication treatment that are FDA approved in the United States for posttraumatic stress disorder.
  - SSRIs have significant benefits in anxiety and depressive symptoms, although studies suggest, as well as our clinical experience corroborates, SSRIs have a significant effect of the posttraumatic stress disorder symptoms in 40%–60% of people taking them.
  - This means that the other 40%–60% of folks, unfortunately, do not have a benefit of posttraumatic stress disorder symptom reduction from the medications when taken alone. The Moncrieff article, as well as the large percentage of people who do not benefit from these medications, points toward other components at play such as the placebo effect.

- Medications such as SSRIs are often used in conjunction with other modalities of treatment for maximal benefit.
- Sertraline, the generic name for Zoloft, is an SSRI, FDA approved for posttraumatic stress disorder.
- Paroxetine, the generic name for Paxil, is the other SSRI that is FDA approved for posttraumatic stress disorder.

## *Pharmacological Options: Other*

■ Off-label medications – at the time of writing the book. The commonly prescribed, non-FDA-approved medications for posttraumatic stress disorder include:
  - SSRI
    • Fluoxetine: the generic name for Prozac.
  - Serotonin and Norepinephrine Reuptake Inhibitor (SNRI)
    • Venlafaxine: the generic name for Effexor
  - Anti-anxiety medications
    • Benzodiazepines
      ■ Benzodiazepines such as lorazepam, the generic for Ativan, and diazepam, the generic for Valium, reduce anxiety, although they are habit forming, cause drowsiness, have serious side effects, lead to withdrawal, are controlled substances, and interact with other medications as well as alcohol and can lead to respiratory depression and even death.
      ■ Think of the benzodiazepines as literally cutting off the anxiogenic stimulus from the anxiety response. While reenacting fear from a memory or severe anxiety that inhibits day-to-day life is problematic and may benefit from the benzodiazepine, current real time concern and fear, and physically responding in an actual fear-inducing situation, such as swerving a car, are lifesaving and may be inhibited by the use of a benzodiazepine.
      ■ These days, prescribers are more reluctant to start someone on this class of medications due to the issues described, although if one is on them, respect them for what they can and cannot do.
      ■ Similar to the SSRIs, they can help start a talk therapy modality, ease into painful areas, and open the door to learning coping and healing mechanisms.
      ■ They are, however, almost too good at reducing anxiety, and with anything that is so effective so quickly, there is always a catch, a downside that must not be ignored.
■ Antipsychotic medications and mood stabilizers
  - There have been a number of studies that have reviewed antipsychotics as well as mood stabilizers, such as those used for bipolar disorder. While the side effects of inducing sleep and relaxation through their sedative properties have been noted, there are no currently FDA approved medications in either of these classes for posttraumatic stress disorder.
  - Antipsychotics work well for psychotic symptoms such as hallucinations.
  - Certain antipsychotics also have serotonergic properties that may alleviate depressive symptoms.

   — Regarding side effect risk to clinical benefit ratio, as with any medication, speak with your prescribing clinician as to exactly which aspects of the trauma-related stress you may be prescribed one of these classes of medications.

## *Writing Prompt*

If you are currently prescribed medications for your mental health, consider writing them in the space below, and noting questions you may have regarding their use, side effect profile, risks, and benefits.

   Consider working with your prescriber to answer every question you have, until you are truly a fully educated, informed, and consenting person.

_____

_____

_____

_____

_____

_____

_____

_____

_____

_____

_____

_____

_____

_____

## Conclusion

It is important to take into consideration the clinical needs of the client, as well as the evidence for treatment modalities available. The severity of symptoms of posttraumatic stress disorder and then the length and time and other factors including access to appropriate health care coverage, willingness to engage in, and ability to participate in care should be evaluated.

   More sessions, more intensive requirements such as added assignments, more complex rules and barriers to entry result in failure to keep appointments and early drop out of treatment course. The goal is to ensure the client continues in treatment and does not drop out or terminate before the ending of the treatment course for adequate outcomes to be gained.

# TOOLS FOR OUR SUCCESS

2

# Chapter 3

---

# Value of Treatment

---

Expose yourself to your deepest fear; after that, fear has no power, and the fear of freedom shrinks and vanishes. You are free.

*– Jim Morrison*

## Introduction

The value of treating pathologies is inherent to the individual suffering. This chapter will discuss the benefits in terms of symptomatic reduction, improvement in quality of life and mental health. We have discussed the identification of trauma and stress related disorders as well as different evidence-based treatment modalities. While we incorporate a multimodal treatment milieu, the focus of this workbook is regarding mindfulness, insight, and expressive writing.

This chapter will look at the values of expressive writing in connection with the mindfulness it fosters. The techniques described within can be used by yourself on your own healing journey and can also be used with your clinician as part of a treatment plan. We will also discuss the financial return on investment from a business management perspective.

Operationally, whether you are running a small business or are a manager on a team in a large organization, there are proven, significant financial benefits to ensuring yourself and your employees are cared for. Specifically, attention to and management of trauma and stress related disorders yields a multiple fold return on investment.

By the end of this section, our intention is that the reader will come away with a different level of appreciation for this modality. Our hope is that the reader will begin to think about the reasons why they have not already begun doing this work. Rather than thinking about the benefits of starting expressive writing therapy, we challenge you to think about the benefits of ignoring expressive writing therapy.

We look forward to hearing from you how investing in and practicing the methods described have benefitted you.

DOI: 10.4324/9781003323815-5

## Prevalence

Pre-COVID, the posttraumatic stress disorder literature suggested that upwards of 70% of men and 50% of women have been or will be subjected to a traumatic event that qualifies in severity for development of posttraumatic stress disorder. COVID became a global equalizer, bringing those numbers unfortunately significantly higher.

Major depressive disorder and posttraumatic stress disorder are among the two mental health diagnoses with the highest prevalence in the population. Major depressive disorder has a 70% lifetime comorbidity in people with posttraumatic stress disorder. The two together increase the already high comorbidity of self-injury and suicide. In the United States, pre-COVID suicide rates had already increased by 25%–30% from 10.5 to 13 per 100,000 people.

Of note, other anxiety disorders such as panic disorder have a 15% lifetime comorbidity. Borderline personality pathology has a 12% lifetime comorbidity with posttraumatic stress disorder.

## Economic Burden

The economic burden of posttraumatic stress disorder in the United States is estimated to be over $3 billion annually. Pre-pandemic reports suggest that depression resulted in 200 million lost work days a year and cost companies up to $44 billion a year.

Data has shown that across the United States, over 60% of people with mental health or substance use issues do not receive clinical care. Posttraumatic stress disorder is known to be linked with a higher risk of comorbid mental health and physical issues, as well as a higher risk of morbidity and mortality.

## Expressive Writing Therapy

This interactive workbook is intended to focus on expressive writing therapies as a therapeutic avenue for trauma and stress related disorder, specifically posttraumatic stress disorder. Techniques, guidance as well as writing prompts will be discussed throughout. This section of the chapter will discuss the evidence-based specificities to this modality.

According to numerous studies, including Sloan et al. (2016), there is value in written exposure therapy as it promotes recovery through writing about the traumatic issues. Of note, based on findings in a prior study by Sloan et al. (2011), their findings suggested that patients with more severe symptoms may not benefit as much from written emotional disclosure as compared to those with less severe symptoms of PTSD.

The authors in the 2011 study also discuss a potential limitation and lack of finding significant benefit for participants, that is they did not include psychoeducation as part of the instructions for the writing exercise.

These findings are indeed consistent with other studies and our own clinical experience as well. More severe, more complex needs of the patient often require multimodal forms of treatment to address the symptom profile.

The values particular to expressive writing therapy are included below. We will be reviewing the physical and physiological, the mental and emotional, the personal, the financial, and the work-related values.

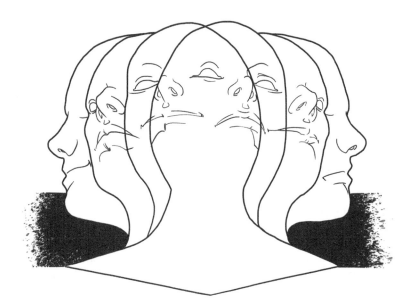

# Benefits: Physical and Physiological

■ First and foremost, we want to emphasize that managing symptoms of trauma through expressive writing therapy has been shown to improve the sense of control over psychosomatic issues. As we pay attention to our bodily sensations, we improve control over them, the associations we make, and what we say about ourselves. This mindfulness allows for a progressive decrease in sensitivity to the stressors and how we react to our triggers.

■ An improved sense of control of one's body and sensations results in a decreased need for healthcare visits, decreased emergency department visits, decreased inpatient medical and psychiatric hospitalizations as well as a decreased need for pharmaceuticals.

■ As the body improves its physiological response, there is a whole host of associated positive consequential benefits.

■ Expressive writing therapy has been shown to:
  - Enhance recovery
  - Decrease blood pressure
  - Regulate breathing
  - Decrease states of arousal and hypervigilance
  - Decrease cortisol and the inflammatory response to traumatic memories
  - Improve immunity

■ Another benefit is that expressive writing therapy allows you to honor your own experience, and therefore, increase awareness to your patterns. It allows you to make decisions, follow and track if you are going through with these decisions. This will in turn increase healthy habits. For instance, with the writing prompts, if you are raising awareness to your sleep disturbance issues, your sleep will also help you regulate your emotions.

■ The decisions you incorporate in your day-to-day life will also have an impact on your hormone levels. Your everyday choices, such as healthy eating, exercising, and sleep hygiene, all the decisions you make through the writing process will help you track your lifestyle and improve your outcomes.

- The study by Zhang et al. (2022) provides evidence for the power of nostalgia and positive memories on our ability to withstand pain and tolerate discomfort.
- At the interaction of mind and body, when one gains awareness of bodily sensations through expressive writing, the inner awareness fosters improvement of empathy as well.
- Training your ability to bring attention to the body, with mindfulness, and label and describe the feelings associated are skills that can be achieved.

## Benefits: Mental and Emotional

- This is about permission; any writing prompt that does not feel interesting or that you do not want to do remember that it is just an offering.
  - In the moment that they do not feel right, skip it.
  - You may go back at a later time to that prompt or may never go back to it.
  - This is all about giving yourself permission and designing your own care.
  - When understanding your past trauma and that things in your life may have been out of control, you also see that these exercises are designed to give the control back to you.
  - You are giving yourself the permission and compassion back to yourself.
  - There is no harshness, no rigidity, no mandate to any of the modalities, or writing prompts or techniques offered in this book.
  - If the writing prompt triggers something or if you find yourself getting off on a tangent, simply continue.
  - There is no right way to complete the exercise.
  - These are to ignite things that were unexpressed.
  - Perhaps the thing needed to be asked was not a specific prompt of question in this book, there may be a writing prompt that gets close to it.
  - You can write what you need to.
  - There are no guidelines, so don't try to stay on topic as there is no topic.
  - Let the ideas and thoughts and feelings flow as you write.
  - It is important also to notice that our old criticisms of grammar and spelling and punctuation do not matter either.
  - In traditional writing and in talk therapy, we are sometimes unable to access the things that these prompts are intended to access.
  - None of the traditional rules apply.
  - You can always go back and clean up a response later on if you want to retain it for some other purpose.
  - This isn't the time to be concerned or overly cautious about your writing skills.
  - It is time to be with yourself and allow compassion to flourish.
- Expressive writing therapy has a large number of significant valuable impacts on mental health and wellbeing. Most significantly, it is evidence based in reducing symptoms of post-traumatic stress disorder.
- Through exposure to and being mindful of the trauma, it has an effect of reducing the fear and inflammatory response to the trauma.
- As the individual works toward improving their health and creates an environment where they are able to focus on expressive writing therapy specifically, there is an additive effect in terms of enhancing their recovery.

- Spending energy working on expressive writing has a clinically significant impact on cognitive restructuring.
  - This methodology gives you the power to re-write your own narrative.
  - There is a greater sense of control, as you are working toward reframing your perceptions.
  - It also has the effect of reducing trauma-related negative beliefs and negative self-talk.
  - As one advances in their writing, one is able to modify the experience of the event.
  - Lastly, it works toward enhancing resilience and provides a new foundational habit to mitigate future stress responses.
- Specific to comorbid psychiatric illnesses, expressive writing therapy has an impact on the following:
  - Decrease in dysphoric mood.
  - Decrease in depressed mood.
  - Decrease in anxious mood.
- The randomized control trial by Meshberg-Cohen et al. (2014) discusses the benefit of decreasing symptom severity of anxiety and depression and posttraumatic stress disorder symptoms in patients with co-occurring substance use disorders.
- The first study and authors to look at the benefits and therapeutic value of expressive writing were Pennebaker et al. (1986), in an article that reviewed writing in context of therapeutic healing. For further information on the origins and the value Pennebaker brings to the field, we have several other resources including his book *Expressive Writing: Words That Heal* (2014) in the references section.
- We include specific space throughout this book for the individual to physically write responses to the writing prompts. The main reason is that there are benefits to activating the mind and memories through the modality of longhand writing.
- Studies including the one by Mueller and Oppenheimer (2014) show that writing longhand as opposed to using word processing leads to deeper processing and understanding, as well as a longer effect on symptomatic reduction of depressive, anxious, and posttraumatic stress disorder symptoms.
- If you are going to be using this textbook in complement to talk therapy with a clinician, consider still writing down your answers and reviewing them in session. The reason for this is that discussing memories aloud, also referred to as narrative therapy, has been shown in studies to yield an even better result in symptom reduction and longevity of reduction of symptoms.
- Insight is promoted through the cognitive restructuring described above as well as the repetitive positive reinforcement.
- Writing gives voice to repressed, suppressed, and blocked memories and builds personal identity.
- When one reads what was written, one may uncover parts of themselves that were difficult to reach. With further experience, the individual becomes able to see the moment the emotions arise and the moment they cease. This then allows for the individual to have increased control.
- Particular to the writing prompts and instructions themselves, the following studies document the value of the method:
  - A study by Sloan et al. (2007) provides further evidence that instructions that include emotional expression of the traumatic event versus cognitive based instructions yield improved results.

- The randomized control trial by Lichtenthal and Cruess (2010) reports evidence of symptomatic benefit when specific instructions to write about making meaning of the traumatic experience are used. This study looked at bereavement in particular and showed significant positive impact on depressive and posttraumatic stress disorder symptoms.

■ Through expressive writing and the mindfulness developed, the user will experience significant improvements in relationship quality and longevity. They will be able to see themselves and empathize with the other.

■ Consider using this skill in the workplace, too, with employees and bosses, customers and vendors.

## Benefits: Personal Reasons

You either learn your way toward writing your own script in life, or you unwittingly become an actor in someone else's script.

— *James Taylor Gatto*

There are a number of reasons why someone would personally choose to do writing therapy in addition to the medical and psychological ones listed above. When you have increased self-awareness and a framework to assess your strengths and weaknesses, you are at an advantage.

If you can identify what makes you happy, what you want more of, and in contrast, what you want less of, you will be in a better position to seek out opportunities to be at the right place at the right time to catch them and be successful.

Personal benefits to expressive writing therapy include the following:

■ It can be done anytime and is flexible enough in that it can be done in most places where concentration can be maintained.

■ Again, this is a unique and highly personalized experience.
   - Some people like to have a scheduled approach to writing.
   - For example, having a reminder set on their phone or a reminder for a specific time in the day.
   - Just know what type of person that you are and when is a good time for you.
   - Some people like to wake up a couple of minutes early, before everyone in the house is awake, and do their writing.
   - Others prefer writing right before going to bed.
   - For some people, none of these work, and they like carrying a journal with them.
   - You can try different things to personalize this experience for you.
   - Try the reminder on your phone or try carrying a journal.
   - You are doing something different and allowing yourself to find what works for you.
   - Allow yourself to discover what your style is.
   - This may come as a surprise, as there may be aspects of your life that you are very regimented and planned, and when you are writing, you may benefit from or prefer a less scheduled approach.
   - When it comes to self-exploration, allow self-compassion to be your guide.

- It has the added advantage of improving expressivity as well as creativity.
- There are minimal to no additional costs once access to the writing prompts is obtained.
- It is easily implemented.
- A clinician can use the techniques and writing prompts and easily distribute them.
- This workbook is currently printed in English and there are plans to translate it to other languages, as expressive writing therapy can be done in one's native language.
- Because it is writing based, there are minimal to no risks or side effects, other than the time commitment.
- Individually, the exercises do not take much time from one's day and provide more benefit than detriment.
- Writing therapy is recommended at times as an alternate to or an adjuvant to clinical psychotherapy, with or without medication management.
  - It is important to remember that self-exploration and expressive writing is supplemental to different types of treatment.
  - You may require group therapy to experience not being alone or medication for a chemical imbalance.
  - Expressive writing is a different route that is in addition to these and not a replacement.
  - Due to the fragmentation and different parts that are affected by trauma, as it affects your body and belief systems differently, there are parts of you that are therefore treated and healed in various ways.
- This modality is Americans with Disabilities Act (ADA) friendly! It can be done easily by people with most physical disabilities, including speech or hearing or language impairments. Certainly, since ambulation isn't required for these exercises, it also mitigates the need to get into a car, travel, or find parking.
- By using this workbook, one can maintain physical distance during tele-mental health appointments.
  - This can be valuable in the setting of communicable diseases, such as respiratory illness, or in vulnerable patients, such as those immunocompromised or with an infection.
  - Similarly, this methodology is easy to use if the person has specific avoidant behaviors or personality traits. One can avoid the clinician or other patients in a clinic altogether.
- If one is doing these writing prompts and following the workbook on their own, it is also a perfect way to maintain anonymity, if so desired.

## Benefits: Financial

Knowledge is power. The building blocks of knowledge of the modality is contained in this book. As the reader becomes better at gathering information about themselves, they inherently add value to themselves and their surroundings.

Improving one's cognitive functioning, mood, and physical health all allow for an improvement in ability to make decisions going forward. We make over 35,000 decisions a day! As you gain insight and control over your emotional and physical responses, you improve your ability to make better decisions and obtain better results. Regardless of the domain, decisions at home, in relationships, or at work all benefit.

The mindfulness practice enhanced by expressive writing therapy allows for improved reflection, focus, and improves self-mastery.

Studies by the American Psychological Association report that currently over half the workforce feels stressed. In Chapter 7, Family, Children, and Resilience, we review the impact of prior traumas and effects in subsequent relationships and at work. The pandemic has exacerbated elements of stress and burnout. Industries such as insurance and banking groups were already seeing the significant return on investment in mental health in the workforce and are now seeing the increase in demand.

Mindfulness programs, including writing therapies, show a 200% return on investment when an improvement of focus, collaboration, and decreased stress can be established. Employee turnover reduces, and increased job satisfaction is reported.

Pre-pandemic, Aetna published that through mindfulness programs, they saw a 28% reduction in stress levels, 20% improvement in sleep quality, and 19% reduction in pain in participants of their program. Aetna saved $2,000 per employee in health savings per year after implementation of their mindfulness program. Aetna gained $3,000 per employee in productivity and calculated their return on investment as 11:1.

Numerous studies, books, and articles have documented the financial value of workplace mental health investments including promotion of health in the workplace. The article by Baxter et al. (2014) demonstrates a clear return on investment when workplace health promotion programs are put in place.

Other companies that have implemented mindfulness-based mental health program include:

- **Coors Brewing Company**: They reported a $6 to $1 return on investment.
- **Equitable Life Insurance Company**: Published positive findings.
- **Citigroup**: Reported improved performance and productivity.
- **Dow Chemical**: Reported improved resiliency, a 50% decrease in employee burnout, as well as a significant improvement in dietary choices. These dietary choices were sustained and improved over six months.
- **Jaguar Land Rover**: Demonstrated significant returns.
- **German Software Company SAP**: Reported a 200% return on investment.
- **Insurer Direct Line Group:** They registered a business growth to 31% in a year, reversing their declining trend.
- **UK Institute iOpener**: Reported a value of increasing happiness in the workplace. They demonstrated a 46% reduction in turnover, reduced cost of sick leave by 19%, spend 40% more on focused tasks, and felt energized 65% more often. Sick leaves were down six fewer days a year, and participants remained at their jobs twice as long.
- Certainly, Silicon Valley companies have incorporated mindfulness into their workforce programs. Apple, Google, Microsoft, Twitter, Salesforce, Facebook, and LinkedIn, to name a few, have increasingly adopted the value of mental health in the workforce.

An engineer at Google named Chade-Meng Tan developed a mindfulness curriculum named Search Inside Yourself that has been used in many companies. The awareness that he brought to the STEM industry regarding mental health is phenomenal, breaking the stigma and improving the quality of employee lives, while also demonstrating a financial return.

In great part due to the examples above, mental health and wellbeing is now a fundamental part of the criteria for awards that recognize organizations as being great places to work at. Cultures that promote mental health reap the benefits of a more engaged workforce, and in turn, greater creativity and productivity.

The research article by Mavranezouli et al. (2020) discusses the cost effectiveness of treatments for posttraumatic stress disorder. Included in this article were the financial benefits of therapies including EMDR (see Chapter 2, Identifying and Treating Trauma), self-help with support, psychoeducation, and trauma focused cognitive behavioral therapy. Notably, after the net monetary benefit of EMDR, the following three interventions were somatic/cognitive therapies, self-help with support, and psychoeducation. These were then followed by the use of medications and other forms of therapies.

Absenteeism, defined as a pattern of staying away from work or school, regardless of reason, decreases with focus on mental health. Presenteeism, a term gaining in popularity, is defined as the loss of productivity when a student or employee is not functioning at their fullest. Presenteeism is also decreased in organizations that implement healthy cultures.

The decrease in absenteeism and presenteeism then improves productivity. Employees have an increased collaboration on teams, are more engaged, and have improved communication. As productivity and concentration improves, the organization can calculate the specific value per employee salary as to the return on investment per person.

A healthier workforce spends less in health care utilization. Healthier employees or health care covered individuals result in decreased medical insurance claims and costs. It also results in reduced sick leave.

People with a history of trauma who are not ready or willing to start traditional forms of treatment often have high fail to keep rates (that is, they do not show up to their appointments) or complete dropout rates.

If the business setting is a clinical office and you are a clinician contemplating implementing expressive writing therapy into your practice, know that benefits incurred by the client result in reduced fail to keep rates. This allows for improved clinician productivity, improved quality of care, and measurable outcomes.

This modality also has a reduced patient dropout rate from this type of treatment. A large portion of those with a history of trauma who do start therapy find that they are overwhelmed by the treatment, exhausted by the flooding of memories, and are unable to handle or process them appropriately, and consequently, drop out of care as well.

Additional reported benefits of expressive writing include:

■ Increased patient satisfaction rates.
■ Higher reported bond with therapist.
■ Observed to be highly effective at treatment end point.
■ As discussed in earlier sections, this modality has a low intervention cost.
■ Similarly, expressive writing can be made readily available and fit around work/life schedules.

# Writing Prompt

Consider using the space below for notes on what caught your attention regarding the values of expressive writing therapy.

_____

_____

_____

_____

_____

_____

_____

_____

_____

_____

_____

_____

_____

_____

_____

_____

## Writing Prompt

What would your personalized expressive writing experience look like? For example, as you intentionally design your experience, how will you design when you write, set reminders, or carry a journal?

_____

_____

_____

_____

_____

_____

_____

_____

_____

_____

_____

_____

# Posttraumatic Growth

There is research suggesting positive aspects in an individual exposed to traumatic events. Posttraumatic growth is paradoxical in that it is defined as improved or better functioning of the person after traumatic exposure.

Studies suggest that some folks experience an improvement in resilience, ability to adapt, sense of independence, and appreciation having experienced some levels of trauma. Elements such as renewed sense of gratitude, decisions to improve on relationships, potentially spiritual changes, decisions to do things they were hesitant to do, or putting off have been observed.

Posttraumatic growth can be achieved as a natural result after the traumatic event, and also in treatment such as psychoeducation and therapy processing, as well as creative and narrative forms of writing therapies.

The spectrum from the stress induced benefits on the individual in the shorter term and having and/or developing resilience is important to be aware of when treating clients, as well as the ability to hold the concepts that stress reactions and growth can happen during the same time.

# Preparing: To Heal

Understand that trauma and history of trauma-related stress are not life sentences and that we are not our symptoms. Whether we have anxiety, or depression, or posttraumatic stress disorder, the symptoms do not identify who we are or how we act in the world, and these are things we can change.

Especially these days, when we are talking so much about identity, it is important to remember that for people who have been traumatized, there may be aspects in their lives that they are thriving in or other aspects that they are suffering in. It is important to acknowledge that the person suffering from trauma may, for example, also be extremely creative and write poems that may move others. Humans are extremely resilient, and it is important to look at individuals from the greater perspective. A traumatized person is someone who still cares for the elderly or drives the city bus. The symptoms are what needs to be focused on, and they can be worked on and changed; they aren't the whole entirety of the person.

There are two types of trauma work. There is the immediate aftermath of the crisis, the acute phase, which requires a very different form of therapy. When in a crisis, one cannot engage in deeper work. This is a time for crisis intervention.

A visual that Duygu shares with her clients is, for example, when you are running for your life, you won't stop at the porta potty, you'll just urinate all over yourself. You won't stop at a gas station to get a candy bar, you'll keep running. In crisis mode, one is unaware of their needs, emotions, or states of being.

When you are actually ready to do deep work, you need to have the ability to be able to dive deep in and go into things that have been avoided. You will visit emotions, states, and dynamics that you have not allowed yourself to visit because you were in survival mode.

By reading this far into the book, you have demonstrated a decision to learn more about the healing journey. Next, we will discuss how the healing occurs in connection with others.

# Preparing: Support Network

Make sure that you have some sort of emotional support network and have identified people you can rely on when needed. Think about your own current coping skills and those of the people you identified.

Part of trauma work is to make sure you and your therapist are able to design a support structure for you. Some therapists teach things like yoga, music, and pet therapy. Find a therapist that suits your needs. As you are identifying your coping skills and the ones you are looking to learn, make them clear. Self-care examples can include a warm bath if that helps you. See Chapter 4, Balan 3-2-1 Method, for detailed discussions on self-care.

Schedule therapy sessions, especially with trauma work, with time afterwards to digest and process. This is also a good transition time to allow for difficult feelings to arise and to understand that, before things get better, they may get worse for a while.

We all have busy lives; it is important that with trauma therapy that consistency is respected. In trauma, everything has a tendency to be out of one's control, which is why the experience of showing up to the same place and sitting with the same person at the same time of the week is extremely valuable. Try to be as regular and consistent as possible without skipping sessions. It is also important for the therapist to realize this and foster a setting for the client to allow for compassion.

Showing up consistently, both for the client and the clinician, will ensure the experience of continuity is gained. It is important to remember that if you want to skip a session, to ask yourself if there is something that you are avoiding, is there something that you don't want to talk about. Is there resistance? And to what?

The therapy session doesn't end when the fifty-minute session is over. The subconscious mind continues to dream, think, and heal. This is another reason why expressive writing is such a great complement to the work of talk therapy. With the questions and experiences that arise in the session, certain things begin to move around in your mind. Things you may have been unaware of come up to your awareness.

When the sessions are spread too far apart, the process of healing gets interrupted. The therapeutic process continues in your dreams and day-to-day actions. If the next time you go to see your therapist is too far apart, every time you meet again, you engage in re-bonding. In relational trauma therapy, you work on the bond and that gets healed with the therapist. If the bond gets broken with longer time in between sessions, it takes longer to re-form the bond, and the treatment itself may take longer.

In therapy, there may be interruptions. You may start and stop and have associated complicated feelings. When that starts to happen, you may have bursts of discomfort from the intrusive memories, feelings of being unsettled. This is a good time to assess readiness to explore further. This is when you start making connections and begin getting curious about these emotions. Reflect on why you are having these thoughts, why you cannot connect, why you quit at a certain level at a job, or why you cannot regulate emotions when these things happen.

When you are getting curious about these things, that is when you are ready to explore.

To make sure that you have a clearer understanding of what additional support networks you may need, discuss this with your clinician. We have also included a list of associations, organizations, hotlines, and helplines toward the end of this workbook.

# Writing Prompt

Consider using the space below to reflect on the following two-part prompt:

1. **Who do you have in your support network?**

_____

_____

_____

_____

_____

_____

_____

_____

_____

_____

_____

_____

2. **Reflect on their strengths and qualities important for you.**

_____

_____

_____

_____

_____

_____

_____

_____

_____

_____

_____

## Preparing: Community

As you work toward preparing your mind, body, and social connections, you must also take inventory of what is available to you in your community. Factors that positively influence an individual and the group collectively include common issues, cultural belonging, and religious cohesion. See Chapter 7, Family, Children, and Resilience, where we further discuss protective factors in detail.

The research article by Rubin et al. (2021) discusses the role of social cohesion that art and culture has on promoting community wellbeing. Take this into consideration as options that may work for you. During a time of a crisis, such as a pandemic, war or systemic racism, art, music, and culture have been shown to have positive benefits. They are associated with decreased stress, reduced sense of isolation, as well as reduction in the perception of the trauma itself.

A community that fosters the bringing of people together and allows for social interaction, by definition, reduces isolation. It enhances belongingness and increases resilience. Cohesive communities improve the individual's sense of self and promote improved physical health and sense of mental health and wellbeing.

## Writing Prompt

Consider using the space below to reflect on the following prompt:

**How do you connect with others?**

_____

_____

_____

_____

_____

_____

_____

_____

_____

_____

_____

_____

_____

_____

## Preparing: Healing Environment

Pacing is key. There is no rush to trauma therapy. One must create a place of trust, physically and mentally. Sometimes to get to the difficult story within, Duygu has worked with people for years before they uncovered their trauma. Allow for the healing to unfold at the appropriate pace and be open for feedback.

Consider and accept offerings from your therapist. Duygu may offer her client a Gestalt therapy empty chair technique, or narrative therapy, or expressive writing and guided imagery. These are all offerings, and there are many different ways to reach and to work through things.

If something does not feel right, let your clinician know. You can try something else or try it at a different time. Nothing is mandated. As you prepare the healing environment, the open space is what is critical.

For our clinician readers, make sure that at the end of a session, there is enough time to ground to life, to wrap up, and to make sure the client has resources and coping skills. Ensure that the client is oriented in the present. Consider using humor to orient, as appropriate.

When working with difficult memories, you may say: "In this moment you are with me, in that moment you were alone. This is not your life today."

Emphasize the client's current strengths, orient them to their present life, and emphasize that you are only taking them back to the moment of the trauma. Perhaps say: "We are just visiting" or "We are getting in the car to drive there, but we are not parking there, we are driving back and parking here."

As part of the foundational healing environment, Duygu will teach the technique of finding something in the room to anchor the client. Choose something that if things get too stressful, you will be anchored to. Try not to choose something that moves like a pet. This helps the client anchor to the space that they are in. Say things like: "Notice the chair, things around you, the arms on the arm rest" or "Notice your breath, notice where you are." Especially if the person experiences flashbacks, have them pick something that can bring them back to the present.

## Preparing: Sea Analogy

You can use this sea analogy for self-guided exploration or with your clinician.

Imagine you are by the ocean shore. The ocean is vast, with creatures underneath the water, an entire universe of life that you are oblivious to. You walk in the sand and find some seaweed; it has roots and goes all the way deep, and it is attached to many things. You look further along the roots, the seaweed is attached to a pack of Doritos chips, a dead fish, a cigarette butt, shells, and the decomposed foot of a seagull.

This is what happens. When you uncover things, slowly other nasty things that you are not ready to look at also get uncovered. We won't throw it back in the water. We put those things by the shore to look at when we are ready. Once we start diving into the old, crusted pain and the old dynamics, we will find more.

This is awareness building, but you have to be ready for it. So, it is OK if a story or a dynamic comes up, or a pain or emotion comes up that you are not ready to process. We frame it and say that we will visit it later. We give it a name or a headline and say we are going to visit it later.

Healing itself can evolve, it is important to honor what healing stage you are in. Sometimes a client will uncover a difficult memory, work through it, and just when they feel they are doing well, they will drop out of therapy. For their evolutionary process, that was what the client could handle. The client comes to a point and that needs to be honored. The client may need to rest there for a bit before going deeper. It is crucial for the therapist to know where the client is. You cannot push someone into a memory before the person is ready.

In therapy, sometimes we stop doing deep work and do more managerial things like coping skills and soothing strategies. Sometimes what seems like chit-chat deepens the relationship. To have the experience of someone who witnesses you in your pain is consistent and always shows up when they say they will is very healing.

As a patient or clinician, if you make a mistake like schedule someone incorrectly or miss an appointment entirely, create an environment where repair can occur and you can own your mistakes. Validate your feelings. With that aspect of the relationship, additional healing happens. Someone else showing curiosity of who you are, be with you, and giving space to your feeling is valuable. To achieve that, any method is valid. You may listen to a song together or show genuine curiosity in the client's art or work. Use your own style however you can, to establish trust, as a patient or clinician.

Physically, we know that working our muscles at the gym is through repetitive movement and physical action. You lift the dumbbell up and down and develop strength repeatedly over time. Training our brain is very similar. Neuroplasticity is a concept that what we do and think and pay attention to actually changes the very structure of our brain. As we train our brains through mindfulness, we are able to acquire skills to further strengthen the things we choose to reinforce.

## Conclusion

Through the methods described above, we allow for the refining of self-knowledge and self-mastery. This in turn allows for new, constructive mental habits and better interactions to take place.

This clinical textbook guides the user to recognize psychological trauma in our current climate and our current stressors. It entails an evidence-based approach to healing and recovery, utilizing the telling, retelling, and processing of the experiences.

Interactive treatment planning elements in this book include specific writing prompts that allow the clinician or individual user to formulate, creatively reframe, and document the concerns. This then allows for introspection, re-writing one's narrative, sharing with the treatment team, and a path to healing.

# Chapter 4

# Balan 3-2-1 Method

Write in recollection and amazement for yourself.

*— Jack Kerouac*

## Introduction

This section will describe the methodology that we have created from our experiences as well as years of clinical patient care. It has been designed to be easily used and remembered, and it will serve for the template that we use throughout the workbook.

As discussed previously regarding written expression of trauma, the values are inherent, from a clinical perspective as well as regarding sustained quality outcomes. The Balan 3-2-1 Method has been used and honed with clients, students, and colleagues and the current iteration is what we will be describing.

We are making the Balan 3-2-1 Method available for use by individuals and clinicians and ask that proper naming credit is given when using it.

The three sequentially decreasing numbers in the title indicate that the focus will be drawn toward the center of the individual during the practice of this method. We chose three easy prompts, numerically in reverse order to facilitate the use of this method.

Throughout this workbook, you will find several writing prompts and space provided to write, as well as reminders for the structure of the Balan 3-2-1 Methodology. This section will go deeper into each component and can be referred to later on during various writing exercises.

DOI: 10.4324/9781003323815-6

There are three parts to the method that work synergistically and are recommended to be done in the order described. The first part, three, reminds the clinician or individual of the three elements of setting the environment. The second part is to begin focusing on the writing prompt itself by diving deeper into two thoughts and two sentences in response to the primed clinical exercise. The last part, one, is to bring the exercise to a close with one affirmation, an intent. Each part will be expanded on below.

## Balan: Three-2-1

There are three elements to this first part, hence the number three:

- The Body
- The Setting
- The Breath

To begin, the intention of completing the writing prompt must be made. Everything starts with our body and our mind, and to get the first element in place, we must set the framework of initiating a writing prompt. Some of the writing exercises may be more emotionally challenging, depending on the individual.

## Balan: Three-2-1: The Body

We will be providing a number of ideas that have worked for our clients; feel free to use them as is or adopt them to however works best for you. To get the body and the mind ready, do something in the name of self-care that you might not feel like you normally would have done. Try to think of something that might be out of your ordinary routine, so that it is linked with this exercise.

The more these pleasant, self-care routines are linked to the writing prompt exercise, the more comfortable they will become. As that develops, the cathartic and emotionally restorative process of these writing prompts will become increasingly evident.

For example, take a full shower, do your makeup, or do your hair. The process of getting your body and mind ready can be decreased into smaller chunks as well. Perhaps wash your face with a cleanser that feels good or put on some lotion.

You might consider changing into a dress that you like or some comfortable clothes. The intention is of self-care toward your body. This can also be anything that prioritizes you, yourself. You could do some yoga; you could go out for a walk.

The main thing that we emphasize for this part is that it should be done with the intention of: "This is what I am doing for my body." Begin getting into the mindset of thinking that you are prioritizing and taking care of yourself.

Consider even repeating: "I am prioritizing taking care of myself."

For those of us responsible for taking care of others, either an adult, relative, or a child, think about creating a space for you to perform the self-care that is truly about yourself. Taking a quick shower while also giving your child a bath is not self-care. Taking a grocery store trip without having the children with you is not self-care. Similarly, taking a simple quick shower is not self-care. These are basic things that everyone does all the time.

Self-care is something like filling the bath and putting salts into it and sitting in it. Self-care can be taking a long shower with the intention to work on yourself. We will talk about intentionally setting up the environment in the next part.

## Writing Prompt

Consider using the space provided to take down notes of what self-care means to you and how you plan to incorporate prioritizing yourself in your routine.

_____

_____

_____

_____

_____

_____

_____

_____

_____

_____

_____

_____

_____

## Balan: Three-2-1: The Setting

Setting the environment in which the writing exercise will be completed will be an important next step. We began by discussing setting the internal environment with the body and mind, and we will end the section with the third part where we discuss the breath.

The external environment chosen must be a safe space. This can be your garden, a dedicated place in your home, or your room. It should be free from distractions. The time dedicated for writing should not also have a list of to-dos hanging over one's head. The environment should be free of technology distractions. Minimize the buzzing, dinging, or ringing of phones or other appliances.

Consider opening a window with the intention of letting negative thoughts that contaminate you out. Let the toxins out of the room and the house. Think about controlling the energy in the space, such as lighting a candle or incense. Choose whatever makes you feel good.

Putting the intention of letting go of anything that tangles you will allow your mind to process the exercise and for the healing to commence. Think about things that block or prevent you from living the life that you want and let those go. Think about the most recent anxieties on your mind and spend effort to let them go as you set the environment with intention.

To further get the body and mind ready, you may wish to have something nourishing. This can be food or drink for your body, or a scent or sound for your senses. In your environment, perhaps you can have a warm cup of your favorite tea or a glass of water with a slice of lemon in it.

As mentioned earlier, this should be something that feels like an extra step, like the self-care examples discussed above. If you are getting water, perhaps not have it be a basic plastic bottle of water. Put intention into getting a glass of water in your favorite cup. The extra step with intentionality is what we are reinforcing here.

The nourishment could come from a smoothie or warm tea. Think of meaning in color and material. It can be a yellow drink with pineapples in it, a tea with turmeric, or a green smoothie. The intention is that it is nourishing your body and heart and soul.

These do not have to be fancy or expensive, although they should be something that is not just a day-to-day thing we do when we are rushed. A glass of water can have intentionality with a slice of a lemon in it or fresh mint. Basic can be nourishing. Remember that we are setting new behaviors, and we want them to be done repeatedly so they become coupled with the experience and the healing from trauma.

As we are further discussing the environment, consider a dedicated space for this work. Possibly incorporate soothing music. Consider something according to your mood. If you are feeling sad, allow something that expresses the sadness. You are not trying to be happy, that is not the goal. The goal is to have the unexpressed emotion find expression. Music is a great tool for some people, although may not be for others. It could be a tune, a gong, or something to do with sound.

Since words have a limited capacity, talk therapy works only to a degree. As discussed in other sections of this book, writing works a bit better and taps into different parts of the brain. We are able to access emotions and memories in different ways including through the body, dance, breathing, and music. Sound accesses preverbal memories as well as experiences.

Build the area you plan to do these writing exercises into an altar. Whatever that word means to you, have it be the equivalent of a space dedicated to the work of healing. Some people like having pictures of those they love, a calming ocean, or a pleasant memory such as a family vacation. Set out books in your space that are inspiring. Books that remind you of your past and those that give you a window into your desired future.

Trinkets or small remembrances can anchor you. Think of symbols or shapes that provide you a sense of wholeness. The environment can be made to be felt sacred. Again, with all that the word sacred means to you as an individual. These components should be heartwarming, for example, a drawing that your daughter made for you.

Consider creating an altar, a tray of things that will remind you of things that you are grateful for in your life. Think of items that will connect you with people that you love or your pleasant memories. These can be things that target different sensations, like lavender or rosemary, other soothing scents, or a book that you love, or a seashell that you brought back from a vacation. Anything that will ground you to the experience of living, to nature, to people will work. Creating an altar that will affect different sense, like a piece of chocolate, or your favorite candy that may remind you of Halloween, a reminder of nourishment and loving connection are all things we encourage you to try.

The setting should be free of distractions. The meta-thought exercise is that you should not let any thought grip you. No to-do lists. Free your mind of distractions of the conversation you are having later on, what you are planning to wear for the fancy dinner, or how annoying your mother-in-law is. (Authors' note: the last example is purely imaginative and not from personal experience.)

Accept the thoughts that come to your consciousness, and like clouds, allow them to float on. The goal is also to not have them. The goal is to let them float away, none of them will have a grip on you. For example, the things you need to do before your next vacation is on your mind or you're having a stressful conversation at work later this week. Do not rush these thoughts away, yet also do not allow them to keep hold of you right now.

The thoughts and to-do list and conversation preparation will all still be there. When it is your time to do the writing exercise, remember and consider saying out loud or to yourself:

"Right now, is my time."

Mentally place the thoughts outside of the space. You can conceptualize that you are leaving the thoughts out of the house, or you can leave the thoughts in your shoes, or in the kitchen. Make it visual.

"They are not with me right now; they will still be there when I am done with this exercise."

As we clear our internal and external settings, another source of distraction is often technology. Do not have any screens or phones or buzzing or blinking devices around. At the same time, give yourself permission to realistically be distracted by an unexpected call or interruption. Do not be self-punishing, go back into your space, and allow yourself to resume the writing process where you left off.

You may have dependents; your child may ask you for something. Interruptions are a part of life. Say to yourself: "I was interrupted, now I am back and allow myself to resume." Anything that pulls on you, the affirmation that should follow is: "I am not letting this grip me."

"Right now, I am here for myself."

Over time, this phrase will become easier to say to yourself or aloud and more automatic. As you learn and train yourself to give yourself permission, you will embody the reality that you are deserving of self-care.

"I deserve to self-indulge."

When you start the practice described above, it may initially be more difficult and seem forced. Outside distractions may cause more interference and complexity in returning to the writing. As you circle your thoughts back to your body and breath, over time, the distractions will be more manageable and occur less and less.

Once what was defined as a distraction will come to feel more like a visitation. It won't be your baseline existence; it will be things that you can accept and control much easier. The more experience you have with this process, the more it will happen, just like anything else.

## Writing Prompt

Consider using the space provided to take down notes on how you envision a calm setting looks like for you and what you will work on to allow yourself an environment for healing.

_____

_____

_____

_____

_____

_____

_____

_____

_____

_____

_____

_____

# Balan: Three-2-1: The Breath

The final part of setting the internal and external environment to ensure an appropriate foundation to heal through the writing exercises is the conscious effort we recommend putting into your breathing. We will be covering several types of techniques. Try them and use the ones that work best for you.

Chapter 6, Brain–Body Connection, discusses the neurological pathways of trauma and response, and it discusses that the act of breathing in involves the parasympathetic nervous system. As you breathe in, your heartbeat slows down, and other elements of the parasympathetic nervous system activate. Essentially, think of the things that activate as those that are opposite to and incompatible with fight-or-flight mode.

Shallow, rapid breaths are a symptom of and can induce or worsen anxiety, panic, and stress. Deeper, controlled breathing elicits calm, reduces signs and symptoms of nervousness and worry, and allows for the mind and body to relax. The concept is that you want to regulate your breathing initially, so your body knows that you are safe.

For each of the following techniques, we recommend that when you are in your setting of choice, free of distraction, that you are comfortably sitting down. If your body and setting permits, consider sitting cross-legged. A chair with your legs comfortably hanging down is alternately fine. Ensure that you have a proper backrest, so that you are not slouched over or bending your neck or spine in a way that may cause strain or harm.

Try incorporating one or more of the following techniques as part of the Balan 3-2-1 Method. Consider doing the breathing exercise for two minutes each time to start with. As your body and mind becomes more comfortable with the technique, you can gradually increase the time by a minute or two.

# Breathing Technique 1

One type of breathing exercise is termed **diaphragmatic breathing**. To begin, place one hand on your belly and the other hand on your chest. Take a couple of moments and breaths to see how both hands feel as you inhale and exhale. Breathe in slowly and notice your lungs expand and your belly also expanding. When you exhale, slow the flow of air through your mouth by making it in the shape of a small "O."

Breathe in and out several times like this, each time focusing on expanding your belly and slowly exhaling. The method of focusing conscious thought and energy like this will yield significant positive outcomes. The value of having your hands on your belly and chest are to emphasize and reinforce the breath going toward your abdomen, in deeper, longer breaths. This is in contrast to shallow breathing that enters and exits quickly at the level of the chest, and this is associated with states of anxiety, stress, and fight-or-flight.

As we recommend with any behavioral change, practice makes permanent. If this is a breathing technique that you enjoy and find calms you better or more sustainably than the others, consider doing so for a couple of minutes longer each time you sit down for a writing exercise.

Not only is there no downside to this, but your mind will also incorporate deep breathing and associate it with reduction of stress, anxiety, and traumatic feelings.

## Writing Prompt

Consider using the space provided to take down notes on how you felt during and after trying the **diaphragmatic breathing** method.

_____

_____

_____

_____

_____

_____

_____

_____

_____

_____

_____

## Breathing Technique 2

A variation on diaphragmatic breathing described above is to do the same technique without holding your hand on your chest and belly. This version is somewhat more intentional and mindful than day-to-day automatic breathing that we do without thought, yet is easily doable in other places besides during the writing exercises. The term for this is **deep breathing**.

## Writing Prompt

Consider using the space provided to take down notes on how you felt during and after trying the **deep breathing** method.

_____

_____

_____

_____

_____

_____
_____
_____
_____
_____

## Breathing Technique 3

The second style we will introduce is an exercise that has the user breathe out like a lion. This technique, known as the **lion's breath**, also works on the muscles in the front and sides of the face. As the name suggests, you will imagine yourself as a lion sitting in your chair with your hands in your lap and body gently leaned forward.

Upon taking a deep breath in, think of the lion, open your mouth very wide, and stick out your tongue. When you exhale, do it with energy, and you may even make the sound "HAAAA" as you breathe out.

As you are spending a lot of energy forcefully breathing out, with your mouth wide open, you will want to rest and breathe at your normal pace and rhythm a couple of times. Then do the same type of breathing with your hands in your lap, chest leaning forward and forcefully breathe out with your mouth open.

## Writing Prompt

Consider using the space provided to take down notes on how you felt during and after trying the **lion's breath** method.

_____
_____
_____
_____
_____
_____
_____
_____
_____
_____
_____

## Breathing Technique 4

The next technique is called **mindful breathing** and involves a word that you can focus on. Some words we have used include love, peace, and calm. The word should elicit a sense of ease and release of tension.

As you settle into your comfortable environment, free of distraction, and are putting your intent to work on your self-care, begin the deep breathing method described above. After a couple of conscious deep breaths, begin to repeat the word that you chose over and over in your mind. As you inhale, repeat the word, and then when you exhale, repeat the word.

Similar to the repetition of one word, you can choose a short phrase for when you inhale and another one for when you exhale. Imagine that you are inhaling positive energy and exhaling out the tension and worry. When you inhale, consider saying something like: "In with the peace," and when you exhale, you may choose to say something like: "Out with the worry."

## Writing Prompt

Consider using the space provided to take down notes on how you felt during and after trying the **mindful breathing** method.

_____

_____

_____

_____

_____

_____

_____

_____

_____

_____

_____

_____

_____

## Breathing Technique 5

An appealing method of breathing that involves directing the airflow to each nostril separately is called **alternate nostril breathing**. As you will be placing your hand and fingers on your face, always consider general hygiene and wash your hands prior to this technique.

This method is sometimes associated with various yoga techniques, although we will describe it as simply as possible. Sitting in your comfortable setting, put your pointer finger and thumb to your nose in a way that if you pinched them, you would close both nostrils.

For the first part, only use your pointer finger to press on one nostril, stopping airflow from that nostril, and breathe in from the other side.

Keep that breath in and use your thumb to close off the other nostril, and let your pointer finger off your first nostril, and exhale from that side.

Continue to alternate between nostrils, closing one off as you breathe in from one and exhaling from the other.

## Writing Prompt

Consider using the space provided to take down notes on how you felt during and after trying the **alternate nostril breathing** method.

_____

_____

_____

_____

_____

_____

_____

_____

_____

_____

_____

_____

_____

_____

## Breathing Technique 6

An interesting technique that works wonders to reduce tension in the muscles of the face while decreasing anxiety is the **humming breath** method. As you are in your setting that has been mindfully organized to be as free of distraction and technology as possible, sit in a comfortable position.

This breath incorporates the deep breathing technique used earlier as well. Take a couple of deep breaths, and then on each exhale, with your mouth closed, begin to hum. You can choose to hum softly or loudly. As the vibrations spread throughout your mouth and throat and up your face and around your head, you will feel the muscle tension alleviate and your sense of calm increase.

## Writing Prompt

Consider using the space provided to take down notes on how you felt during and after trying the **humming breath** method.

_____

_____

_____

_____

_____

_____

_____

_____

_____

_____

_____

## Breathing Technique 7

The final method we use and teach is called **box breathing**. Imagine a box with all sides being the same length. Our breaths as we inhale and exhale will all be the same duration.

In your comfortable seating position, as you are preparing your intent to do the writing exercise, this form of breathing is simple to do with significant calming benefits.

To begin, we suggest inhaling for four seconds, and holding it in. This is where the box with equal sides comes in; hold your breath for four seconds. Then exhale for four seconds and stay still with the breath exhaled for another four seconds.

There is a rhythm to this that allows for the mind to spend energy on the breath and counting, and after several repetitions, will yield its positive outcomes of reduced anxiety, tension, and worry.

## Writing Prompt

Consider using the space provided to take down notes on how you felt during and after trying the **box breathing** method.

_____

_____

_____

_____

_____

_____

_____

_____

_____

_____

_____

_____

## Writing Prompt

Consider using the space provided to take down notes on what you felt overall doing these breathing techniques and which method you enjoyed the most.

_____

_____

_____

_____

_____

_____

_____

_____

_____

_____

_____

_____

_____

## Balan: 3-Two-1

The second portion of the 3-2-1 method is simply the number two to remind the individual of the written work ahead. Throughout this workbook, we provide writing prompts in relation to the section and topic covered.

Depending on the prompt, you will have space to write down your thoughts. The number two is to frame the exercise. It is purposefully a low number, so as not to overwhelm and to create boundaries within the scope of the process.

You can write two thoughts. They can be as simple as two sentences or two paragraphs. The purpose is to focus less on the quantity or content and more on the process, which should be free of external and internal distraction to focus and work toward healing.

This part and the next will comprise the writing exercise, and you can choose to keep them private, or share and incorporate into part of your therapeutic treatment planning with your clinician.

## Balan: 3-2-One

Lastly, we align our thoughts and conclude the writing exercise with the final element. The number one signifies the singular remaining piece, as well as the oneness of yourself. This can be one affirmation, one desired intent, one wish, or one outcome you would like to see following this journey.

Gratitude is frequently something we discuss with clients. There is room for gratitude in this section as well. You can think of substantial things that you are grateful for, as well as abstract things. You can be grateful for the connections you have.

Consider the inner qualities you have that you are grateful for. You may be grateful for the awakening and self-awareness journey you are taking, or the realization of or integration of your past.

You may be grateful for the healing work you are doing by reading this book, with your intention to connect with a loved one, or keep working with your therapist. You may be grateful for taking the time for self-nourishment and your courage to take on self-care.

Think about something that has to do with you and your own qualities. You may be grateful for your heart that is beating, your lungs that are breathing, and your muscles in your body that are moving. This gratitude directed inwards is very powerful and reframes how you center yourself and enhance your calm.

As the wise person that you are today, protecting and empowering your past hurt self, consider saying the following to yourself or out loud:

"I deserve connection."
"I won't make anything, or anyone give me permission to love or take care of myself."
"I will make sure that I have the safety for self-care."

What do you imagine for yourself? These thoughts could go in this part of the writing exercise. When using an affirmation, stay away from negative words. For example, don't say: "I don't want to get sick." Instead consider rephrasing it as. "I want to get healthy."

Always use positive words. Allow yourself to dream. Whenever you notice that you have a critical voice telling you something is "too much for you" or that you "don't deserve grandiose dreams," accept the thought and let it also float away. Allow yourself to think of and dream the most magnificent, magical thing ever.

You want to be a bestselling author? Write that down. You want to open a business or have a romantic relationship that sweeps you off your feet? Write that down. You want to buy that beautiful house? Not only write it down, imagine that all of these already happened.

Imagine your relationship in the future, that you are on the vacation of your dreams and are with the person you love, and are having dinner, and laughing in conversation. Visualize it. Make it real. If it is that you want a job or success in your career, or an award, visualize it. Write it down.

When the critical voice comes, tell the voice that it is just a dream and that you can dream as high and magnificently as possible. We are all in a dream. We are all dreamers. Everything is a dream.

Imagine what kind of qualities you want to possess. How do you want to feel? What inspires you? How are you nourished? How do you envision to be healthy and strong? Imagine all these things, visualize them. What would it be like if you were inspired? What would it be like if you had a job that energized you?

Sum these up in a sentence. Condense the thoughts. Say something like: "I deserve to have a job that is inspiring, energizing, fulfilling, gives me prosperity, and gives me connection."

The sentence does not have to be grammatically correct, may be a run on, or incomplete. Allow yourself to think and write.

Some final ideas that may help you get started may include:

"I am good enough the way that I am."

"My body is beautiful the way that it is."

"In this moment, I deserve everything only because I am alive."

"I am breathing, my heart is beating, and I deserve to live my life to the fullest."

"I am the way that I am in this moment, and in this moment, everything is the way it is supposed to be."

## Writing Prompt

Consider using the space provided to take down notes on some of the ideas you may have for an intention or wish for yourself.

_____

_____

_____

_____

_____

_____

_____

_____

_____

_____

_____

# BAL2AN

## Balan 3-2-1: Summary

In summary, the Balan 3-2-1 Method incorporates the following:

3. Three elements to set the stage for healing and align the mind and body for the healing power of the writing exercise: The Body, The Setting, and The Breath.

    We will provide prompts and space for the three elements to be written down. From exercise to exercise, these three elements may be different depending on location and individual need, or they may be consistent and similar. The purpose is to bring attention and mindfulness as to the intention of the process. There are no right or wrong ways to complete this exercise. You yourself will know what is working for you and your situation.

2. Secondly, there will be space for the two thoughts to be written down as per the writing prompt.

1. Lastly, there will be space for the one intention/affirmation to be documented.

There are no time limits for how long an exercise should take to be completed. Also, there is no rule on having to complete the entirety in one sitting. Life and responsibilities may get in the way. Alternately, you may want to think about the writing prompt and return when you feel more open, creative, and receptive to your thoughts and feelings.

> If you evade suffering, you also evade the chance of joy. Pleasure you may get, or pleasures, but you will not be fulfilled. You will not know what it is to come home.
>
> *– Ursula K. Le Guin*

## Analysis

The analysis of one's written exercises is valuable for a couple of reasons. The product serves as a memorial to the time and mind frame that it was written in. It can be reviewed on one's own or with a clinician. It can be analyzed shortly after having been written or later on.

We include elements that can be explored, discussed, and delved deeper into. These are suggestions and guidelines based on professional writing analyst's techniques. They do not convey rightness or wrongness, as the writing exercises are personal. They do, however, allow for the individual and clinician to have an additional layer of specificity with which to focus on the produced work.

As we review written text, we are looking at patterns and the meaning imbued to them by the author themselves. Look for consistency, ambiguity, contrast, or confusion.

Upon completion of writing, suggestions for exploration and discussion include the following:

- While the exercise isn't about being grammatically correct, take notice of errors, or inconsistencies in choice of spelling, abbreviations, and any shortcuts.
- Pay attention to the pronouns used. Specifically, use of first person, singular (I, me) versus plural (we, us) pronouns.
- Be alert to the usage of point of view. Did the author use the inside self, as opposed to seeing events happening as if watching someone else experiencing the events described? This is similar, although distinct enough from the next item below.
- In the written narrative, explore if the individual was involved as a central character that has some level of power/control over the events, or if the events simply happen to them. The locus of control is critical in the retelling and reframing of one's narrative. As mentioned above, we are looking for patterns, and we can use these observations in writing style and preferences as additional points to explore and uncover.
- Pay attention to the tenses used by the author. Was the text completed in past tense, present tense, or future tense? Were there consistency and continuity gaps in the way it was described?
- Regarding emotionality and tone of voice used, see if there are descriptors that can be used. For example, is the tone sterile or pedantic? Is it serious or aggressive? When does the tone shift to being childlike or shameful? The purpose is more to draw attention to and discuss whether choices are intentional, conscious, or otherwise. There are no points for grammar or correctness or accuracy, nothing is awarded or taken away. The value is the exercise itself, and any subsequent analysis is for the continued enhancement of mindfulness of the author and participant.
- When reading for deeper meaning and content, keep focused on resolved versus unresolved elements of the narrative.
- Similarly, the written style and content can point in the direction of processed and yet to be processed aspects of the trauma. Depending on the level of connection in therapy, these may be held onto for future exploration.
- Writing openly and creatively with intent and emotionality takes time for some, and it comes immediately naturally for others. Look at the amount of data and information provided versus emotional descriptors. It may feel less intrusive to discuss sterile data like a date or location of an event. Conversely, it may be more challenging to document the associated feeling with an event. These findings may be great opportunities for further exploration in the therapeutic environment.
- As we review the completed written exercises, a first pass of the text may not reveal details such as the adjectives used. Upon repeated examination, look for patterns in descriptors and meaning held to the words used.
- Which part of the individual do they spend more or less time on describing? Where is the attention focused on? Are there any feelings or emotions connected?
- Are there aspects that are reported as being forgotten or difficult to remember? How are forgotten or repressed memories dealt with in the narrative form? Is there evidence of desire to uncover and remember, or is it brushed over as not important?

- Regarding patterns and consistency, pay attention to the use of types of words such as positive words versus negative words. Is there a tendency to look at the world glass half full, or is there an inherent pessimism and sarcasm associated with the writing?
- Similarly, are there trauma specific words that the author uses versus those that they avoid? If there is description of the traumatic event, are there trigger words, and if so, what are they! How does the author circumvent uncomfortable terms and descriptors?
- Aesthetic and stylistically, especially if written by hand, look at penmanship, any alternating or changes in style, emphasis, and/or size of characters written.
- Look at the use of punctuation, use of capitals, and when and where these are chosen.
- Additionally look for any other markings on the page, doodles, arrows, and any potential meaning behind extemporaneous markings.

As discussed, no one finding will be significant on its own. Consistencies, themes, and patterns are the more valuable aspects to bring to the forefront.

If you are using this workbook in a self-guided manner, realize that there are no right or wrong ways to go about this work. Maintain your support network and congratulate yourself for working so hard to continue to better yourself!

## Writing Prompt

Within the framework of the Balan 3-2-1 Method, consider your response to the following:

**How do I know I am alive?**

3. With intention, set your internal and external environment.
   - **The body**: What mindfulness techniques are you choosing to allow your body to heal?

   _____

   _____

   _____

   _____

   - **The setting**: How are you intentionally influencing your setting?

   _____

   _____

   _____

   _____

   - **The breath**: Which breathing technique will you use as you prepare for this exercise?

   _____

   _____

   _____

   _____

2. What are your thoughts and feelings in response to the writing prompt above?

_____

_____

_____

_____

_____

_____

_____

_____

_____

_____

1. What is your one intent or affirmation in context of the writing prompt above?

_____

_____

_____

_____

## Writing Prompt

Within the framework of the Balan 3-2-1 Method, consider your response to the following:

**What areas would I like to heal?**

3. With intention, set your internal and external environment.
   - **The body:** What mindfulness techniques are you choosing to allow your body to heal?

_____

_____

_____

   - **The setting:** How are you intentionally influencing your setting?

_____

_____

_____

— **The breath**: Which breathing technique will you use as you prepare for this exercise?

_____

_____

_____

_____

_____

2. What are your thoughts and feelings in response to the writing prompt above?

_____

_____

_____

_____

_____

_____

_____

_____

_____

1. What is your one intent or affirmation in context of the writing prompt above?

_____

_____

_____

_____

_____

_____

_____

_____

_____

# DOOR TO OUR MIND 3

# Chapter 5

---

# Language of Mind and Body

---

> There is a brokenness out of which comes the unbroken, a shatteredness out of which blooms the unshatterable.

> – *Excerpt from* The Unbroken *by Rashani Rea*

## Language and Culture

Both of us have lived in different countries for years. We have gone to school in Germany, Turkey, and numerous states in America. We have studied in various languages and are fluent in several of them.

Throughout the spectrum of ages of our lives, from our formative early developmental stages before we met, to our years in Istanbul, Turkey where we began dating, to now living in the Bay Area in the United States, we have remained anthropologically curious and intellectually hungry. Basic survival, let alone thriving in a culture of different languages and religions, requires an open mindedness and level of sensitivity to messaging and nuance.

Different languages have different letters that don't exist in the other, some are written and read left to right, while others right to left. Some have pronouns indicating separate genders, others are all "they." Some languages have definite articles used before a noun for masculinity or femininity. Some have formal conjugation of words to denote age and respect.

The proper written structure of a language versus learning the common vernacular based on where you are living can also be dramatically different. Slang and curse words of the language are often picked up first, according to Yener, while Duygu focuses on interactive words and phrases early on.

We have reflected on when we realized we first started dreaming in the new language, as well as the numerous, often hilarious, mistakes Yener makes when communicating in a different language. Being able to ask for a basic need such as where the bathroom is, or how to purchase a food item are important beginner steps, although when living in a community, the ability to convey information and relating requires a deeper understanding. Body language such as how to present yourself in deference to someone older than you in certain cultures is important and a show of respect.

DOI: 10.4324/9781003323815-8

In context of the above discussion, we must also remember that our cultures are not things that restrict or necessarily bind us. We can reframe our perspectives and choices to aspects that enrich us. We have the freedom to choose what things of our culture we want to embrace, as well as the ones we want to let go of.

When we visit different cultures, whether through friendships or when we travel, we explore and understand that there are numerous different ways of living. We can choose the things and adopt things from cultures that are geographically far from us and make them ours. For example, these can be elements such as the way things are celebrated, or what is celebrated, or the role of the mother or father. There are so many definitions, it is important to remember that there are teachings and customs in cultures that may work for you and those that may not work for you at this time.

## Writing Prompt

Consider using the space below to reflect on the following two-part prompt:

1. **What aspects of your cultural background do you want to let go of?**

_____

_____

_____

_____

_____

_____

_____

_____

_____

_____

2. **What aspects of your cultural background do you value and want to embrace?**

_____

_____

_____

_____

_____

_____

_____

_____

_____

_____

_____

_____

## Writing Prompt

Consider using the space below to reflect on the following prompt:

**What customs, what cultures would you like to make yours?**

_____

_____

_____

_____

_____

_____

_____

_____

_____

_____

_____

_____

_____

_____

_____

_____

_____

_____

_____

_____

_____

_____

## Connecting

All these are examples of the first step of conveying a need and receiving basic responses in return. The deeper appreciation comes when one reflects on the mental models that language, cultures, political influences, and religions instill. Gross gestures mean different things in different communities, as do subtle facial mimics. Nodding the head up and down in one country means yes, while in another literally means no.

Being able to be in touch with one's emotions and convey that to another is challenging in one's mother tongue, let alone in a second or third language. Idioms and sayings in general are fascinatingly culturally specific, and the ones regarding expressing feelings, sensations, and emotions are very telling.

Sensations in the human body, regardless of language or ethnicity one is born into, are all uniform. We are all made of the same building blocks, have the same hormones and neurotransmitters sloshing around our bodies, see Chapter 6, Brain–Body Connection, and have the same skeletal and organ structures. The data from the muscles to the brain or from the nervous system to the intestines are always the same for every human. That is how we are.

What is different, therefore, is not the signal, rather the decoding and perception of the information. Certainly, people from different cultures will have different perceptions and explanations for bodily stimuli. People within the same culture, heritage, background often also interpret sensations differently. Even within the same person, over time, or after certain experiences, the same data can be thought of in a different light.

## Messaging

From a very young age, we are taught mental models and narratives by our caregivers. Some families rely on stories encapsulated by a religious context, while others refer to other cultural and societal information. Parents themselves are products of their upbringing and environment and impart what they think is appropriate onto their offspring.

At any given moment, we are bombarded with messaging, commercial marketing, trending latest social norms, influencers on social media as well as political propaganda. How does one learn to take in what is healthy and valuable while filtering out the rest? How does one detect external cues that are overtly malicious versus insidious over time?

Even at our peak performance, fully rested, well fed, and content in relationships, family, and career, humans are devastatingly ill equipped at sorting out appropriate healthy messaging from information designed to misinform, create addiction, or take advantage. Marketing works because it is designed to tap into the primal brain.

The addictive natures of video games and social media are designed by scientists that have studied the human mind and psychology to explicitly create these addictions. The developers openly admit this, and yet the use of social media and consumption of digital detritus is at an all-time high.

Basic connections between the visual stimuli and the emotions they elicit are fully taken advantage of to ensure the organization delivering the message wins. That is the business model. Just as deliberately as we are detailing the neuroanatomy and psychology behind certain processes for the betterment of the individual in this workbook, other clinicians have malevolently chosen to trade their pledge of "first do no harm" for a lucrative paycheck in manipulating masses, propagandizing, and deceiving.

It is now even more important that we have the ability to learn the language of mind and body. We must learn to appreciate the signals our physical organs are sending, and how our emotional and thinking selves are connecting.

## A New Mental Model

In the last three years, we have tragically seen a significant increase in the inability to focus and pay attention to our bodies and minds. Globally, humanity has been increasingly preoccupied, told what to do, how to act, how to think, what to be afraid of, what to avoid, what to buy, what to wear, how to interact, and how to avoid others.

Even in the before times, pre-pandemic, attention deficit disorders were on a dramatic rise for children, adolescents, and adults. Depressive disorders were increasing, as were anxiety disorders. Addictions in general and behavioral addictions such as social media and online gaming were already at pandemic proportions.

We were distracted and thought we were loving it. Each ding notification from an app needed to be reviewed and responded to immediately. Buried in our cell phones, we missed so much of day-to-day life. Yener had to teach our son that his phone with the brown leather case was his personal phone and the one with the black case was for work. Dad can occasionally be interrupted during usage of the brown cased phone. What a strange model for a child to grow up seeing everyone around them behind a glowing screen. There are now baby toy cell phones! We are teaching our children the culture we know.

With the advent of the global COVID pandemic, focus went to one topic, the virus, although the ability to focus at all went down the drain. Fear, panic, and terror all lead to compulsive checking of media, identical discussions on the news, and political messaging.

Humans flocked to toilet paper, the wrong type of mask, then the right type of mask, socially distanced, and then called it physical distancing. Not all heroes wore capes, and the lowest waged folks in supermarkets were deemed essential. Administrators enjoyed the future of the workplace being their homes, while mom and pop businesses closed, and new businesses based on testing, sanitizing, and general fear porn emerged.

We venerated the coordinated clapping of first responders and mocked anyone that had a different view than what we were told to have. We tried to have online drink dates and cursed when we couldn't angle the camera correctly during online board game nights. Tragically, we caught the virus, many people died, and we all mourned.

We celebrated the introduction of the vaccine, then some of the heroes that didn't wear capes were fired for choosing not to get the shot. Numerous political uprisings and movements occurred throughout the world, and yet we all saw the same images online on social media and seemingly all had similar conversations. Masses were told which protests were sanctioned and appropriate, while others were deemed terroristic and punished.

Pandemic pods burst when people realized they couldn't tolerate one another, then alcoholism increased when people realized they couldn't tolerate themselves. Working from home, schooling from home, and deferring all plans to this new normal, which was supposed to last only two weeks to flatten the curve, has lasted for years and years.

These all continue to result in dulling, numbing, brain fog, burnout, and eventually the abrogation of one's self-identity.

## Making Sense and Moving On

How did we allow this to happen? To ourselves? To our children? Have we all dissociated and are all now post-post traumatized?

Are there some individuals, cultures, or set of values people have that enabled resilience and protected them from this global whirlwind? The answer is yes.

What about those that have been sucked into the vortex and want to learn to re-write their narrative and take a better grasp on their mind and body? To elicit the answers to these, we suggest learning the language of yourself.

We never have a moment to just be. We cannot remember the last time we were even bored, especially after becoming parents who both work, and our son's extracurricular activities surpass the number of hours in a day. Duygu explains to our son that boredom leads to creativity, and it is a luxury to be bored. He hears his mother say this, although it is unclear if it can be attained.

How do we "just be." How can we bring on boredom, a peaceful calm that will lead to a creative, healthier mind?

As you read the next section, consider finding a quiet place, as free of distraction as possible. The discussion will be on the mind body connection and learning to hear your body. Once you are able to hear what your physical sensations are telling you, you will learn to listen. Understanding will come as you become more adept at listening and make connections that are aligned with how you want to feel.

You will learn to appreciate the reasons why you have been feeling the way you have, in part due to the connections that were made before and will learn to undo them, slowly. The habits of misinterpretation of bodily stimuli did not happen overnight, and the healing will similarly be gradual.

A mentor told Yener to think of these new connections as a new pathway in a garden. We have been going down one road on our bike for months and years. It is rote and well-traveled. It is the effortless instinctual path, although one that you want to change.

In order to do this, we must bike down a new route, which may be grassy and bumpy. The newly created trail won't be as smooth and easy to go down as the other one. Initially. Although with time and practice, it will become familiar and continued to be reinforced as the positive connection is solidified, and you are achieving your goals.

## Mind and Body

As a clinician, the therapist is trained to observe physical attributes, behavior patterns as well as gestures, gait, choices, and vocalizations made during session. As the individual, one may not be consciously aware one is sitting the way they are or making similar movements habitually. The therapist is also trained to notice changes, as the healing occurs. Depending on the modality of treatment, the clinician will point this out to reinforce healthy change as well as to educate for sustained gains.

The clinician is further trained to link these physical observations to internal states: Smiling as a sign of happiness and frowning as a sign of sadness or anger. Those are straightforward and relatively easy to detect.

The more subtler cues of shame or helplessness are nuanced and individual specific, requiring a foundational rapport and trust in the clinical setting. Once established, these valuable interpretations are shared, and reactions of the patient are observed and discussed.

Imagine this continued feedback loop between clinician and patient. And all these are separate from the content of what is being discussed! An experienced clinician will know how their patient is doing, even during silence. In fact, some of the silent times during a therapy session can be pregnant pauses, filled with information eager to be delivered.

The physical signs and signals within us are there to tell us what is going on. Our brain, organs, and muscles are in constant communication throughout the day and night. We have control over some of the processes in our body like lifting our hand or kicking a ball.

Some processes, however, are not in our conscious control, like digesting food or fighting off bacteria in our blood stream. Other processes occur without us having to think about them, such as breathing or blinking, although we can override them – to a degree – on command.

Quick, sneaky tip to mess up someone's golf game: just as your opponent is getting ready to swing the golf club, ask them if they inhale or exhale during the swing. This will switch their involuntary breathing pattern to the forefront of their mind. Mental focus and energy will be diverted to the breathing, and the swing of the golf club will suffer.

Do we smile because we are happy or are we happy because we smile? There have been numerous neurophysiological studies looking at the time the electrical impulse goes from the muscles in the face to the brain and the corresponding emotion they elicit.

Clinically, we know that even if you are not feeling specifically happy and tell yourself to smile, the resulting release of neurotransmitters, as well as your brain's interpretation of the smile as being associated with being happy, gets triggered.

Go ahead and try it right now. Smile.

How do you feel?

Similarly, the frown can elicit feelings of unhappiness or anger. These scientific discoveries and related findings are ridiculously complex yet yield such a simple trick to essentially hack one's mind body connection.

If you are working on these exercises by yourself or with a clinician, the attention is initially to be brought to the act of observation.

> Language alone protects us from the scariness of things with no names. Language alone is meditation.
>
> – *Toni Morrison*

## How Do You Feel?

For the range of emotions such as anxiety, anger, sadness, happiness, fear, shame, helplessness, where in your body do you feel them? Are there descriptive words such as feeling open, or closed, or passive that you would use?

The physical sensations and feelings in various parts of our body have different ways of being described. It is important to have words available to connect with the feeling. The label will allow for the sensation itself to be isolated. The cause or ways to remedy the feeling come later.

## Writing Prompt

In an effort to help start this journey, some examples of sensations by body part are included, consider adding ones that better describe your own experiences.

- The HEAD may feel:
  - Achy, dizzy, dull, floating, full, light, numb, sharp pain, spinning, throbbing, tight, tingly, tired, heavy, crowded, foggy
  - add your own: _____
- Our EYES can get:
  - Scratchy, tired, blurry, tearful, achy, tingly, out of focus, painful, swollen, itchy, dry
  - add your own: _____
- Our EARS sometimes are:
  - Tingly, ringing, warm, cold, muffled, painful, achy, clogged
  - add your own: _____
- The NOSE can feel:
  - Stuffy, runny, clogged, dry, itchy, sneezy, tingly, congested
  - add your own: _____
- Our MOUTH and TEETH may become:
  - Dry, achy, itchy, gagging, tingly, sensitive, painful, clenched, salivating
  - add your own: _____
- The NECK can be:
  - Stiff, painful, crooked, tight, tired
  - add your own: _____
- The THROAT may feel:
  - Dry, scratchy, tense, tender, achy, closing up, lump in throat, painful
  - add your own: _____
- The SHOULDERS can become:
  - Slouched, slumped, crooked, achy, tired, hunched
  - add your own: _____
- Our CHEST may feel:
  - Open, closed, painful, tight, tension, heavy-hearted, constricted
  - add your own: _____
- Our LUNGS can feel:
  - Cough feeling, painful shallow breaths, anxious rapid breaths, scratchy, itchy, dry, congested
  - add your own: _____
- The STOMACH and INTESTINES may feel:
  - Achy, grumbling, hungry, tense, protruding, gassy, empty, full, fluttery, anxious, need to go to the bathroom, painful, tender, nauseous
  - add your own: _____
- Our ARMS and LEGS sometimes feel:
  - Achy, sharp pain, dull pain, itchy, joint pain, tingly, jittery, cold, tired, heavy, numb
  - add your own: _____

## Interpreting

Now that we have started the path down observing and labeling sensations, we can begin to think of how we interpret them, followed by what we do to make ourselves feel a certain way in an effort to soothe, comfort, and heal.

We recommend the clinician to become comfortable with asking their client what the client thinks is going on with them. More often than not, the individual has been dealing with these sensations for a while, and regardless of adaptive or maladaptive interpretation, the client can tell you what they notice. That information can lead to marked clinical value.

Just as we are practicing the art of listening to the language of oneself, we also suggest that everyone learn to be a better listener in general. If you ask a question of your body, a friend, or a client, wait for the response. Genuinely wait for the answer and pay attention to what is being said. Then you can return with a follow-up response or statement. The act of asking a question and not listening is useless and takes away from the interaction. It is a wasted opportunity.

Practice this act of asking a question and waiting for the response. Do it when you ask your spouse "how are you?" or when you are looking in the mirror, anxiously trying to listen to what is happening in your mind.

We are working toward integrating where an emotion is felt for you specifically. Similar to putting a name and label to the physical sensation, it is important to identify the association between a mental state and its physical manifestation.

Just like we can cause ourselves to blink or suppress blinking for a bit, we can also learn to manage how we react to symptoms as we learn they are linked to an emotional state.

A tragically comic example is during the first several months of the global pandemic, Yener was certain he had the virus. During the day, he would check his throat, breathing, other psychosomatic symptoms, blood oxygenation, and temperature. Thankfully he remained physically at baseline, with no observable or measurable change in anatomy or vital signs. He was anxious and repeatedly would monitor himself.

On any given evening after work and completing his parenting duties, he would have a beer, and all of a sudden, all the symptoms he thought he had would dissipate. This happened on numerous evenings, and while continuing to practice all appropriate screening and health precautions, he recognized the clear link. Marital and clinical note: Duygu maintains she knew this connection much earlier than Yener realized it for himself.

Alcohol reduces anxiety while drinking, it is also a common substance of abuse as it is addicting, socially acceptable, and readily available. Once the person stops drinking, and as the body withdraws from alcohol, that process actually causes anxiety, depressed mood, and can make an anxiety, depressive disorder, or panic disorder even worse. Not to mention all the other psychological detriments of drinking such as blacking out, amnesia, decreased judgment, worsened impulse control, increased risk-taking behavior. The physical harmful effects of alcohol include blood pressure changes, effects on the heart, the stomach, intestines, brain, nervous system, sexual functioning, sleep cycle, known carcinogenicity, teratogenicity (harm for unborn baby), damage to baby while breastfeeding and many, many others.

Obviously, drinking is not a recommended solution for anything and always entails more harmful sequalae than good. Although it was during a moment of humorous clarity that he noted that it was more his anxiety than anything else.

If a delicious hazy IPA cured COVID, things would have been much simpler. It doesn't. But recognizing this experience pushed him further to work on his mind and body and reconnect the symptoms and causes.

## Writing Prompt

Practice thinking of your own emotional palette. What are the range of feelings you have experienced?

Think about the following as a starter set upon which you can add your own.

Put a check mark next to the emotions and feelings you have felt in your lifetime. Consider using the space by each word to add personal sensations and memories attached to these emotions, feelings, and states of being.

☐ Acceptance _____

☐ Adoration _____

☐ Aesthetic appreciation _____

☐ Affection _____

☐ Afraid _____

☐ Aggressive _____

☐ Agitated _____

☐ Agony _____

☐ Alarmed _____

☐ Alienated _____

☐ Amusement _____

☐ Anger _____

☐ Annoyed _____

☐ Anticipating _____

☐ Anxiety _____

☐ Arrogant _____

☐ Attraction _____

☐ Aversion _____

☐ Awe _____

☐ Awkwardness _____

☐ Baffled _____

☐ Bemused _____

☐ Better _____

☐ Bitter _____

☐ Boisterous _____

☐ Boredom _____

☐ Burned out _____

☐ Calm _____

☐ Caring _____

☐ Cheated _____

☐ Cheerful _____

☐ Comfortable _____

☐ Compassionate _____

☐ Confident _____

☐ Confusion _____

☐ Connected _____

☐ Content _____

☐ Coping _____

☐ Courageous _____

☐ Cowardly _____

☐ Craving _____

☐ Curious _____

☐ Cynicism

☐ Defeated

☐ Deflated

☐ Delighted

☐ Depression

☐ Desire

☐ Desperate

☐ Detached

☐ Determined

☐ Devastated

☐ Disappointment

☐ Discomfort

☐ Discouraged

☐ Disgusted

☐ Dislike

☐ Disoriented

☐ Disturbed

☐ Distracted

☐ Doubtful

☐ Eager

☐ Ecstasy

☐ Embarrassment

☐ Empathy

☐ Enjoyment

☐ Envy

☐ Euphoria

☐ Excitement

☐ Exhaustion

☐ Exposed

☐ Fascinated

☐ Fear

☐ Friendly

☐ Frustrated

☐ Fury

☐ Gaslit

☐ Glad

☐ Gloomy

☐ Gratitude

☐ Grief

☐ Grumpy

☐ Guilty

☐ Happiness

☐ Hatred

☐ Heart broken

☐ Heartache

☐ Helplessness

☐ Homesick

- [ ] Hopelessness _____
- [ ] Horny _____
- [ ] Horrified _____
- [ ] Hostile _____
- [ ] Humble _____
- [ ] Humiliated _____
- [ ] Hungry _____
- [ ] Hurt _____
- [ ] Impatient _____
- [ ] Indifferent _____
- [ ] Infuriated _____
- [ ] Insecure _____
- [ ] Insulted _____
- [ ] Interested _____
- [ ] Irritated _____
- [ ] Isolated _____
- [ ] Jealousy _____
- [ ] Joy _____
- [ ] Kind _____
- [ ] Lazy _____
- [ ] Limited _____
- [ ] Loathing _____
- [ ] Lonely _____
- [ ] Lost _____
- [ ] Love _____
- [ ] Loyal _____
- [ ] Lust _____
- [ ] Mad _____
- [ ] Meaningful _____
- [ ] Melancholy _____
- [ ] Miserable _____
- [ ] Modest _____
- [ ] Moody _____
- [ ] Morbid _____
- [ ] Mourning _____
- [ ] Nauseated _____
- [ ] Negative _____
- [ ] Neglect _____
- [ ] Nervous _____
- [ ] Nostalgic _____
- [ ] Numb _____
- [ ] Offended _____
- [ ] Optimistic _____
- [ ] Outrage _____
- [ ] Overstimulated _____
- [ ] Overwhelmed _____
- [ ] Pain _____

☐ Panic _____

☐ Paranoid _____

☐ Peaceful _____

☐ Perverse _____

☐ Pessimistic _____

☐ Pity _____

☐ Pleased _____

☐ Positive _____

☐ Pride _____

☐ Puzzled _____

☐ Questioning _____

☐ Rage _____

☐ Regret _____

☐ Relaxed _____

☐ Relief _____

☐ Reluctant _____

☐ Remorseful _____

☐ Resentful _____

☐ Revulsion _____

☐ Romantic _____

☐ Ruthless _____

☐ Sadness _____

☐ Safe _____

☐ Satiated _____

☐ Satisfied _____

☐ Secure _____

☐ Sedated _____

☐ Self-aware _____

☐ Self-caring _____

☐ Self-compassion _____

☐ Self-pity _____

☐ Self-respecting _____

☐ Serenity _____

☐ Sexual desire _____

☐ Shame _____

☐ Shocked _____

☐ Shy _____

☐ Smug _____

☐ Sorrow _____

☐ Stressed _____

☐ Stuck _____

☐ Suffering _____

☐ Surprised _____

☐ Suspicious _____

☐ Sympathy _____

☐ Tension _____

☐ Terrified _____

☐ Terror
☐ Thankful
☐ Thrilled
☐ Timid
☐ Tolerance
☐ Traumatized
☐ Troubled
☐ Trust
☐ Uncertainty
☐ Uncomfortable
☐ Undermined
☐ Unsettled
☐ Upset
☐ Vengeful
☐ Vicious
☐ Vulnerable
☐ Warm
☐ Weak
☐ Withdrawn
☐ Worried
☐ Wrath
☐ Yearning
☐ Zealous
☐ Zen

Consider using the space below to add any additional emotions, feelings, and states of being that are personal to you, and personal sensations and memories associated with them.

# Synthesizing

Now that we have spent time identifying parts of our body, how we feel in those parts, as well as naming the list of emotions, it is time to combine the information. Again, if you are doing this exercise alone, use the provided space to write your thoughts. You can return to them later for continued progress. If you are working with a clinician, this exercise will also work better if you write them down and share with your clinician as appropriate.

For the first part of the sentence, we will introduce the physical sensation, such as "tingling." Then indicate where in the body it is being felt, such as "around my mouth." Then think of what happens when you notice that physical sensation in that part of your body.

For example, tingling around one's mouth could be associated also with rapid breathing, blowing off carbon dioxide from the lungs, causing the actual sensation of tingling around the mouth and lips. A real physical sensation with real pathophysiology tied behind it.

Now, is the body anxious after which it breathes in and out rapidly before experiencing the sensation around the lips? Or, is it the other way around? Is the sensation around the mouth initially noticed by the conscious brain and then the person thinks it is associated with their prior anxiety and panic patterns, and thinks they therefore must be anxious?

Interesting chicken or the egg thought exercises, and we would recommend you take the time to do this. You can either read these passages now while reading this section or you can bookmark them and come back to them when you encounter the experiences and have time to notate them.

# Writing Prompt

Consider the following streamlined template to complete this exercise:

### Example 5.1

When I feel *waves of dull pain* (physical sensation) in my *gut and stomach* (body part), I feel *grief and sadness* (emotion/feeling/associated thoughts).

### Example 5.2

When I feel *tightness* (physical sensation) in my *right shoulder* (body part), I feel *anxious* (emotion/feeling/associated thoughts).

Personal experiences:

1. When I feel _____ (physical sensation),
   in my _____ (body part),
   I feel _____ (emotion/feeling/thoughts).

2. When I feel _____ (physical sensation),
   in my _____ (body part),
   I feel _____ (emotion/feeling/thoughts).

3. When I feel _____ (physical sensation),
   in my _____ (body part),
   I feel _____ (emotion/feeling/thoughts).

4. When I feel _____ (physical sensation),
   in my _____ (body part),
   I feel _____ (emotion/feeling/thoughts).

5. When I feel _____ (physical sensation),
   in my _____ (body part),
   I feel _____ (emotion/feeling/thoughts).

6. When I feel _____ (physical sensation),
   in my _____ (body part),
   I feel _____ (emotion/feeling/thoughts).

## Writing Prompt

Within the framework of the Balan 3-2-1 Method, consider your response to the following:

**If your pain dissolved in your sleep, what kind of a day would you wake up to?**

3. With intention, set your internal and external environment.
   - **The body**: What mindfulness techniques are you choosing to allow your body to heal?

   _____
   _____
   _____
   _____

   - **The setting**: How are you intentionally influencing your setting?

   _____
   _____
   _____
   _____

   - **The breath**: Which breathing technique will you use as you prepare for this exercise?

   _____
   _____
   _____
   _____

2. What are your thoughts and feelings in response to the writing prompt above?

   _____
   _____
   _____
   _____

1. What is your one intent or affirmation in context of the writing prompt above?

_____

_____

_____

_____

## Centering and Mindfulness

As we build upon what we have learned in this section, we now turn our attention to centering techniques and increased mindfulness.

While distracting oneself with errands or a mindless TV show or flooding the brain with chemicals such as alcohol or cannabis may temporarily push the feelings away, they are not being dealt with. In addition to therapy, day-to-day exercises can be used to help center and train oneself to productively overcome the unwanted, pathological feelings and thoughts.

The chapter that introduced the Balan 3-2-1 Method includes numerous breathing techniques. The biologic pathways with which these breathing exercises impact the mind are described in Chapter 6, Brain–Body Connection. A centralized component of preparing for mindfulness is the breath. We stimulate the systems involved with reducing the arousal state and allow for connection with the body.

Earlier in this chapter, we discussed bodily sensations. Begin incorporating the breathing techniques as you are aware of and identify the feelings in your body. Practice being with them. Practice tolerating them. Certainly, concerning or otherwise unrelenting discomfort should be consulted with your medical doctor. We are referring to the day-to-day sensations of existing.

## Mindfulness Exercise

A deceptively simple mindfulness method that we employ ourselves as well as with clients is a finger tapping exercise. To practice this method, follow our steps below:

- Look at your fingers on one hand. It doesn't matter which hand.
- Look at them and position your hand as if you are holding a ball upwards with the tips of your fingers.
- Begin by tapping your pointer finger with your thumb.
- Release and then tap your middle finger with your thumb.
- Release and then tap your ring finger with your thumb.
- Release and then tap your pinky finger with your thumb.
- You can repeat the steps in reverse from pinky to pointer and then back again, several times.
- Simply focus on each finger at a time. Maintain your line of sight on your fingers.
- As distractions come up, redirect your attention to your fingers and the rhythmic tapping of each finger in order.
- Notice and acknowledge thoughts and bodily sensations as they arise.
- Welcome these feelings and continue your mindful focus on your fingers as you tap each finger.

- Do this for thirty seconds initially. Not even a full minute. Then discontinue and resume your other activities.
- As you desire, you can increase the duration of each mindfulness session.
- Consider practicing this method when you find a time that you are already calm.
- Upon several days of practicing this, try doing it when at a slightly elevated level of intense emotions, such as mild anxiety.

As you do this, you are learning to be with these more intense feelings. You are generating feedback loops inherently and learning that you are able to tolerate sensations, survive them, and build a handy skill (pun intended) for future use.

## Gratitude

Gratitude is a concept most people feel they inherently understand yet find difficult to describe. It has been discussed in the literature as both an emotion as well as a cognitive process. It is connected to appreciation, although exists separately. It has its roots in empathy and being able to have the capability to understand the other.

Acknowledging and being thankful are elements of gratitude and are mechanisms with which to measure it. One's behaviors and attitude while interacting can show the levels of gratitude one has.

There are certainly selfish and calculated reasons that are reinforced, which is the cognitive aspect of willingness and choice to continue being grateful. It can also be viewed as a chess game, where the individual thinks of the steps forward, how their actions will affect the other, and how in turn they will be treated. There are also prosocial elements that provide a feedback loop of positivity through meaningful relationships.

The parts of the brain that are involved with gratitude are linked with the ability to interpret other people's intentions. While twin studies have shown a potential for genetic heritability of gratitude, the link between expression of oxytocin secretion that enhances connectedness with others, and gratitude is even more fascinating.

We can teach, model, and reinforce gratitude as parents to our children as well as in social encounters with our peers. There are proven benefits to one's physical and mental health, success in friendships, romantic relationships, school, on organized sports teams, as well as at work.

Emphasizing gratitude in writing exercises has also been shown in studies to provide the benefits outlined above.

Expressive writing that incorporates gratitude:

- Enhances well-being
- Increases optimism
- Improves mood
- Decreases symptoms of depression
- Decreases symptoms of anxiety
- Decreases negative thinking
- Promotes posttraumatic growth
- Improves cognitive processing
- Improves insight
- Increases patience

- Increases humility
- Allows one to rethink priorities
- Focuses the individual on plans going forward
- Improves productivity
- Improves creativity
- Decreases and buffers against burnout
- Improves relationships
- Improves conflict resolution skills
- Improves satisfaction with life
- Decreases materialism, a known barrier to gratitude
- Increases level of physical activity
- Improves sleep patterns
- Improves dietary choices and habits
- Increases adherence to prescribed medication regimen
- Decreases inflammation
- Decreases HbA1c, associated with blood sugar levels and diabetes
- Assists in treatment of substance use disorders

Similar to the way we outlined the values of expressive writing therapy earlier in this book, you will notice the parallels with gratitude in particular. There are no costs associated with thinking about and expressing gratitude. It takes nothing away from you and has the potential to provide so much. Of course, this should all continue to be in conjunction with any medical therapeutics prescribed by your clinician.

Of note, there are known barriers to gratitude, materialism being one mentioned earlier. The others include cynicism as well as narcissism. These make sense when you understand the pathway to gratitude as discussed above, and they can be buffered against once they are identified and done intentionally.

## Writing Example: Gratitude

Below is an article that Yener wrote in 2018.

## Gratitude, One Step at a Time

Our journey in life is directly affected by how we perceive our experiences and continue to move forward. This is my story of resilience and gratitude.

I was born with a rare, non-hereditary congenital defect: proximal femoral focal deficiency. My left hip bone was malformed, left leg shortened, and left foot severely deformed. My parents learned of this the moment I was born and were swept into a whirlwind of emotions and questions.

They were required to become educated on the condition, the prognosis, options that would affect my life, and most importantly, coping mechanisms. They learned skills required to raise a child that could not walk unassisted, to support, buffer and withstand the fears, and bullying, and to emotionally "normalize" the experience for me. Their mission suddenly became to ensure I grew up with the ability to cope and overcome this physical shortcoming.

My first step was delayed to eighteen months of age, when I received my first prosthetic leg. I remember requiring a new leg every year, as I grew in height, to minimize the imbalance in my hip and gait. At age 6, my parents elected to have my left foot amputated to allow for the prosthetic leg to accommodate a knee joint and bend like a "normal" leg.

Imagine trying to get used to a new pair of dress shoes, and multiply that by many times, in physical discomfort and pain, but also add the psychic reminder of true dependency, disability, and being "different." Neither the pain nor the emotional burden has been eliminated, and they likely never will.

It has been easier to cope with the physical prompts of pain – every step I take affects both of my legs, back, and neck. It has only been recently that I have been better able to come to terms with the emotional internalization.

My father would take me to the doctors' appointments – they were bittersweet times I had with him alone – hundreds of hours together over the years, to learn from him, to build my confidence, and to develop my sense of humor and resilience. The experiences were highlighted by the train rides to and from the doctors; the waiting in the prosthetist's fitting rooms; interactions with the treating teams; and secretly confiding my sadness, disappointment, and worries to him.

My father was a deeply funny man, quick and sharp of wit, unapologetic and acerbic at times, yet comforting. He would debrief my mother when we arrived home, and the warmth and love she provided helped solidify the realization that they were doing their best and loved me unconditionally.

As a child I knew I had an obvious difference – at home with my siblings, at school with friends – unable to participate fully in routine activities. My parents raised me telling me I am no different – that if I wanted to ride a skateboard or a bike, that I could – and they supported me when I tried. This notion of being the same, an equal, was empowering, and allayed impulses of inferiority and self-pity.

The proverb "fall down seven times, get up eight" was precisely how my parents coached me. I buckled, tripped, and fell many times, and still do. And I get up. I feel I have no other option, and I am grateful for what my father and mother have instilled in me.

Seven years ago, when my wife was pregnant with our first child, I had a true existential panic. I had no idea how my son would react to me not having a leg, walking differently, and even worse, not being able to play sports with him. I resorted to what I learned, that I would "normalize" it and that would be the only thing he knows. It was my wife that taught me to rejoice in my difference, to embrace my perceived weakness as a strength, and model my endurance and ability to overcome obstacles to our son.

That concept was foreign and in fact scary to me. I have always employed humor and have been outgoing with peers, but always private about my own journey. I felt as if being open and honest was overcompensating and perhaps even cheesy.

It has only been in the last year following the death of my father, that I have consciously decided to speak about my struggles, how I developed my sense of self, and my promise to be the best father I can be. My difference is my strength, and I try to develop that sense in my son. I am grateful for my wife, for her love and wisdom, and for my son, for pushing the boundaries of my emotional and physical abilities even further.

I am also grateful for my treating providers. Thanks to my experiences of how they bettered my life with their kindness and empathy because of which I chose to study medicine and care for my patients in a similar manner.

Humor has been a great defense mechanism for me, and gratitude has been my salve. Studies demonstrate the physical and psychological benefits of expressing gratitude – that it improves the balance of neurotransmitters that regulate mood and our sense of connection with others.

As an emergency room psychiatrist, I have cared for thousands of patients many a time on the worst day of their lives. My promise to my patients has always been to empathetically listen, provide hope in their wellness journey, and teach resilience. I am grateful for each and every one of my patients, past and future, for what they teach me, knowing that we are all on our own journeys, together.

> I am grateful for these human connections that have enabled me to get up when I fall, and that keep me going, one step at a time.
>
> *– Yener Balan (2018)*

## Writing Prompt

Within the framework of the Balan 3-2-1 Method, consider your response to the following:

**What qualities about yourself are you grateful for?**

3. With intention, set your internal and external environment.
   - **The body**: What mindfulness techniques are you choosing to allow your body to heal?

   _____

   _____

   _____

   _____

   - **The setting**: How are you intentionally influencing your setting?

   _____

   _____

   _____

   - **The breath**: Which breathing technique will you use as you prepare for this exercise?

   _____

   _____

   _____

   _____

2. What are your thoughts and feelings in response to the writing prompt above?

   _____

   _____

_____

_____

_____

_____

_____

_____

_____

_____

_____

_____

1. What is your one intent or affirmation in context of the writing prompt above?

_____

_____

_____

## Writing Prompt

Within the framework of the Balan 3-2-1 Method, consider your response to the following:

**What mistake have you made that ultimately lead to growth or healing?**

3. With intention, set your internal and external environment.
   - **The body**: What mindfulness techniques are you choosing to allow your body to heal?

_____

_____

_____

_____

   - **The setting**: How are you intentionally influencing your setting?

_____

_____

_____

_____

    — **The breath**: Which breathing technique will you use as you prepare for this exercise?

_____

_____

_____

_____

2. What are your thoughts and feelings in response to the writing prompt above?

_____

_____

_____

_____

_____

_____

_____

_____

_____

1. What is your one intent or affirmation in context of the writing prompt above?

_____

_____

_____

_____

## Chapter 6

# Brain–Body Connection

Reality exists in the human mind, and nowhere else.

*– George Orwell*

## Introduction

This chapter dives deeper into the specifics of the biological mechanisms that are integral to our understanding of trauma. We cover specific regions in the brain as well as connections among them.

We also review the current understanding of their intended function and what impact experiencing trauma has on them. This chapter also includes risks of acute physical trauma and medical consequences of traumatic stress.

## Limbic System

The limbic system provides the structures for memory and emotions including pleasure. Its functions include recalling events and details based on the emotional aspects of the experience as well as our intrinsic drives and motivation.

The main physiological components of the limbic system include the following:

- Thalamus
- Amygdala
- Hypothalamus
- Hippocampus

DOI: 10.4324/9781003323815-9

# Thalamus

The thalamus acts as a relay and connection hub of regions. Sensory fibers including those from vision, taste, hearing, and physical touch sensations connect and relay through the thalamus and go to their respective areas of the brain.

# Thalamus: Function

The thalamus receives information in the relay station described above, such as what we see, hear, taste, feel, and sends the information to the amygdala.

The thalamus also functions in concentrating. It helps sort between what you need to pay attention to and focus on. It conversely also allows you to filter out what you can ignore. This allows for learning.

States of being awake and alert are also functions of the thalamus, as are elements of consciousness and sleep states.

# Thalamus: Impact of Trauma

It is not uncommon for people with posttraumatic stress disorder to encode their traumatic memories as separate pieces of information. The thalamus, under healthy circumstances, acts as a relay station. One current understanding of the impact of trauma is that this function gets disrupted, and rather than the entirety of the event being remembered, the individual recalls discrete portions of the trauma. For example, the sights and what they saw will be a separate memory, and the sensations a separate one.

# Amygdala

The sensations described from the thalamus above are then processed through the amygdala. Perception of the received stimuli results in a behavioral and emotional response. For example, stimuli that suggest danger or a threat influence the individual's response, such as anxiety or fear and running away.

# Amygdala: Function

The majority of research currently available regarding the amygdala is based on fear and threat responses. There is an increasing amount of research done into the amygdala, and we are now uncovering roles that it plays in the intensity of emotions as well.

This workbook focuses on trauma and healing. We know that trauma and the associated fear responses are often very intense, and they trigger the pathways described. The role the amygdala plays in the intensity of negative as well as positive emotions is now better understood. There is literature to suggest that intense positive emotions are also processed, and that (classical) conditioning is developed via the amygdala as well.

Once the information is received by the amygdala, the signal is then sent to the cortex to realize what the threat is. For example, is the loud banging sound coming from outside the window a gunshot or fireworks?

If a threat is detected by the cortex via the amygdala, that information is sent to the hypothalamus and then to the pituitary gland, then the sympathetic nervous system, and then to the adrenal glands. The fight-or-flight response, described below, by the autonomic nervous system then goes into effect.

As introduced above, the amygdala also allows for the connection of the stimulus and a corresponding response. Classical conditioning occurs, where something that was not connected with a negative or intense response before becomes connected to an intense response when experienced together during the traumatic event. Associations are formed during events, such as a sight or sound that occurred during the traumatic event, and then can later on trigger a fear/threat response itself in the absence of a true threat.

## Amygdala: Impact of Trauma

For people who have posttraumatic stress disorder, the amygdala continues to act as if the threat, the traumatic event, was persistent, triggering the same pathways. The constant release of these stress hormones, including adrenaline and cortisol, leads to a chronic traumatized state, and it has significant negative impact on the body. See Chapter 3, Value of Treatment, where the physical and mental health impacts of traumatic stress are discussed.

People who have flashbacks will have similar fight-or-flight responses described below in the absence of an actual, physical, current threat.

## Hypothalamic Pituitary Adrenal (HPA) Axis

The pathways and function described above all are parts of the HPA axis. We know the HPA axis involves what the body and brain do when there is perception of a threat. Information goes from the hypothalamus to the pituitary gland and then the adrenal gland, resulting in the secretion of neurotransmitters and hormones.

As indicated in the name, the HPA axis is comprised of the following:

- Hypothalamus
- Pituitary gland
- Adrenal glands

## Hypothalamus

One can imagine the hypothalamus as the main control system for the autonomic nervous system described below. The hypothalamus receives information encoded with the emotions from the amygdala, and in response, triggers the secretion of neurotransmitters and hormones.

## Adrenal Glands

The adrenal glands are responsible for the secretion of norepinephrine, epinephrine (adrenaline), and cortisol. During normal functioning and response, adrenaline and cortisol are beneficial and can protect the individual. Examples include allowing the person to run away in face of a threat.

In pathological states, when the HPA axis is inappropriately stimulated, states of chronic stress and damage occur to the body and mind.

## Hippocampus

The hippocampus has three main functions: the formation of new memories, making long-term memories, and spatial memory.

1. **Formation of new memories**

   The hippocampus receives information from the senses, from the thalamus, and stores information into memories. Signals from the hippocampus also go to the anterior cingulate cortex and then to the prefrontal cortex.

   Information such as what happened, when it happened, and sensations including sight, smell, hearing, temperature, feeling are all received and processed by the hippocampus.

   For example, I wore a red bathing suit to the sunny beach, yesterday. These are explicit memories in that you need to spend conscious energy to recall them. They are autobiographical – I wore a red bathing suit at the beach – and semantic, which includes dates and other general knowledge.

2. **Making long-term memories**

   When we think about a memory, an event, repeatedly, including the details, there is a higher likelihood of it becoming encoded and consolidated as a long-term memory. From the example above, if I think of the things that happened, the sights, smells, and feelings associated with them, such as how warm it was on the sunny beach, my new red bathing suit, and how happy I was to finally go on vacation and be with my brother who I haven't seen in months, I am furthering the chance that it will be retained longer term.

   These connections, in turn, allow for our ability to remember things later on. Interestingly, when we remember an event that has high emotional intensity, the associated, encoded sensations, such as the feelings and things we saw or smelled or heard, are also brought to the forefront.

3. **Spatial memory**

   We have the ability to close our eyes and remember where we are, and for the most part, where things are in the room we are in. We can also imagine the grocery store we have been to numerous times and remember where the vegetable aisle is as opposed to the bread aisle. This spatial memory is a function that works in concert with the other functions described above.

## Hippocampus: Impact of Trauma

People with posttraumatic stress disorder are sometimes found to have distorted understanding of input from their surrounding environment. This can result in the misinterpreting of stimuli as threats and danger.

Studies have shown decreased hippocampal volume in individuals with history of abuse and traumatic stress. Clinically, this in turn has been associated with subsequent development of other psychiatric disorders including personality pathology.

## Prefrontal Cortex

The prefrontal cortex receives information from the above pathways and is the area that is responsible for making sense of things. The prefrontal cortex also helps plan and understand the signals received.

## Prefrontal Cortex: Function

Unlike the other areas of the brain discussed earlier, the prefrontal cortex adds a layer of processing and functions to prevent the person from displaying behaviors not compatible with their surroundings.

It allows for a conscious decision, a choice to be made, and to help regulate, as appropriate, the signals being sent throughout the brain and body that were initially activated by the amygdala.

## Prefrontal Cortex: Impact of Trauma

Studies have shown a reduction in volume of prefrontal cortex in individuals with history of abuse and posttraumatic stress disorder. This in turn impacts the ability to process information and react accordingly.

## Autonomic Nervous System

In medical school, we were taught the mnemonic the "four F's" to remember the functions of the Autonomic Nervous System: Fight, Flight, Fear and F%$! (a not nice way to say "make love").

The ANS is involved with blood circulation, muscle tone, endocrine activity, cognitive arousal, hormonal activity, and emotions.

There are two parts of the autonomic nervous system, the sympathetic and the parasympathetic nervous systems.

## ANS: Sympathetic Nervous System

The sympathetic nervous system is responsible for the fight-or-flight aspect of response. This arousal occurs before we are even aware of what we are doing or how we are responding to the perceived threats, i.e., the signals from the amygdala described earlier.

When the sympathetic nervous system is activated, the following bodily changes occur:

- Metabolism elevates
- Heart rate elevates
- Alertness increases
- Breathing becomes faster and more shallow, sending more oxygen to the brain
- Pupils dilate
- Sweating occurs
- The stress hormone cortisol releases
- Blood vessels to the gastrointestinal tract constrict, thereby decreasing gastrointestinal movement. This conserves unnecessary activity and use of energy like digestion to preserve for places that need the energy the most to run away or engage in protecting the body
- Rise in blood sugar to help with increasing energy for fight or flight
- Blood vessels to skin constrict
- Blood vessels to muscles dilate, providing more blood to be able to move around, run away, or fight the threat

These responses throughout the body go back to their normal baseline after the perceived threat is no longer present. In other words, the heart rate goes back to normal, breathing rate goes back to normal, etc.

In response to a stressor over time, the body may fail to recover to normal, resulting in a chronically activated HPA axis response.

## ANS: Parasympathetic Nervous System

Counter to the sympathetic nervous system, the parasympathetic nervous system can be remembered by the rhyme "Rest and Digest."

The parasympathetic nervous system serves to save energy, slows many bodily functions down, and allows for the following:

- Decreases heart rate
- Decreases breathing rate to baseline
- Decreases metabolism
- Relaxes the muscles
- Constricts the pupils
- Increases digestion and movement of the gastrointestinal tract
- Acts on nerves and blood vessels responsible for penile erection

## Serotonin

Serotonin is a neurotransmitter that influences:

- Emotions such as
  - Mood
  - Anxiety
  - Fear
- The encoding of memories that have an emotional component to them
- Sleep disturbances
- Appetite
- Aggressive behaviors including violence directed outwards
- Violence directed inwards including suicidality and self-injurious behaviors
- Impulsive behaviors
- Personality pathology such as borderline personality disorder

Studies indicate that serotonin has an inhibitory effect on the effect of norepinephrine. This means that serotonin decreases the effect of norepinephrine. In other words, serotonin has the effect of calming fear, decreasing arousal states, such as hypervigilance, as well as the impact of intrusive traumatic memories.

While the umbrella review by Moncrieff et al. (2022) demonstrated that there was no support for the link between low serotonin and depression, the current FDA approved treatment for posttraumatic stress disorder is the serotonergic medications.

It is hypothesized that serotonin plays a key role in the development of and impact of the symptomatology of posttraumatic stress disorder. Depressive disorders, anxiety disorders, personality pathology suicidality are all found to be comorbid in patients with posttraumatic stress disorder. See Chapter 2, Identifying and Treating Trauma, for types of treatment available for more information on serotonergic pharmacologic options available.

## Acute Physical Trauma

A recent study by Joseph et al. (2021) suggests that a quarter of hospitalized trauma patients screened met criteria for posttraumatic stress disorder. They also report that independent risk factors for posttraumatic stress disorder include younger age, being a victim of a crime, and being struck by a motor vehicle.

Other studies indicate that there is up to a 50% prevalence in patients experiencing medical trauma. This is interesting and concerning in that trauma is typically unexpected, sudden, frightful, and stressful.

The event followed by going to the hospital in an ambulance, the sights, sounds, and motions all in the frightened state exacerbate the experiencing and coupling of the event and the body's response. The fact that half of these victims develop posttraumatic stress disorder needs to be common knowledge on every medical trauma treatment team.

Studies in children show a slightly lower rate of developing traumatic stress at around 30% in the setting of acute medical trauma resulting in need for medical and/or surgical intervention.

We are all too familiar with the significant emotions, including terror, brought on by medical interventions. Over the past several years, we have been introduced to new forms of medical stress, testing, stigma, and forced avoidance. See Chapter 10, Covid, Disasters, and Loss, specifically discussing the impact of the pandemic on our collective lives.

Those with motor vehicle accidents and other types of orthopedic injuries are also at elevated risk. The study of veterans by Franklin et al. (2018), requiring medical and surgical intervention demonstrates they are at a clear risk for developing serious psychological symptoms. The conclusion is that acute physical trauma victims may benefit from screening, proper early identification, as well as appropriate clinical intervention.

Patients of trauma and those receiving medical interventions such as surgery or intensive care unit stays are the primary focus of this section, although we must note the impact of this experience on the partners, close friends, and spouses. The literature suggests "we" language to remind the treating team and the patients that the experience, the disease, and the healing journey are shared. The mental health of the close family and caregivers must also be taken into consideration.

We must emphasize that clinically, we know that the majority of trauma survivors, around two-thirds, do recover psychologically without psychiatric intervention. This information, therefore, makes it clear that appropriate screening and identification is key prior to administering an intervention.

## Medical Consequences

Studies show that stress and impaired mental health can impact the healing of wounds, as well as immunity in general. Increased levels of stress can result in inflammatory states which are itself linked with metabolic and cardiac illnesses.

Associated medical comorbidities with posttraumatic stress disorder include:

- Heightened perception of pain
- Increased use of healthcare
- Increased use of medications
- More chronic illnesses
- Poor physical function
- Delayed return to work
- Low patient satisfaction

Compare this list to the impact of treating trauma discussed previously in this book and note the compounding impact of how intertwined the mind and body is.

## Writing Prompt

Consider using the space below to reflect on the following two-part prompt:

1. **Do you remember an experience when you had a medical or physical trauma? If so, write about this trauma as if it was a news report. Just tell the facts of the event.**

_____

_____

_____

_____

_____

_____

_____

_____

_____

_____

_____

_____

_____

2. **Now, describe the emotional and sensational elements of the event, along with any other memories and details attached to it.**

_____

_____

_____

_____

_____

_____

_____

_____

_____

_____

_____

_____

_____

# WINDOW TO OUR SOUL

## 4

# Chapter 7

# Family, Children, and Resilience

The wound is the place where the light enters you.

*– Rumi*

## Introduction

This section is dedicated to reviewing factors within a family setting, the development of relationships, and bonding of the child with the adult. We also explore how the family system interacts and the impacts of traumatic experiences.

We will be reviewing factors of resiliency as they relate to the individual, the nuclear family unit as well as the community in general. Aspects of traumatic experiences will be examined, and the concept of adverse childhood experiences (ACEs) will be discussed.

The long-term impact of being witness to or experiencing singular or ongoing, prolonged trauma will be discussed. We also provide a deep dive into mitigating and protective factors as well as writing prompts and exercises that can be conducted on an individual basis, or with the family as a unit.

As discussed in other sections of this workbook, psychological as well as physiological reactions to traumatic events and their aftereffects vary by individual and can vary overtime within the same individual. This section also looks at the family, exploring components of protective factors of resilience within the family system.

This section can be used on its own and also in conjunction with a treating provider toward a clinical treatment plan.

DOI: 10.4324/9781003323815-11

# Creating Connections: Attachment Theory

It is important to understand the concept of attachment theory and how personal identity is developed. The ability and desire for humans as soon as they're born to develop connections with others is innate.

The mother's or caregiver's desire to connect with their newborn is also instinctual and rewarded through pleasant reactions caused by neurotransmitters when that contact occurs. For the most part, when the child is able to understand that when they call out to their mother, she consistently and reliably reacts and responds appropriately, the child develops a pattern of relationships that are otherwise healthy.

There is an inborn desire to be close to warmth and love. All throughout our lives we continue to seek positive reinforcement in the form of safe and secure boundaries. Evolutionarily, on the part of the newborn, the value of this is self-evident. A decrease in risk, physical and emotional safety as well as a source of food is critical to the ongoing survival of the species.

Our sense of identity, who we are, the concept of ourselves develops during these connections and interactions with others. Patterns of relationships we experience early on in childhood form the lens through which we view future relationships.

Another way of saying this is the way attachment is formed creates the foundation upon which our ability to navigate social interactions and manage relationships is built.

Now imagine disturbances in the patterns of the child's ability to call out for help, resulting in confusion and the inability of the mother to attend to the child. Alternately, imagine the child being able to call out for help during a time of distress or need for comfort and the mother's inability to receive that information appropriately due to their own mental illness or their own distractions such as substance use or general absence.

Deviance from the norm, while may cause short-term distress, typically if short-lasting, and mild in intensity, typically does not result in long-lasting attachment injury. A pattern of consistent attachment behaviors, conversely a pattern of inconsistent or pathological attachment behaviors on the part of the caregiver, does however result in long-lasting sequelae.

The prolonged separation or abrupt, unplanned, separation of the caregiver and child, as well as the loss of a caregiver also result in emotional detachment of the child. After a crisis, both the mother's as well as the child's sense of security may be severely affected, resulting in difficulty receiving or reciprocating emotional signals.

The emotional distress after separation and how the individual feels searching for their attachment figure unsuccessfully are of particular importance to note, especially for one that has a pathological pattern of attachment.

Children learn about the world from their caregiver's facial expressions, gaze and eye contact. The messages about love, relationships, and safety are transferred through the gaze. That is why you will see an infant or child always making eye contact with their caregiver. And they will smile. If they smile and the caregiver smiles back, it soothes the kid. If the expression of the mother is angry, the child will get dysregulated and the message will be that the world is unsafe, that they are not safe or loved.

When the facial expression is neutral, there isn't a way that we can understand that we are loved or that we can trust the person. The flat affect or neutral, unresponsive affect, such as those found in depressed caregivers, can be deleterious. Flat affect is automatically dysregulating; you see that in the child, they get unsettled, frazzled, and dismayed. The message of "you can trust me," "I will keep you safe," or "I love you" can never be conveyed with a neutral affect.

# Volatility Early On: Adverse Childhood Experiences (ACEs)

The Centers for Disease Control and Prevention (CDC) conducted one of the largest investigations resulting in a pivotal study that ended in 1997, in partnership with Kaiser Permanente, a major healthcare organization, to study childhood abuse, neglect, and subsequent consequences on later development.

Interestingly, the origins of this study were when Dr. Felitti, Chief of Preventive Medicine at Kaiser Permanente in Southern California, was working with patients in his obesity clinic. He was working to figure out why more than half of his patients were leaving the program just as they had begun to lose weight. While this weight loss was part of their treatment plan and their desired outcome, patients were dropping out of care.

Numerous clinical interviews and astute observations lead to what is now referred to as the ACEs Study. The findings have changed the way we care for people, understand developmental sequelae of ACEs, and need for focus on prevention and appropriate clinical interventions.

The study by the CDC and Kaiser Permanente was groundbreaking. They discovered that childhood trauma leads to adult onset of chronic diseases and depression as well as other mental health issues, violence, being a victim of violence as well as financial and social problems.

The identification of the ACEs allowed for researchers and clinicians the ability to understand and impact millions of people going forward. The impact has resulted in changes in practice patterns from the pediatrician's office to human resources in the workplace environment.

ACEs that were measured included physical, sexual, and verbal abuses.

- Physical abuse is defined as a parent or adult pushing, grabbing, or hitting in a way that injury was sustained.
- Emotional abuse is defined as a parent or adult insulting or acting in a way that made the individual fear for their safety.
- Sexual abuse is defined as a parent or adult making physical contact in a sexual way or trying to have intercourse with the person.

Neglect in the form of physical or emotional neglect was also measured.

- Neglect is defined as being never or rarely helped or loved, lacking support for emotional or physical needs such as food insecurity, not attending medical appointments, having unstable housing or clothing.

Other questions were related to exposure to family members with mental illness, a family member that attempted suicide, exposure to family members with substance use issues, and exposure to crime.

Additional traumatic experiences included having witnessed intimate partner violence, exposure to firearm related violence, witnessing a sibling being abused, and witnessing violence outside of the home.

Experiences such as loss and separation included having suffered a parental loss or separation such as divorce, imprisonment, or deportation. Other environmental factors such as having lived in a war zone or an unsafe neighborhood were also added onto the list of adverse experiences.

Gun violence and stress related to firearms also have a significant effect on ACEs in communities.

# ACEs: Impact on the Individual and Society

The extended and prolonged presence of stress and these ACEs can result in what is termed as toxic stress. The culmination of these then impact the development of the individual's body, brain, and immune system.

In addition to the mental and behavioral impact of ACEs, follow-up studies have revealed that ACEs also lead to the adult onset of chronic diseases.

As the field of researching ACEs grew, we have come to learn that two-thirds of adults have experienced one or more types of ACEs. Even more disconcerting is that over 10% of adults have experienced four or more ACEs.

Of those, over 80% have experienced two or more types of ACEs. In other words, ACEs usually do not happen in isolation.

ACEs do not discriminate, and they occur across demographics, races, and socioeconomic status. No one subset of the population is immune.

Lastly, the more ACEs one experiences, the higher the risks of mental, physical as well as social problems as an adult are.

Functional imaging and brain scans of individuals who have experienced ACEs reveal diminished activity as well as temporal lobe dysfunction. The temporal lobes regulate emotions (see Chapter 6, Brain–Body Connection) and receive input from the senses.

The impact of our experiences come from where we live and what we witness, and oftentimes, we can outweigh inborn resilience and our capacity for healing.

The individual that grows in context of ACEs, resulting in diminished temporal lobe functioning, will suffer from cognitive as well as emotional difficulties. The damage to the system causes much of the burden of our chronic disease, mental illness, and most violence turned out-wards that we see in our societies.

Important, and while seemingly unrelated, long-lasting impacts of adverse experiences include increased rates of physical trauma (such as car accidents), brain injury, fractures, and burns.

Unsafe sex, unintended pregnancies, as well as complications during pregnancy and delivery such as the demise of the unborn child are also increased. Sexually transmitted infections such as HIV and others have also been found at increased rates in those with ACEs.

Childhood sexual abuse is very much linked with unsafe sexual behaviors. This pattern of not being able to protect their boundaries with the same reason that no one taught them this, and they don't have the belief that their body is worth protecting. This is further reason for why survivors of incest experience rape later on in life. Sexually transmitted infections as a result of promiscuous and unsafe sex patterns are experienced in these populations. Also associated with this constellation of issues is alcohol and substance misuse.

Chronic illnesses such as heart disease, diabetes, autoimmune disorders, and cancer have been linked to ACEs. As mentioned earlier, the higher the number of ACEs, the increased likelihood of onset of serious chronic medical conditions and also the need for more drug prescriptions.

Subsequent mental health and substance use issues have also been linked, such as an increased incidence of depression, anxiety, posttraumatic stress disorder, self-injurious behaviors, suicide, as well as alcohol and other drug use.

ACEs also impact longevity in general. Studies suggest that those with significant ACEs-related morbidity die up to twenty years sooner than their counterparts with less or no ACEs!

## ACEs: Emotional Abuse

Another aspect that needs to be addressed is the impact of emotional abuse. At times, the impact of this type of abuse can be more severe than other types. It has the propensity to be recognized less and taken action against at a lower rate. An unpredictable parent who in one moment can be loving, kind, and playful and the next moment be aggressive and say mean things can be confusing and damaging for the child.

Sometimes the threat of physical abuse is used, like "you will get a spanking," or sometimes the threat of abandonment, such as "I will give you away," or "I'm leaving," or even "I will give you to an orphanage." It is important to remember that the threat itself has the same effect of the actual act.

When the kid envisions the mother leaving him without protection, abandoning him alone, by himself, that is the same as it actually happening. The body reacts to it in that way because brain visualizes it, he experiences the helplessness and fear as if it were occurring. The brain doesn't know if something is imagined or something is real. This is why therapy visualization, and psychodrama work, as well as expressive writing. They work in similar mechanisms.

These verbal, emotionally abusive threats that are viewed by many as harmless and used thoughtlessly can have severe long-term consequences and cause dysregulation, poor coping mechanisms, insecurity, and injury in the ability to form bonds, trust, and attachments.

A parent that says discouraging things like "you can't do this," or name calling or things that are disguised under teasing that are considered acceptable but are actually hurtful, can have long-lasting impacts. These experiences can damage the child's ability to use his voice to protect himself. The perception of the young girl, for example, and their boundaries are also affected. This type of ACE is way too common. It happens in school settings from a teacher or in a sport setting from a coach, where the children may get discouraged and belittled, or they may even be called names.

Circumstances such as the child being subjected to fulfill the parent's emotional needs, feeling responsible for the parent's anger, for the parent's sadness or additions, or exhaustion from work are all destructive. The child internalizes the feelings of guilt, or worthlessness, or the concept of "I am a burden." These are all aspects of ACEs that do not get much attention. Even things like comparing siblings to one another or preferring one sibling versus another are detrimental in excess.

## Case Example: The Other Daughter

This is an example of twin girls, one who looked exactly like the mother and the other who did not. From the time of birth, the mother took the child that looked like her into her bed, breast fed her more often, and even smiled at her more often. The other child who didn't look like the mother progressively became distressed and began to act out.

In contrast, the one that looked like the mother worked to please the mother more, adopted the mother's interests, and they formed a bond that excluded the other twin. As she was excluded, she acted out in ways that caused even more exclusion and punishment.

This in turn leads the girl to emotional eating, gaining weight, and acting out in school, where her grades and performance suffered.

This comparison of the two from birth puts a wedge between the girls and made it near impossible for a relationship between them to be formed. The twin that looked like mom aligned with mom and the siblinghood was poisoned. This created a tremendous amount of emotional pain and hurt for the other twin.

## Writing Prompt

Within the framework of the Balan 3-2-1 Method, consider your response to the following:

**What kinds of things, such as thoughts or emotions, can you let go of?**

3. With intention, set your internal and external environment.
   – **The body**: What mindfulness techniques are you choosing to allow your body to heal?

   _____

   _____

   _____

   _____

   – **The setting**: How are you intentionally influencing your setting?

   _____

   _____

   _____

   _____

   – **The breath**: Which breathing technique will you use as you prepare for this exercise?

   _____

   _____

   _____

   _____

2. What are your thoughts and feelings in response to the writing prompt above?

   _____

   _____

   _____

   _____

   _____

   _____

_____

_____

_____

_____

1. What is your one intent or affirmation in context of the writing prompt above?

_____

_____

_____

_____

# ACEs: Neglect

Neglect in the form of not caring for the child's physical needs, their social needs, and emotional needs are all aspects that impact the individual. Not taking the kid out for a playdate or to the park, not showing up to school events, or neglecting hygiene gets internalized. The child begins to think "I am worthless," and the feeling of invisibility, not being seen, becomes a part of their narrative.

This in turn makes it so that when things are too difficult to feel, the child doesn't feel anything. When they are neglected, they begin to neglect themselves, too.

For example, if a mother doesn't take care of the child and make sure she is appropriately dressed, is wearing rainboots, a jacket or a hat, the kid doesn't develop the ability to assess the needs of their own body. The person grows up unable to see if they are cold or even think about asking themselves that question.

A similar scenario occurs with food. If the parent doesn't give food that tastes different or comes from different cultures, or if they are not given the opportunity to share a meal or learn what they like or do not like, the child doesn't develop an understanding of the nourishment of food.

If the child doesn't know what their own preferences are and their needs are not met, they don't understand how to detect or feel. They then are unable to advocate for their own needs. It becomes second nature for the child to neglect their own needs as well.

If, for example, bedtime isn't prioritized or a routine is not set, respected, or observed, the child is impacted. If the environment isn't quiet, the kid doesn't learn to settle into sleep, or a clear transition from daytime to nighttime isn't respected, the child doesn't learn the importance of sleep hygiene. This becomes internalized and the child is not in tune with their bodily needs. This causes the same effect that other traumas cause where the defense is to shut down. A non-feeling defensive response.

Later in life, when feelings become too difficult, the person reverts back to their learned defenses. Either that or the neglected child acts out. This is how the memories get stored. It can be very triggering for a child who comes from neglect when they experience something that reminds them of when they were neglected.

# Case Example: Neglected Boy

This is an example of an individual who in childhood was neglected, was sent to school with dirty clothes, hair, and nails. As a result, he was bullied, which led to his withdrawal and social isolation. He described the feelings of inability and inadequacy of making friends.

Later in adulthood, this person became overly controlling and obsessed with their outer appearance. He always tried to make sure he was dressed to perfection, following the latest fashion trends and styles. He got gratification when he was praised at work for his outfits and looks. He would spend enormous amount of time with his hair and appearance, to the point that it interfered with his day-to-day activities.

When any time there was an imperfection, like a wrinkled shirt or a pimple on his face, he would get severely anxious and remove himself from social situations. In those moments, he wasn't the adult with the wrinkled shirt, he was the eight-year-old boy who went to school with his dirty clothes.

At the time, the memory was incomplete and not stored properly. At the time, the little boy had no control. In this moment, as an adult, although he technically has control, he feels like he doesn't. The adult man time traveled and found himself transported in time to his childhood self. The trigger of the wrinkled shirt caused him to feel like his young self.

This self-discovery took quite some time for him to discover. Initially, and for a while, he did not even realize the connection or know that when he felt like his clothes weren't exactly right, that would cause him an extreme anxiety and panic attack. He hadn't linked his feeling uncomfortable in his adult life with the issues described.

Through therapy, he was able to make the connection that those things were triggers and then realization and awareness was built. Once the foundation of self-awareness was built, he worked on self-compassion, and he was able to soothe the child. He was able to tell the child that he no longer needed to go to school with dirty clothes and that he has an adult that took care of him. His adult, wise self took care of him, washed and ironed his clothes, and the kid did not need to worry about it anymore.

Through talking to his inner child and role-playing and soothing that eight-year-old boy and allowing for that child to express the pain that the neglect caused, he was able to feel more at peace with himself and his appearance.

# ACEs: Isolation and Stigma

When we are kids, we are egocentric. Everything that happens to us is because of us, in our minds. When there is abuse, children internalize it and believe it is their fault. In relational trauma, for example, such as divorce, if children are not met with affection, compassion, and age and developmentally appropriate explanation of what is occurring, they believe that mom and dad are fighting because of them. When there is physical abuse or neglect, or abandonment, the same thing happens. "My dad left because I'm not worth staying for," or "I'm not loveable," or "Mom is hitting me because I deserve it," or "I'm a bad girl."

These narratives get absorbed into our identity and become part of our narrative. We believe that we deserve to be left, we aren't good enough to be loved, or our bodies are not worth respecting. For example, in sexual abuse, the narrative that we are deserving of what we are getting is a theme we encounter.

In abuse, there are statements such as "you are a bad kid" or "you are a difficult kid," and these get internalized, too. What that happens, there is shame attached to it, and the belief that they were at fault, defective, and not good enough, and that is why they got abused, sets in. When people believe that and it gets internalized in their identity, that narrative gets repeated, and the individual finds themselves in similar stories.

A lot of isolation also comes with these narratives. Instead of being vulnerable and being able to accept compassion and care, the individual with these internalized narratives puts themselves in situations where the abuse repeats.

We discussed the concept of egocentric thinking of "the abuse happens because of me," and now will focus on the thinking of "it is only happening to me." Isolation occurs, especially in the context of other people's lives.

Exposure to curated, filtered, social media posts, happy people eating meals together, causes us to assume that everyone's life is beautiful and functional, and they have happy families. The person with traumatic stressors views this and thinks that their life is malfunctioning, incomplete, has holes in it, and only they are dealing with these issues.

It is important to address isolation and address these narratives in therapy. One of the ways of doing this may be self-disclosure in therapy. Obviously in a way that will therapeutically serve the client. Another way is self-disclosure in books, where people write about their struggles, abuse, their weight issues, having an addiction, or being a child of an addicted family member.

Groups are also helpful in breaking this isolation. For example, children of families of alcoholics have similar tendencies and similar patterns that happen to them from their past. The person witnesses violence, or they are neglected and make themselves either really small or really large. They either submit to the aggressor or act out depending on the situation. Many of these cyclical patterns repeat throughout their lives. It is helpful when people go through groups of families of alcoholics or families of people with mental illness.

Another example is of early pregnancy loss or groups for those who lose a child. When a child dies or a mother loses a baby, the internalization of "it is my fault" gets activated. Group therapy where people who suffered similar losses unite and share their pain is really helpful in healing. Offering each other support and coping mechanisms, and the idea that all this suffering is a part of life, and is a part of being a human, and does not inflict us alone, are valuable experiences.

## ACEs: Issues at School and Work

As can be imagined, ACEs have an impact on school and work performance, and research has supported this. Other behavioral and cognitive effects include decreased school attendance and secondary and professional level school completion rates. These all then have an impact on entry to the workforce, as well as performance and attendance in a professional setting, in addition to all the aforementioned interpersonal issues.

Consider the individual with a history of ACEs, toxic stress, impacted brain and stress response and nervous systems with the ability to navigate school or workplace environments. The ability to sustain attention, make decisions, and gain new information are all impacted. The effects on impulse control, self-regulation, and ability to engage influence every system the individual encounters going forward.

Now, as the reader, whether clinician or not, think about all your interactions in any given day and any issues you may have had trying to communicate. We work with individuals and organizations to understand the impact of ACEs, as well as work toward communication styles to allow for empathy and compassion.

With such a high rate of ACEs and such a large number of people having gone through these experiences, there is a zero percent chance that you have never encountered someone with a history of an ACE.

We must therefore exercise open mindedness, work toward reducing stigma, and reflect on expectations and empathy in its truest sense. How is the other across from you experiencing the world? How can we work to appreciate other's abilities to ensure students are able to learn at school and employees can maintain productivity?

The Centers for Disease Control and Prevention suggests that the prevention of ACEs could lower the impact of massive economic burdens such as heart disease by 1.9 million cases, as well as lower the incidence of depression cases by 21 million. The cost estimate of the effects of ACEs is estimated to be over $500 billion a year in the United States alone!

## ACEs: Care and Management

Prevention, recognition, and treatment are key elements to managing the impact of ACEs. Approaches such as the factors in resiliency discussed in this chapter are proven to be effective. In a school or workplace setting, having specific policies and procedures relating to strengthening support to the individual, family, and community is beneficial.

As discussed throughout this book, early identification, early engagement, and early treatment with families and individuals yield the most benefit. Access to medical and mental health care services is critical. Many pediatrician's offices are providing ACEs screening questions to parents as they wait before an appointment for their child.

In some ways, the perception of ACEs and how physical punishment is accepted in some cultures needs to be addressed. Hitting a child is never acceptable, yet we see that in certain cultures, certain types of abuse are normalized.

There are certain behaviors for certain genders that are normalized, which make them not discussed or not brought up, and the individuals don't seek out help. The culture and family reinforce to learn to live with it, which creates more and more unhealthy behaviors, such as substance use and the repetition of abuse and these behaviors. This is precisely why it is important, going back to the cultural discussion, that we as humans want to feed from our cultures and traditions, yet should strive to evolve and move further.

With corporal punishment, raising the awareness and talking about parental training of positive discipline and other methods of discipline is important. We should always aim to be better than our preceding generations. We do not want to say: "it is OK in this culture" or "it is acceptable to hit like this in our family." We want to grow and live in societies where children are cared for in a safe and secure way, a way they need to grow and thrive.

School-based interventions and the education of teachers and other adults in the child's and family's community are necessary. There has been an increase in recent funding for early childhood home visitation programs as well as education campaigns and the raising of awareness.

Mindfulness and emotional intelligence are innate with some having a propensity toward higher empathy. These skills and techniques, however, can also be learned. Healthy ways to interact, healthy ways to socialize and develop relationships, as well as parenting, can all be encouraged, modeled, and taught. Decreasing stigma, promoting pro-social behaviors, and providing avenues to discuss these issues are very valuable.

Social and community-based approaches include education and legislative measures. Thankfully they have been gaining favorable traction over the last several years in the United States. Key factors to address include housing and food insecurity, as well as income inequality.

Strengthening economic support, such as tax credits, and general safety and wellbeing has been an increased focus, especially in impoverished and underserved communities. Violence and safety in the community are all impacted and targets for mitigating ACEs as well.

In summary, reducing and preventing ACEs and trauma during childhood will dramatically reduce the development of mental health issues in adulthood. So many of the psychological and psychiatric pathologies we encounter today could have been prevented.

## Protective Factors in the Family System

We discussed the individual's forming of connections with their caregivers and then the devastating effects of ACEs. The next section will discuss protective factors, evidence-based interventions, and observations based on behavioral patterns.

The main elements of protective factors revolve around communication patterns among members of the family, the disposition of individuals and their methods of relating with one another, as well as deliberate attempts to build guardrails around the family. External structural support such as community involvement and the strength of bonds created outside of the family are also essential.

The purpose of listing out and discussing these protective factors is to appreciate how innate temperaments affect the individual as well as the dynamics within the family setting. There are indeed many elements on the list discussed below that can be learned, practiced, and deliberately reinforced.

In addition to providing a primary barrier of resilience, these protective factors also have the effect of mitigating worsening symptoms of acute stress and posttraumatic stress disorder in a family system.

The focus on communication styles within the family is important to understand the way health and resilience is formed as well as potential areas of opportunity regarding maladaptive patterns that may be ingrained. During times of relative calm and stability, these patterns often solidify and create a culture specific to that family.

The definition of family can be as varied, as complex, or as simple and straight-forward as the imagination allows. In a system that involves adults only, communication styles are of a certain maturity level. In a family system that involves adults as caregivers to children, the dynamics are as different as the number of connection points between individuals.

Having a loving adult figure, whether a grandmother, a teacher, or an aunt who doesn't necessarily have to be a parent, is another protective factor. If there is a person that shows the child affection and care and genuine unconditional love, that is a protective factor that goes a long way.

Another protective factor is the coping mechanisms and structures available to the child such as church services, other community services, or extracurricular activities such as being on a sports team.

Other creative outlets of expression such as art, drama, painting, writing, music, movement, or dance are critical to have available in the community. There are programs that help children of sexual abuse or children of other ACEs that incorporate drama that are extremely effective. These modalities end up being a creative way of allowing the child to express themselves and also to re-write their stories. Programs that allow children to be together, to express and move with safe adults are very valuable.

The roles that we play within a family be it parent, father, mother, child, sibling, grandparent, or grandchild also affect the way we look at one another. See Chapter 8, Culture, Identity, and Society, for a discussion and a case example on roles in context of traumatic stressors. Studies suggest that marital status, specifically being married, correlates with increased resilience, ability to overcome adversity, and decreased symptom severity of posttraumatic stress disorder. Our identity is shaped based on how we view ourselves within a system.

Communication styles within families are certainly influenced by the maturity of emotional expression as well as the length of time people within the family have spent with one another. Certainly, based on age, the ability to understand and process experiences, especially trauma, will vary.

In the context of the traumatic events such as a disaster or pandemic, younger children may not realize the long-term effects of the experience.

Under the age of five, the concept of death is fluid and there isn't the understanding of irreversibility. As the child gets older, they begin to understand the aspects of cause and effect as well as become more observant of their surroundings. They can tell when something is missing or misplaced. Later on, they can tell subtleties of communication styles and rhetoric.

While there is a shift from concrete thinking and magical thinking that things can manifest from fantasy, as the child gets older, they realize that real-world actions have short- and longer-term consequences.

Younger children with limited outside exposure and fewer friends typically are closest to and communicate most with the adult in the home, the mother, father, or caregiver. During the adolescent and teenage years, they might not want to share as much with their parents or other adults in the house and are more likely to share with their peers.

The maturity of emotional expression and having the tools to be able to identify and describe as well as discuss what they're going through depends on the developmental stage and the age of the child. Individuals with developmental disabilities, expressive or receptive language disorders, autism spectrum disorders will have communication styles and requirements unique to the individual, especially in context of traumatic events.

Sensory impairments such as blindness or deafness must also be taken into consideration given patterns embedded within the family.

In short, individuals must be able to openly communicate information that is simple, as well as age, and developmentally appropriate.

## Case Example: Young Couple

All identifying personal information has been significantly changed. The purpose is to illustrate attachment injuries that are triggered in a young couple.

Twenty-four-year-old Elijah and his twenty-four-year-old wife Victoria came to therapy with the chief complaint of desire to improve their communication and their intimacy.

Victoria was four years old when her father abandoned her and was raised by her mother as a single parent. Growing up, Victoria quickly learned the skills necessary to take care of herself and others. Her coping pattern of putting herself secondary to caring for others was further exacerbated when her mother fell ill with an autoimmune disorder when Victoria was sixteen years old.

Victoria became responsible for all aspects of home care including the groceries and laundry in addition to caring for her sick mother.

Elijah came from a home where he was exposed to his father's alcoholism. Every night his father would drink and become aggressive and physically and verbally abusive. His family has the burden of generational abuse, as both Elijah's mother and father came from poverty and physical violence.

When Elijah's father would drink at nights, he would beat him. Elijah's mother would sometimes try to interfere and stop her husband, although was unable to. His father would sometimes beat his mother as well. She was never able to protect Elijah.

He grew up witnessing his mother's helplessness, her crying and abuse. In addition to trying to protect himself physically from his father and emotionally from his mother, he also had to learn not to show his sadness to his mother for fear that she would become even more depressed.

The similarities in both Victoria and Elijah are that they both grew up feeling the need to protect their mothers. For Elijah, not being able to protect his mother was a trigger. He blamed her for that. Upon becoming an adult and in a relationship with Victoria, whenever Elijah felt stressed or issues came up at work or with his aging mother, he would dissociate and find ways to escape. Through therapy, he was able to understand and see the connections as being triggers from the past.

Victoria expressed that she enjoyed being needed, being around people, and preparing meals for guests and neighbors. Elijah reported that he was more introverted. Using the Psychobiological Approach to Couples Therapy (PACT) approach, when Elijah goes within and disappears in his introverted character, this is referred to as the island. Victoria's approach of pursuing him is referred to as the wave.

Whenever Elijah was going through something, he would retreat. Victoria would always perceive this as abandonment. When she experienced this as rejection and abandonment, she would pursue him and repeatedly ask him questions. Elijah felt she was pestering him and he would retreat even further. In turn, Victoria would thus become increasingly emotional and cry. Elijah would then shut down even further. At times he would even become explosive, angry, and resentful.

Seeing someone's sadness would remind Elijah of his mother's inability to protect him, and his mother's sadness that became more of a burden to him. When he was victimized, he would also try to make his mother feel better. In his wounding, he would end up also consoling his mother. Because of that, whenever he subsequently saw someone emotional or upset, especially if they were upset at him or because of him, he became reactive.

Both Victoria and Elijah experienced difficulty in asking for and needing help. Victoria always felt the need to give and to socialize, although unable to verbalize this as a need of her own. Elijah was unable to ask for what he needed, as he learned growing up that no one cared about his pain, and that in order to move forward, he had to bottle up his needs and face things alone. When he had obstacles in his life, instead of partnering with his wife and attempting to work together, Elijah would try to handle them himself. When that would not work or solve the issue, he would retreat in alcohol and music.

The external incident that brought the couple to counseling was when they learned that Elijah's mother was diagnosed with end stage cancer and was hospitalized. The numerous procedures she underwent, in addition to Elijah needing to be ever present were triggering. He had to go back and forth to his old home, flooding him with old haunting memories.

During this time, Elijah completely shut down to his wife. He reported being very distraught and that he did not want to speak with her or anyone. This upset Victoria, and she threatened separation and eventually divorce. That was the incident within the relationship that brought them to therapy.

In counseling that is trauma focused, you explore how people support one another in attachment injuries and how people heal one another in their trauma. You have the couple talk with one another and gain insight into what they learned.

For example, you have the couple sit down facing one another. The intention is for their two nervous systems to interact. The goal is for the nervous systems to regulate one another.

For example, in this case, they trigger each other's attachment wounding. Elijah triggered abandonment and rejection in Victoria. Victoria, in turn, triggered the trauma memories as well as feelings of avoidance in Elijah.

During the couples counseling session, you have the couple face one another, and teach them to regulate themselves as they regulate their partner. Have them focus on each other's eyes, and micro expressions, and their body posture and their hands. Don't have them talk just yet.

Have them move to one another, get their chairs closer, and then ask how they feel. Have them touch one another, then have them sit close, and instruct them not to touch one another. Have them experience one another in relation to their bodies.

Have them figure out how they arouse one another. When you find out how they arouse one another, you can also begin working on how they can soothe one another.

We know that the gaze is one of the first forms of communications we have as an infant. The baby attaches to the mother with their gaze and makes decisions on love and security. Similarly, as adults, the gaze is critical for relationships and intimacy and love. Have the couple pay attention to each other's gaze.

Then have them pay attention to their emotions.

When Victoria brought her chair too close, Elijah said that he felt threatened, that he felt he wanted to move his chair away. In this scenario, you have Elijah move his chair away, and then ask Victoria what that meant for her, how she felt when he said he felt intruded upon and crowded. In this instance, Victoria said that she felt rejected and began crying.

You then start talking further about what happened, where Victoria remembered this feeling from. She went into the story of her memory of when her father was putting his things in a moving truck. Raise awareness to that and discuss the old memories that become triggered in the present.

When Elijah retreated, this triggered her old memories. Then bring awareness to Elijah about this and what else could he do when he moved away. He volunteered to put his hand on Victoria's knee. Ask her how that feels. She said it felt warm and good.

As the therapist, you communicate and teach them ways that make sense and feels comforting to them. You teach them to navigate connecting with one another, within each other's capacity, in ways that feels doable for them. You also thereby help them understand their own triggers.

When Victoria cried, the therapist can ask Elijah what he sees in her eyes, where he saw this before. He replied saying "in my mom's eyes." You build awareness and bring the family history and injury into the session. You ask each person what would be helpful in that moment. How can you support them?

For Elijah, he reported feeling more supported when Victoria put her arms around him from behind, held him, asked him no questions, and allowed him to just be still. He said that felt more supportive to him. Victoria said that she can do that.

Then you ask Elijah, when Victoria felt upset that he was moving away, what can he do. He said that he could play music as that was a coping mechanism pattern for him. Victoria said that it worked for her as well.

As the therapist, you teach the couple ways to navigate and support in ways that won't be triggering or threatening. This takes time, practice, and repeated effort.

The basic understanding is that before you can have rational conversations, you have to connect with one another in body. In this example, playing music was comforting and brought their heart rates down. Hugging from the back was soothing, decreased the breathing rate, and relieved tension in the muscles. Connecting with one's own body, being able to describe it to the other, and learning empathy and acting on it with the other allow for healing as a couple.

## Writing Prompt

Consider using the space provided to reflect on the following:

**What kind of things do you need to hear to be able to connect with another person?**

_____

_____

_____

_____

_____

_____

_____

_____

_____

_____

_____

_____

_____

## Writing Prompt

Within the framework of the Balan 3-2-1 Method, consider your response to the following:

**In a relationship, what kind of patterns do you fall into?**

3. With intention, set your internal and external environment.
   - **The body**: What mindfulness techniques are you choosing to allow your body to heal?

_____

_____

_____

_____

    — **The setting**: How are you intentionally influencing your setting?

_____

_____

_____

    — **The breath**: Which breathing technique will you use as you prepare for this exercise?

_____

_____

_____

_____

2. What are your thoughts and feelings in response to the writing prompt above?

_____

_____

_____

_____

_____

_____

_____

_____

_____

_____

1. What is your one intent or affirmation in context of the writing prompt above?

_____

_____

_____

_____

## Protective Factors: Parenting Style

Research indicates that an authoritative parenting style allows for resilience and sets the foundation for many other patterns of interactions and communication styles. This type of parenting, as opposed to permissive, uninvolved, or authoritarian styles, yields self-reliant, cooperative, and self-controlled children.

Households that have worked on and adopted this type of nurturing and responsive interactions yield the benefit of a supportive environment where consistency is the foundation and firm boundaries and limits for the children are maintained.

Within the realm of nurturance and love, the concept of self-love and love for others develops. Aspects such as shaming or threatening the child are avoided, and therefore, the child is able to learn how to solve complex problems without inwardly focusing on frustrations or dwelling on toxic negativity.

Authoritative parenting involves the use of positive reinforcement as well as reasoning while combining sensitivity and warmth. In general, punishments or even threats are not used, rather collaborative problem solving is encouraged.

The locus of control and sense of power is dramatically different in authoritative parenting styles versus the others mentioned earlier. Parents who realize that they must work toward incorporating environments conducive of mental health and wellbeing model as well as teach the behavior and skills for the child to be able to manage difficult emotions during stressful times.

Studies have shown that these children have significantly better outcomes and have healthier coping mechanisms when experiencing trauma. This also provides for an interconnectedness of the family unit which further mitigates the harmful and acute stressors of a traumatic event which then also reduces posttraumatic stress disorders.

These children have a decreased incidence of major depression and anxiety. They also have a lower likelihood of engaging in pathological substance use. These individuals are also more likely to become independent and successful academically as well as in their careers.

## Writing Prompt

In summary, if one is working toward improving their parenting styles, consider incorporating several of the following listed below. We are also including space for the reader to add thoughts on what they can implement while engaging with their loved ones.

- ■ Encourage the child to speak about their feelings.
  - – Foster an environment where they come to the parent when feeling sad or scared.

_____

_____

_____

_____

_____

_____

_____

_____

_____

_____

■ Allow for time with a child to express their needs and wishes in the way they are able to developmentally.
  – Consider avoiding jumping in, putting words in their mouth, or dismissing the child, especially when trying to express their feelings.

_____

_____

_____

_____

_____

_____

_____

_____

_____

_____

■ Maintain firm boundaries and stick to previously agreed upon decisions.
  – Some examples could be things like responsibilities around the house such as cleaning their room.
  – Ensure that something that you said as the parent or caregiver has meaning and is consistent in message.
  – Consistency regarding routines, bedtimes, mealtimes should be held sacred. We all benefit from reliable consistency, and the safety of being able to expect something and it actually happening, every time, is critical.

_____

_____

_____

_____

_____

_____

_____

_____

_____

_____

■ Consider the times when you are reacting in response to something, regardless of cause, if the child is around, and think about how you are modeling your reactions.
  - Specifically work toward avoiding extreme levels anger or negative excitement around the child.

_____

_____

_____

_____

_____

_____

_____

_____

_____

■ If needed, prepare a consequence rather than a punishment.
  - Think about reinforcing behaviors that you want to be continued while teaching the child to appreciate why consequences exist.
  - Consequences should be real-world based and as a direct result of the action or inaction on behalf of the child. They should be temporally close to the event of concern and discussed as to why it is occurring.

_____

_____

_____

_____

_____

_____

_____

_____

_____

_____

## Protective Factors: Family Dynamics

Openness and the ability to feel comfortable within a safe space to express emotions as well as being able to be honest are critical. Trust within the family system ranks among the more valuable factors predictive of resilience.

As discussed earlier, the family that is aware that they have some sense of control of decision making and planning that can be done in the home typically does better. Levels of resilience in a family are directly related to the capacity to adapt to new routines.

The ability to look back at previous experiences and incorporate them into the new situations they find themselves in allows for a greater sense of control. For example, after a disaster such as an earthquake, the need for displacement, or the current pandemic, everyone has been subject to many new changes in their routines.

Families that have the skill to collaboratively solve problems and explain how they are working toward defining and creating these solutions are considered healthier.

The ability to successfully solve the problem requires being able to see events and situations from multiple angles. This by nature requires a certain level of flexibility as well as open minded-ness. These are all protective factors when it comes to resilience.

The capability to compromise when either a solution doesn't fit or to be able to integrate the thoughts and feelings of others is another protective factor. A family that is able to make meaning from adversity, such as incorporating previous experiences, cultures, and values to what they are currently dealing with, as well as be able to discuss it and work toward overcoming it, typically fare better.

We have discussed mindfulness throughout this book. Clearly an element of resilience includes the ability to engage and be in the present moment. Freedom from judgment, or at least, the conscious awareness of thoughts or feelings that judge and working toward resolving them is key.

Yener was invited to speak with the Mayor of Oakland, California, at a town hall with the city. This was during 2020, the first year of the pandemic, around the holidays. He was asked to address elements of resilience in the community, especially regarding the impact on youth. In addition to some of the aforementioned elements of resilience, he spoke to the impact of hope.

A positive disposition coupled with a healthy outlook on life events has been shown to diminish the impact of external stressors. Being future oriented and planning activities together as a family allow each individual to contribute and to ideate a world that continues to exist. Something to look forward to, even a simple entry on a calendar for a future date gives the entire family, especially the children, a concrete reminder that life goes on.

## Writing Prompt: Family

Within the framework of the Balan 3-2-1 Method, consider your response to the following:

**When I am fully present with my family, what does that look and feel like?**

3. With intention, set your internal and external environment.
   - **The body:** What mindfulness techniques are you choosing to allow your body to heal?

_____

_____

_____

_____

— **The setting**: How are you intentionally influencing your setting?

_____

_____

_____

_____

_____

— **The breath**: Which breathing technique will you use as you prepare for this exercise?

_____

_____

_____

_____

_____

2. What are your thoughts and feelings in response to the writing prompt above?

_____

_____

_____

_____

_____

_____

_____

_____

_____

_____

1. What is your one intent or affirmation in context of the writing prompt above?

_____

_____

_____

_____

_____

# Creative Prompt: Family Crest

A creative family activity that we have engaged in and have recommended to clients and colleagues is the concept of creating a family crest. Imagine historically, the shields or coat of arms, and symbols families would create to wear and display. These would be developed to demonstrate belonging as well as pride. Values, accomplishments, morals, and other important elements would be incorporated. Even in current times, you may have seen some universities that have crests with symbols and words on them in Greek or Latin.

The color and shape and chosen symbols, for this exercise, are all up to you and your family. Symbols can be simple line drawings of something like an animal, a plant, or depicting a hobby. Words such as the name chosen for your family and/or other phrases that you would like to display that is meaningful to you can be added.

For the exercise we are recommending, especially in the context of the family chapter dealing with trauma and resilience, we suggest initially thinking of who is in your family. It can be biological family, chosen family, folks you live with, or those loved ones further away.

1. Consider listing those you identify as being part of your family below:

_____

_____

_____

_____

_____

_____

_____

_____

2. Discuss this exercise with those listed above and begin brainstorming together your collective family values, morals, things you are proud of, and concepts that make you all feel you belong as part of the family. Consider listing those identified below, you can use single words or phrases to describe them.

_____

_____

_____

_____

_____

_____

_____

_____

_____

3. We have divided the template family crest into four, although feel free to use as many or as few of the items listed above in your personal crest. Using the space provided below, now think with your family about how you will depict and draw or write the elements that symbolize your family. A classic example could be something like a lion for bravery or a heart for love. The value in this exercise is less the artistic quality of the product and more the process of discussing and creating together.

_____

_____

_____

_____

_____

_____

_____

_____

_____

4. Now take turns together, using pencils, markers, crayons, and colors of your choosing to begin your family crest.

# Example: Balan Family Crest

As a family, we also created our family crest. We began this exercise during the first year of the pandemic and found it to be very valuable as a communication tool. Our son was eight at the time, and we wanted to model some of the elements discussed in this chapter, as well as work together as parents to sit down and discuss what our values are.

During the uncertainty and evolving anxiety and traumas we all witnessed, we wanted to have a shared exercise, something we could hold on to and see with our eyes, keep on the fridge, and discuss together.

As discussed in the creative prompt above, the three of us sat down and began brainstorming our values. The first word our son said was "nice." So, we wrote that down. Then came "respect" and "brave." Yener suggested "gratitude" and Duygu added "love."

We love playing board games and the theater, and we wrote those down. In fact, Duygu and Yener spent many years together in Istanbul in their high school theater, so that was an added personal element. We are from Turkey and thought of somehow characterizing that as well. We cooperate with one another, work hard, and feel at peace when we are together. Humor and being "funny" is another thing we all agreed on as well.

Once we collected those concepts, we thought about how to symbolize them. How can we show peace? Love came easily when our son drew the heart in one part of the crest. Yener wanted a dragon to show gaming as well as bravery. Duygu drew the honeycombs for hard work and cooperation, and our son added the small bee to one side, because he said the honeycombs needed a bee.

When we searched online for a symbol for theater, the classic two masks came up, one smiling and the other frowning. We chose to include the smiling one, with the other half shaded behind it. The roles we play and the masks we wear also were discussed. The peace sign was an obvious one, then we thought of Turkey and the olive trees that grow in that climate as well as in California, and we realized that the olive branch can represent them all.

We certainly had fun completing it, kept it colorless, although may color it someday. When we look at the crest, it reminds us of where we are from, our current values, and some truths we hold sacred. It is inherently personal and is meaningful for us as a family, yet when shared with others, as we are doing in this workbook, may be of value as well.

## Protective Factors: Culture and Community

Cultural identity, and how the community one is in, and the level of acceptance of the traumatic experience by others can also be protective factors. See Chapter 8, Culture, Identity, and Society, with culturally specific information. Depending on the traumatic event, faith based and/or religious approaches have also been correlated with positive outcomes.

Having witnessed or having been through a traumatic experience in the past adds another dynamic. Either an individual within the smaller family circle or folks in the greater community as a whole can add generational wisdom to the experience. Their firsthand knowledge and post-traumatic growth experiences can be the scaffolding needed while rebuilding the mental landscape after trauma.

The level of education of an individual, as well as those advising and supporting the family after an event, has also been correlated with increased resilience and decreased severity of symptoms. Specifically, higher levels of education, bachelors and above, according to studies, add elements of resilience.

Similarly, socioeconomic status has an impact. The lower the socioeconomic status, the more problems such as housing and food insecurity become prevalent after a traumatic event, especially during a (natural) disaster.

The less resources available pre-crisis, the less likely the individual or family is to obtain resources and support from organizations such as a bank or insurance company to help rebuild or relocate.

The appreciation of reciprocal importance and value in a community, in other words, that the family unit matters to the community and vice versa is protective. Knowing of the availability of support systems to turn to in the event of a tragedy, crisis, or time in extreme need is invaluable.

Having appropriate support systems in times of traumatic events has been shown to decrease negative self-coping mechanisms such as substance use to self-medicate or other risk-taking behaviors. Supportive school engagement, more on that further in this section, is another source of protection.

Obviously, availability and access to mental and physical health care is paramount when medically indicated. The safety net component of support from a community such as getting information, receiving emotional support as well as being able to exchange ideas or resources is extremely valuable.

## Writing Prompt

Consider using the space below to reflect on the following three-part prompt:

1. What does it mean to you to be in a community?

_____

_____

_____

_____

_____

_____

_____

2. Who can be in your life that can give you the sense that you are in a community?

_____

_____

_____

_____

_____

_____

3. Who can you ask for support?

_____

_____

_____

_____

_____

_____

# Stressors

Family systems are subject to their own specific stressors and intimate partner violence is among the most severe ones. Unfortunately, during the pandemic, we have seen a dramatic increase in intimate partner violence (IPV), mostly of men perpetrating violence toward women.

IPV has been a serious public health problem worldwide. According to the National Intimate Partner and Sexual Violence Survey in 2010, reported by Black et al. (2011), the highest prevalence of physical and sexual violence is seen in Native American, multiracial, and Black non-Hispanic women and men, compared to White non-Hispanic, Hispanic, and Asian Pacific Islander women and men.

In terms of gender, rates of IPV are similar at lifetime rates of around 30% for men and women. Comorbid psychological risks of IPV include posttraumatic stress disorder, anxiety, substance use disorder, and physical health risks including numerous chronic health conditions.

Literature indicates that IPV then often leads to posttraumatic stress disorder, and if the individual is a mother, the traumatic stress and symptomatology directly influence the child.

In the first study of its kind using follow-up design, clinicians and researchers (Glaus et al., 2021) discuss the associations between posttraumatic stress disorder of the mother and effects of the toddler growing into a school aged child. Per the findings in the article, children who witness intimate partner violence and mothers with or without posttraumatic stress disorder are at increased risk of symptoms of attention deficit hyperactivity disorder, anxiety, depression as well as conduct and oppositional defiant disorders. See Chapter 10, COVID, Disasters, and Loss, for more information on peripartum issues and mental health effects of the pandemic.

The study by Voith et al. (2020) finds strong correlation between higher number of ACEs score as a predictor of increased rates for self-reported IPV, both perpetration and victimization. The study looks at marginalized men, those in racial and ethnic minority groups, as well as those of low income. The study provides valuable insight and reasoning for increasing awareness of and development of programs for the aforementioned minority and underserved groups with high unmet clinical needs.

# Youth: Post Trauma

After a natural disaster, pandemic, or an isolated traumatic event such as a school shooting, the reactions of children can have a myriad of different short- as well as long-term effects. While time allows for healing, those involved with a child, family, school, or clinician should pay close attention to the duration of signs and symptoms displayed.

If available, especially to a clinician, it is important to know the baseline of the child, how they were doing, and their level of wellness prior to the trauma. If pathologies or other vulnerabilities existed, the treatment will be different.

In the event of a natural disaster or war, the loss of a home has additional complications. The loss of rootedness, the despair, and isolation caused enhance the stress reaction on the child. Having things that used to be reliable, that the youth could count on, guardrails that were in place all of a sudden being lost or damaged leads to shifts in mindset.

The mental model of the world of people can change, and the community may no longer be seen as a safe space. The sense of self and the identity can also be affected. Perceptions, bodily expressions, as well as self-image change. The meaning of life and relationships is questioned.

Children impacted by trauma, such as during the COVID pandemic, become acutely aware of their surroundings and the cause and effect of how people react. Especially when one's guard is down, in a disaster, one's world views and approach to negotiating relationships change.

Individuals typically do not know how they will react during an acute crisis, and it is important to reflect on this, as suggested in the above writing exercise, so as to be as prepared as possible. The reactionary helplessness, depression, and grief that is often unfiltered in the acute phases are witnessed by the children in the family.

When there is confusion, disorientation, and even disintegration, the loss of routines is heavily felt. Family dynamics change when anchors are lost, and environmental and social boundaries are irreparably blurred.

## Youth: Traumatic Stress

Traumatic stress in children leads to a number of varying symptoms. The environments in which they interact and information gathered will provide a more complete picture of the impact on the child. Places such as the home, school, a friend's house, the neighbors, a relative's house, a church or other place of worship, as well as doctor's appointments can all be surveyed. How the child interacts, how they play, how they express themselves may all be impacted.

On a longer term, children may have difficulty making new relationships. A part of this may be related to the inability or blocking of thinking of the future or making plans. Again, the writing exercise above will foster a more in-depth appreciation of what the specific family can address.

Signs and symptoms can include emotional arousal, such as a heightened state of awareness, feeling jumpy or jittery, as well as an increased startle reaction. This may be in addition to or separate from sleep disturbances. Child and family clinicians regularly become aware of sleep being impacted at any stage of the sleep cycle. Children (as well as adults) can have difficulty falling asleep, waking up during the night, having nightmares, night terrors, the need/desire to sleep with someone else, or keep the lights on.

Decreased external activities, either as a cluster of anhedonia, despondency or depression, or general withdrawal from others, can also occur. Patterns of decreased communication or not wanting to participate in activities are common. Depending on the environment, dropping grades at school or decreased productivity and difficulty concentrating at school or work are all linked.

As touched upon earlier, there may be a preponderance of physiological reactivities as well. The fear elicited during the event may become generalized to loud noises such as thunder, lighting, or car alarms. Irritability, crying, anger, and rage may also be seen. Pattern changes in eating may also occur. Decrease in appetite or compulsive eating may develop. Of note, studies suggest that during the pandemic, eating disorders have significantly increased in adolescents and young adults.

Psychosomatic, bodily complaints such as headaches, heart palpitations, stomach aches, and eating problems can occur. Sensory disturbances, especially in younger children, such as trouble seeing or hearing are also manifestations of stress reactions. Depending on maturity level and the ability to communicate, the child may be more in tune with bodily sensations and less aware of the psychological impact on physical manifestations.

Regression to younger aged type behaviors may be seen. Behaviors can include reverting back to or a new development of whining or clinging, fearfulness, bedwetting, screaming, night terrors, or thumb sucking.

The outward appearance of defenses may be in the avoidance end of the spectrum or the aggressivity turned outwards end. Extreme defensiveness, such as portraying a lack of emotions and appearing uncaring or dismissive, may all be seen.

Avoiding or not wanting to do the things they previously enjoyed is symptom of depression as well as a reaction to traumatic stress. In contrast, acting out behaviors such as physicality at school or with siblings, fighting, or stealing may occur. Sexuality, sexualized responses, and emotional acting out as well as substance use may develop.

As discussed in the section on effects of the COVID pandemic, depending on the type of traumatic event, youth may suffer from the loss of the lives of loved ones. Grief reactions may be short lived or become pathological. Symptoms of mourning may appear similar to those described earlier, although will benefit from a different approach as a family and clinically if indicated.

Lastly, the aggressivity and angst may turn inwards, and signs and symptoms of severe depression such as suicidal ideation, self-injury, and suicide attempts may occur. Decreased insight and a decrease in judgment and impulse control are all key factors in how the youth reacts and responds to stressors.

# Schools

Another essential puzzle piece in the response and recovery phase of the aftermath of trauma is the school community. They have the ability to provide emergency planning before a crisis, including training and interventions in place, as well as for after the acute crisis.

As schools constitute a majority of the time where children spend their time and develop complex relationships, it also is a location of traumatic incidents. Administrators and staff have had to cope with school violence, vandalism, attacks with and without weapons for decades. Physical and sexual attacks as well as robbery and bomb threats unfortunately are at a level that cannot be ignored. Similarly, the complications of substance use, overdose, and legal involvement related to aforementioned offenses all end up looping the school community in as well.

Schools are also a place that copes with individual crises that impact the greater group. Suicides are complicated and emotionally challenging events, and children and families affected by suicide often turn to teachers, counselors, and administration for guidance and support.

There has been significant advancement in the maturity of crisis intervention teams put together by schools over the past several decades. They typically are comprised of the parent teacher association, administration, staff, guidance counselors, school nurse, school psychologist, and volunteers. In addition to providing preparatory planning information and structure, they are available for acute interventions as the traumatic stressor unfolds, as well as trauma-informed debriefing in the aftermath.

Schools serve as a community hub and can provide connection to other community agencies. Post disaster engagement such as activities and routines can be made available. Often times the school campus is a place of congregation and a safe remembrance of life before the trauma.

Community engagement and including the families and children during emergency preparations such as drills and distributing information typically happen through schools. Resources may be available as well as connections to onsite or other forms of counseling.

Schools can help restore a new sense of calm for the children, as well as for the faculty and staff, while a new normal, new rhythm, and boundaries of expectations are established. The school is in a position to provide pedagogically minded interpretations of what is being shown on the news and social media and allow for an emotionally and physically safe environment to process issues.

# Schools: Pandemic

The COVID pandemic has been an extreme challenge for schools, their administrators, and staff throughout the world. The once sacred and safe institution of a school turned upside down, and in many countries, especially the United States, abandoned the most vulnerable overnight.

Switching from in person one day, with promises that couldn't be kept, haphazard and ill-fitting remedies, such as virtual or self-guided, asynchronous learning, had the most deleterious effects on the youth.

The burden on the staff and administrators was also heavily felt, as everyone has been dealing with their own personal issues at home. Individual as well as family member responsibilities magnified in intensity, while preexisting anxieties and newly developing obsessions and fears blossomed into panic and terror.

School staffing suffered from absenteeism and presenteeism. The quality of education dropped through an already substandard floor. Accountability and responsibility let alone oversight of education diminished to near nonexistence. The education responsibility was shifted instantly to the caregiver, and only the children fortunate to have an adult that could afford to spend time with them during the day were attended to.

Administrations experienced and continue to see higher turnover rates coupled with difficulty filling positions. Teaching has always been a calling, similar to health care, and over the course of the pandemic became a repellant. Dramatically underpaid teachers and staff had a chance to reevaluate their needs, financial, physical, and mental health goals, and have responded in the above-mentioned ways. Consciously, or not, in an organized way such as labor activity or quietly on an individual level, there has been no person or unit that has not suffered.

As discussed in Chapter 10, COVID, Disasters, and Loss, depression and anxiety have skyrocketed. Teachers and staff have not been spared. Decreased morale and decreased productivity have all been consequences. Substance use has also increased, and schools are having to cope with this major impact as well.

Students, as well as their families, have also reacted in different ways. Acting out in person or while conducting virtual lessons has been a common distractor. These have all lead to a decreased ability to teach and learn.

We anticipate a wave of significantly delayed or regressed testing scores in mathematics and reading. The reflection of the inability to teach and manage classroom systems and the apathy and burnout felt in school systems are palpable, even while writing this book, in the third year of the pandemic.

# Post Trauma: Caregiving

Caregiving during and after a traumatic event, such as the pandemic, is a concerted effort to re-organize and re-assemble a disorganized and disrupted life. One goal is to provide structure to the sequelae on mental and physical health.

We acknowledge that not everything we thought was correct at the beginning of the pandemic was appropriate. The closing of schools, a dramatic shift in lifestyle, and changes in the routines of caregivers and children have had significant impacts on everyone.

While there was sentiment that children and adolescents are resilient and would be able to bounce back from school closures and separations from peers and classmates for months on end, we now know better. The already phenomenally problematic youth mental health crisis is now significantly more alarming.

## Post Trauma: Goals

The key to any effective intervention is the preparation and planning for different outcomes. As you read this section, consider how you and your loved ones can prepare for an emergency.

## Writing Prompt

We have included a list to work from as well as space to include anything for contingency planning that may be relevant.

- A bag or box for materials that can be removed from the home as quickly as possible.
  - Consider something durable and water resistant, with a zipper such as a backpack.
  - Plastic sealing baggies can hold paper documents and small electronics to keep them water resistant.

_____

_____

_____

_____

_____

_____

- List of contacts
  - Emergency contact name and cell phone numbers, and addresses.
    - Family members
    - Neighbors, friends, babysitter
    - Workplace and School information
    - Designated place to meet in case of emergency

_____

_____

_____

_____

_____

_____

- Medical and other Special needs
  - If anyone in family has special needs, such as durable medical equipment, a brace, or medical supplies, having a plan to retrieve them or having a spare set.
  - Information on where to obtain equipment and replacements when needed.
  - Spare glasses and contact lenses.

– Medications, schedule for taking them, plan to obtain refills and replacements.

_____

_____

_____

_____

_____

■ Critical information
  – Insurance information
    • Health insurance contact information
    • Home and car or other insurance information
  – Passports and identification cards

_____

_____

_____

_____

_____

■ Crucial items
  – Cash on hand
  – Credit and other banking cards
  – Food for several days
  – Water for several days
  – Warm clothes, socks, and shoes
  – Blankets
  – Batteries
  – Chargers
  – Radio
  – Lighter or matches
  – Gasoline for your vehicle

_____

_____

_____

_____

_____

_____

- Pet-related items
  - Food
  - Bedding
  - Toiletries

_____

_____

_____

_____

_____

_____

# Conclusion

Wholistically, the framework for addressing the needs of a person, family, or community involve a combination of the following actions. Early identification is very important. Knowing who is at risk, who has the vulnerabilities, and who is of need will determine how to allocate resources and which direction to point them in.

Once identified, early intervention, as appropriate, will foster a framework for healing. The reduction of risk in general, at home, especially to youth is paramount. Knowing that reducing the exposure to things like violence especially intimate partner violence is important.

Studies show that if the severity and length of exposure is higher, then there is an increase in resulting severity of symptoms of mental health issues such as depression, anxiety, and post-traumatic stress disorder in the child. Mitigating the effects of exposure of trauma on children serves to minimize mental health harm, as was discussed in the ACEs section earlier, minimizing subsequent physical health harm as well.

Education of the families, either through a school system or the healthcare system, is another avenue of support. The more appropriate the information, social and community level resources, and education the individual and family has, the better. They can become more connected, feel more comfortable navigating community resources, reaching out and asking for help and support. Education can provide a framework from which they can synthesize the occurring events.

The desire is to prevent the passing on of trauma through the generations. Research and real-world experience point toward the clinical value of reducing exposure of pregnant mothers to violence and trauma. Studies such as the review done by Toso et al. (2020) suggest this may be correlated with neurodevelopmental disabilities such as development of autism spectrum disorders in the unborn child. We know that in utero exposure is also correlated with behavioral issues later in life.

Going back full circle to the start of this section, it is important to appropriately screen and assess the child. Pediatricians as well as maternal child clinicians will often offer structured assessments of the home environment in attempts to mitigate, reduce, and intervene as appropriate. Studies have shown that the younger the child exposed to traumatic environments, the more susceptible they are to the mental health effects of these events.

# Chapter 8

# Culture, Identity, and Society

A mind is like a parachute, it doesn't work if it is not open.

*– Frank Zappa*

## Introduction

This chapter discusses culture in the setting of trauma informed care. The evidence-based and real-world observations in this chapter provide an empathic approach to understanding the journeys we face. Specific identity-related topics as they pertain to and are affected by traumatic stressors are reviewed including LGBTQIA+, racism, and intergenerational trauma. Populations with heightened risk factors including pregnancy- and peripartum-related trauma, occupations and their specific traumas, displaced persons as well as victimization of cyber bullying are discussed.

## Culturally Sensitive Approach

Psychopathology and sequelae of traumatic events vary across cultures. The treating clinician must be respectful, humble, intellectually curious, aware of, and sensitive to the cultural aspects of their client. The dynamic nature of culture across countries and time is important to keep in mind. It never hurts to simply directly ask the person across from you, if you are wondering and believe the response will help foster the therapeutic relationship.

Aspects included below must all be taken into consideration by the treating provider:

- When and the reason why someone begins treatment
- Religious factors relevant to the individual and their family
- Spiritual and related factors
- Linguistic as well as other communication preferences and considerations
- Based on location, country of origin, the amount of trauma exposed the individual and community is witness to and subjected to

DOI: 10.4324/9781003323815-12

- For example, neighborhood settings with violence or poverty
- The impact of living through or experiencing a war, terrorism, or natural disaster
■ How the individual or family asks for help
■ The impact of racism and racial discrimination on the individual, leading to hesitance to trust a system such as healthcare
■ How they describe the trauma, words and descriptors used
■ How the individual experiences the trauma – where in the body, mind, spirit, and other culturally relevant elements
■ Coping mechanisms based on their family and culture
■ How the family and community experience the trauma (e.g., miscarriage, rape, IPV, child abuse)
■ How their culture views shame, stigma, and discrimination
■ How death is viewed
■ Rituals, ceremonies around death, burial, and ceremonies such as funerals
■ How they experience and interpret the concept of flashbacks
■ The structure and composure of their social support networks

Duygu and Yonur have worked in acute inpatient and emergency department settings as well as outpatient care on the East Coast and West Coast of the United States. Not surprisingly, the populations and cultures of folks we cared for were vastly different in each setting, even within the same country.

Our conscious effort to study and inquire about aspects of our clients and their families was critical in the success of caring for them. Coming from different countries and speaking several different languages, we are acutely aware of the many barriers to treatment. Trauma-related care is sensitive even when speaking the same language, let alone when there are linguistic challenges.

And that is only the beginning.

Communicating effectively entails being able to transmit and receive information in a way that is relevant and resonates. Working in a busy, loud emergency room is far from ideal for any type of treatment, let alone to appreciate the subtleties of cultural nuances, although it was essential for us to overcome.

In our practices in outpatient settings, we have had the ability to spend even more time with the individual and family unit, and to work with various cultures, familiarities as well as hesitancies to treatment.

One of our reasons for putting this workbook together is to provide an alternate, an additional form of care and connecting. Depending on the background of the individual, writing and other forms of expressive creativity can create bridges.

The consequences of not being culturally sensitive include missing out on connecting and forming a trusting relationship with the client, early drop out from treatment, and lack of clinical outcomes. The concerns would range from being a waste of everyone's time to potentially discriminatory, hurtful and negligent, damaging reputation and opportunities to help.

## Identity Trauma

It is important to acknowledge that we are all going to have moments of not being accepted for who we are. In certain communities or race or gender, this experience is unfortunately more likely. Resilience building is critical, and for it not to be turned into a traumatic experience, it is important for it to be met with notes of acceptance. Even if this acceptance comes from one person, the individual can internalize phrases and sentiments such as "you are beautiful the way you are" or "differences should be celebrated." The supported and validated person can then use that strength to build resilience.

For example, if a child who grows up in a predominantly Caucasian community gets confronted with racist remarks, his parents acknowledge his pain. The caregivers that let the child know and make him feel protected and seen and teach him that people like the aggressors exist in life help him learn effective coping skills. The act of advocating for oneself, recognizing the adversity and challenges, as well as learning to ask for support from the community is crucial. Later on in life when this child is faced with different racist remarks, he will be able to advocate for himself in the way he was taught.

When racist or discrimination is ignored, normalized, or even approached with an irregular emotional expression such as violence, opportunities are missed. If effective tools are never shown or utilized, then it has a greater chance of turning into identity injury and will create trauma that will result in repetition and the same identity trauma down the line. That person will go on feeling as "the other," that they do not feel as if they belong in the community. They will feel unseen and unheard.

If the child's parents model advocating for themselves and advocating for the child, the child becomes empowered and has the belief that what he says and what he feels matter, and realize that he has a voice.

## Writing Prompt

Within the framework of the Balan 3-2-1 Method, consider your response to the following:

**When were times that you felt you were discriminated against or invalidated? How did you cope?**

3. With intention, set your internal and external environment.
   – **The body**: What mindfulness techniques are you choosing to allow your body to heal?

   _____

   _____

   _____

   _____

   _____

   – **The setting**: How are you intentionally influencing your setting?

   _____

   _____

   _____

   _____

   _____

— **The breath:** Which breathing technique will you use as you prepare for this exercise?

_____

_____

_____

_____

_____

2. What are your thoughts and feelings in response to the writing prompt above?

_____

_____

_____

_____

_____

_____

_____

_____

_____

1. What is your one intent or affirmation in context of the writing prompt above?

_____

_____

_____

_____

_____

_____

_____

_____

_____

Especially for individuals who are raised in non-diverse communities, having access to material that celebrates different cultures, ethnicities, lifestyles, and religious backgrounds is extremely important. Information conveyed in the context of a safe space to explore, that discusses these differences as a richness, where there is not one way of doing things, that we can grow as humans, and learn from different backgrounds will only yield positive growth. When we learn to celebrate differences rather than use differences for isolation or hurt or collective traumatization, we expand our minds and embrace an empathic approach.

It is important for educators, healers, and parents to incorporate teachings of diversity and multiculturalism on a daily basis. In places like California, we might take some of these for granted, because we are daily exposed to people who come from different places than we do. Even still, however, we notice a certain amount of agreement in California, the Bay Area in specific, an air of invalidation of anything that is not California. We find that there is an air of pretending to be diverse in ideology, belief systems, lifestyles, but there actually are so many other lifestyles that exist, that folks even in the Bay Area can be judgmental toward.

It is essential to remember that people come from different communities and are exposed to different styles of coping and adaptation and lifestyles. Here in California, we might have an understanding of diversity from a perspective of race or gender affirming approach, although we must still keep in mind that there is a broader view of diversity outside of California or any of our respective bubbles, too.

## Writing Prompt

Within the framework of the Balan 3-2-1 Method, consider your response to the following:

**What are some elements of your identity?**

3. With intention, set your internal and external environment.
   - **The body**: What mindfulness techniques are you choosing to allow your body to heal?

   _____

   _____

   _____

   _____

   _____

   - **The setting**: How are you intentionally influencing your setting?

   _____

   _____

   _____

   _____

   - **The breath**: Which breathing technique will you use as you prepare for this exercise?

   _____

   _____

   _____

   _____

   _____

2. What are your thoughts and feelings in response to the writing prompt above?

_____

_____

_____

_____

_____

_____

_____

_____

_____

_____

1. What is your one intent or affirmation in context of the writing prompt above?

_____

_____

_____

_____

_____

## Roles

We discussed identity and trauma and provided several writing prompts regarding identity in specific. We now switch to roles, chosen or assigned, and their impacts on our identity.

For example, Duygu identifies her roles as being a mother, a daughter, a sister, a therapist, being Turkish, an immigrant, from the Middle East, a wife, an author, a wannabe dancer, a healer, soul worker, a searcher, and a traveler.

## Writing Prompt

Consider using the space below to reflect on your roles.

_____

_____

_____

_____

_____

_____

_____

_____

_____

_____

_____

When we think about our roles as a sister, father, healer, or artist, what does that mean in the context of our society? How our roles are portrayed in society, the expectations around them, and what we are being told they must look like all impact us.

For example, what does it look like to be in a family, what characteristics are associated with motherhood or fatherhood? What does being a sister entail? How are holidays celebrated in families? There is a certain ideal around these things, celebrations, vacations, or holidays. It is important to remember that people come from complex backgrounds.

There is no one-size-fits-all fathering. People come from wounded relationships. For some, holidays can be quite triggering as that is the time their abusive parent is home. For some, sister-hood is parentified and really complex. There may not be a bond like those portrayed in social media or TV or in movies.

There are relationships that are difficult, where the people who were supposed to protect us were the ones that hurt us the most. In terms of motherhood, the idea of what a family looks like, with a mom and a dad, isn't consistent with reality. It likely never was and certainly is not applicable today. There are families that are blended, that are highly functional, and those that look like they popped out of a drug store greetings card from the 1960s that are toxic and dysfunctional.

What we thrive for is not a cookie-cutter model of what our roles look like, but more around healthy roles. When we are healthy in our roles, that is what we vibrate and emanate to those around us. We create healthy bonds and connections, and health is what continues.

Some mothers feel very restricted and bound by the feminine role. Breast feeding is one of these highly charged issues. Unfortunately, there continues to be a lot of stigma around mothers who choose not to breastfeed, or mothers who work when their babies are very young, or mothers who travel. The understanding is the mother should be all sacrificing, should adjust their life and needs according to the baby, and should be the home maker. We know now that in our society that this is not true, that fathers are also crucial, as are coparents and other caregivers. They can offer richness, playtime, nourish, and care for their infants as well.

A decade ago, in New York City, as the Medical Director at a prestigious hospital system, when our son was born, Yener was allotted one official day for paternity leave, twenty four hours likely being the least legally allowable at the time. This speaks to the value our society and organizations placed on paternal bonding, connection, support of the birthing parent, etc.

Another example is when our son was in kindergarten, there were some parents who were stay at home moms and had more opportunities to be a class volunteer, and there were mothers who worked who could not do that. There was some guilt, as the working mothers are still guilted for not participating in pick up or drop off, or the school bake or book fairs.

Thankfully the whole understanding of motherhood and fatherhood roles is slowly beginning to break and change. There is still some societal understanding of what a mother and father's roles are, and they are still somewhat gender specific; even though it is shifting a bit, it still isn't rapid enough.

## Case Example: Contracts

The following is a clinical case example of re-writing dysfunctional contracts in relationships.

When our cell phone carrier doesn't provide us with what we need, we find another provider and sign a contract that suits our desires. Similarly at work, we either renegotiate a contract or leave altogether and sign one with another company.

Within relationships, there are also contracts. Agreements and roles within a family, among a couple, with our children can all be reassessed, re-evaluated, and changed.

This case is of a young woman who came into therapy to work on her family dynamics, conflicts, and feeling of intense guilt around her relationship with her sister.

In therapy, when Duygu asked how old the feeling of guilt and feeling of resentment felt, the client said since the age of five. As Duygu explored the relationship with her sister growing up, the client reported that the sister had many allergies as a child. The sister had sensitivities, and there were several occasions the sister was hospitalized.

Their mother and father were constantly anxious, burdened with the sibling's multiple medical issues, requiring attention, trips to doctor's visits, and vigilance around the home. The client was always given the responsibility to care for and make sure the sister was safe and cared for. This gave the client a sense of resentment in her body, and she describes her neck and shoulders are becoming tense. She describes hearing over and over again: "watch out for your sister" and "take care of your sister."

Since the sister had numerous food allergies, there were so many foods the client was unable to have in the house. The client had to modify her life and was not allowed to have certain experiences in order to meet the sister's health needs.

This created an imbalanced relationship, and she had a feeling of being responsible for and being saddled with a responsibility that actually wasn't hers.

As the client got older, the sister with the sensitivities who had learned to lean on the client constantly asked for support. When she moved to NYC, she asked the client to help her find an apartment. The client supported her with shopping and cleaning supplies, due to her chemical sensitivities, and finding her a suitable place to rent.

That was in their contract. It was implicitly stated that client would be the caretaker in the relationship.

Once the client had her own child and had needs of her own as a new mother, she reported the resentment she felt increased. She was sleep deprived, without much support of her own to care for her newborn and still trapped in a demanding contract.

Throughout all the years, the sister learned the client would be there, and never learned to consider the client's needs, or that she would have desires or wishes that were different than hers. This began to create a lot of friction in their relationship.

In this case, their old contract and their old agreement of "I will take care of you" and "I will adjust my needs in accordance with yours" wasn't working anymore.

After some work around boundary setting and identifying what the client needed and wished for the relationship with her sister to look like, she was able to give her burden back to the sister.

The client was able to have a more even, peaceful sisterhood, where both were individuals. The client was released from the obligation and job that wasn't hers.

In therapy, one of the affirmations used was: "that's not your job, your job is to be yourself and have fun with your sister." The messages worked on in therapy were: "you can't take care of your sister because you are a child yourself," "you can eat whatever cookie or peanut butter sandwich you want, because you are not the one with the allergies," and "you have the freedom to live your life."

The client was able to set boundaries with her sister and over time was able to create an environment where they were able to spend time together and enjoy each other's company. The sister then learned to take responsibility of being a peer to the sister, an aunt, and a support system herself.

Their dynamics and contract were re-written and fair.

## Writing Prompt

Based on the prompts of identity and roles you identified above, consider using the space below to reflect on how these parts of you impact your day-to-day life?

1. **How are you restricted by parts of you?**

_____

_____

_____

_____

_____

_____

_____

_____

_____

2. **How do you celebrate each part of you?**

_____

_____

_____

_____

_____

_____

_____

_____

_____

We have discussed identity and role, and we will add more regarding specific examples. There are many studies on the impact of trauma on ethnicity, race, and identity, and in the following section, we will explore other examples in further detail.

## Trauma: LGBTQIA+

The study by Keating and Muller (2020) discusses discrimination as a form of trauma in LGBTQ+ individuals. The study provides support for the hypothesis that those with discrimination as part of their trauma experience had increased emotional dysregulation, anxiety, attachment avoidance, increased symptoms of posttraumatic stress disorder as well as dissociative symptoms.

Identity based physical attacks are another source of trauma in the LGBTQ+ community. Homophobia and transphobia are concerns to be addressed and explored as potential sources of trauma in the individual. These identity-related abuses cause long-lasting effects including physical and mental trauma. Those discriminated against also are impacted financially and from various social circles including previous support networks.

The article by Johnson et al. (2021) describes patterns of microaggressions and victim-blaming, secondary microaggressions in populations, and the harmful effects they result in. The high prevalence of microaggressions in marginalized populations increases their vulnerability and subsequent mental health and physical health risks.

The spiral of health-related concerns due to these targeted attacks is caused by and exacerbated by the traumatic effects of these interactions. There is a significant correlation between identity-related abuse and depression, self-injury, and suicide attempts.

Caregivers such as parents and advocates, as well as loved ones of those targeted due to their identity are also susceptible to and targets of gaslighting and traumatic attacks. These range from the general political and societal to the specific ostracization, bullying, and direct attacking of the individuals.

This becomes particularly troublesome when parents and caregivers are at a time in their transgender child's life and working with clinical teams to plan a path forward for their child. The shame, distress, mental health burden, delays and even refusal of treatment when this occurs results in widening of inequity, worsening of stigma, and leaves the people looking for compassion left alone and betrayed.

## Racial Discrimination

Studies by Bird et al. (2021) and Mekawi et al. (2020) review racial discrimination and discuss the associated posttraumatic stress symptoms, emotional dysregulation, and positive correlation with predictor of future severity of posttraumatic stress disorder symptoms. Emotional dysregulation in this context is defined as inability to manage emotions in reaction to discrimination.

Some studies in the literature suggest that African Americans are at higher risk of developing posttraumatic stress disorder, more severe symptoms, and experience them longer, leading to chronic posttraumatic stress disorder more often. Other studies do not support this and suggest that there aren't predisposing factors based on ethnicity alone in developing posttraumatic stress disorder.

What is important to take away from such conflicting data is that the events and experiences the individual has been exposed to in the past, determines how they understand, make sense of and react when witnessing a traumatic event.

Effects of racial discrimination range from the psychological, such as shame, to the physical such as direct bodily attacks, and more insidious medical harms of elevated stress states. The authors of the Mekawi et al. (2020) study suggest that even if racial discrimination is not a main presenting issue during treatment, that it be a part of the differential and ruled out.

Hankerson et al. (2022) discuss how structural racism and cumulative trauma impacts the intergenerational transmission of depression. The conclusions raise the important issue of access and awareness of these risk factors to ensure timely assessment and treatment as appropriate.

# Occupation Specific Hazards

## *Healthcare Providers*

The occupational hazards of being a healthcare provider as well as the associated mental and physical health burdens have been known to clinicians and organizations well before the pandemic. They include:

- Acute and posttraumatic stress disorders
- Alcohol and substance use disorders
- Anxiety disorders
- Burnout, absenteeism, presenteeism
- Depression disorders
- Fatigue
- Self-injury and suicide
- Sleep disturbances

Dealing with electronic medical records and charting, threats of being sued, compliance and regulatory burdens of managed care, long hours, inflexibility of work hours, minimal control of case load or mix, exposure to infectious illnesses, exposure to traumatic situations and life stories are some of the factors.

The essential worker nature of the healthcare provider during the pandemic further exacerbated an already stressed model of care and has had significantly deleterious mental and physical health consequences.

While absenteeism, burnout, turnover, and staffing shortages were present pre-pandemic, the impact on health care during the pandemic has been tremendous.

Even in the absence of a global infectious disease, being a healthcare worker has always come with associated issues that have also affected the family of the clinician. While being a clinician is deeply rewarding and we are continuously grateful for all our past and current experiences, we realize the impact it has had on our bodies and minds. Thankfully there are protective factors also associated with being in healthcare. They are similar to the general protective factors such as belonging in a community, pride in the work provided, as well as above average income and access to world-class mental and physical healthcare.

Working in some of the busiest emergency departments in the United States, Yener has seen the effect firsthand of stress and how emergency room clinicians are routinely victims of trauma themselves. The ER is a high-risk place for developing acute stress reactions as well as posttraumatic stress disorder due to the nature of illnesses and conditions we care for, as well as the repetitive nature, the unpredictable aspects, and the societal implications of the care provided.

Studies indicate a higher prevalence of posttraumatic stress disorder in emergency department clinicians than general population. Clinicians who have experienced traumatic events may be more reluctant to share their experiences with others. They become withdrawn, less talkative, and we have witnessed an increase in desensitization. While there is an associated level of emotional fortitude by nature of those attracted to clinical positions with higher predilection to witnessing trauma, those clinicians also suffer.

Reports demonstrate, as well as our anecdotal experience of patients and colleagues, that there tends to be a higher incidence of psychosomatic illnesses in these populations. The physical manifestation of their stress reaction, coupled with masking their decreased desire to communicate their issues, share their problems or experiences, and reluctance to debrief, results in a more challenging group to even begin helping. This is especially true if the clinicians or first responders are delivering higher hours of care due to a pandemic or an emergency response such as an earthquake or fire. They may feel less inclined to burden others such as mental health clinicians, while taking time away from their calling and their professional roles.

As one can imagine, the longer the unaddressed stress reactions last, the higher the likelihood that it becomes more difficult to treat.

There may also be concerns regarding inability to share sensitive information. For example, early on in the pandemic, there were supply chain issues and global lack of availability of personal protective equipment, as well as hospital equipment such as ventilators to help patients breathe. There were clinicians working with administrators as well as medical ethicists in every country, and healthcare system that had to specifically come up with a process of how to allocate resources. For most clinicians, especially those in the United States, the concept of even thinking about rationing care was devastatingly novel and nauseatingly too close to home.

Clinicians on panels that determined these workflows were often unable to share the work being done or the selection criteria, if it ever came to a decision of who gets lifesaving intervention and who may not. That psychological burden took significant tolls on the individuals working in these groups that added onto the already high levels of stress of the virus itself.

Of note, surgeons have similar levels of posttraumatic stress disorder as ER clinicians, especially trauma surgeons. Interestingly, studies show that posttraumatic stress disorder symptomatology of trainees is higher than those post training. Medically treating an acutely ill person, dealing with loss, and then working with families of the patient is the job and also immensely stressful.

For more information on our experience and expert recommendations on emergency department psychiatric care, as well as individual and team-based approach to care that have stress mitigating elements, we invite you to read our best-selling previous book titled: *Big Book of Emergency Department Psychiatry* by Balan et al. (2018).

During her years of work with underserved and unhoused populations, Duygu was witness to indescribable existential tragedies. Part of our professional clinical training in mental health included our own individual therapy as well as group therapy. We both continue to have mentors and consultations groups we attend to further enhance our care for ourselves and others.

Stress and burnout were always risk factors for clinicians on the front line, especially those in the emergency department and intensive care units. The symptoms of burnout, the tiredness, irritability, presenteeism are well known, and for decades, human resources and hospitals have worked to get ahead and identify the issues early on, so as to preserve the clinician and role they play in the system. During the pandemic, while every industry and every individual were experiencing stress reactions simultaneously, the aftereffects of burnout in hospital and clinical care are now slowly coming to light.

Clinicians who work in high-stress, high-volume environments like prison systems and emergency departments on a day-to-day basis have to deal with mental illness and addictions and are faced with threats and violence. They also have moments where their work environments feel unsafe.

## Writing Prompt

Consider using the space below to reflect on the following:

**Has there ever been a situation at work that has made you feel unsafe? How did you cope with that?**

_____

_____

_____

_____

_____

_____

_____

_____

_____

_____

_____

When these kinds of attacks, assaults, traumatic stressors happen in employment, oftentimes when that job entails that kind of work, minimizing occurs. "What did you expect, you're working in a prison system" or "happens to everyone, just deal with it" are said, the stressor is dismissed and feelings are invalidated. As clinicians, supervisors, or any other role we play, it is important that we do not underestimate the impact of threats. When we are under threat, the danger is real.

When someone is unable to derive satisfaction or pride anymore in their work, they are constantly fatigued from working longer, more stressful hours, and without a doubt, it has an effect on the patients they care for.

While the use of face masks is cited as a common reason why general patient satisfaction has seen a decline during the pandemic, we also know the emotional connections or lack thereof, and the general sense of unease of the systems and the clinicians had an impact on the patient.

The end users of the healthcare system, patients and clinicians, have suffered throughout.

Taking this to the next step of concerns regarding burnout and the distracted clinician begs the question of medical errors, complications, and direct or indirect harm to the patient. Burnout as well as acute stress reactions lead to impairments in insight and impairments of judgment. Clinical decision making became impaired. We also know that alcoholism and substance use increased during the pandemic.

We are yet to see formal studies of medical errors attributable to dereliction of duty of the clinician, which is the four "d"s that add up to a successful medical malpractice lawsuit. We likely will not see anything of the sort, as it will implicate the clinician, and en masse may be difficult to prove direct causation, although we are certain this occurred.

The mass amounts of disease and death our colleagues have witnessed during the last several years of the pandemic are tragic. Folks didn't have the time to regroup and reenergize from one crisis to the next and added onto their stress and personal symptoms of trauma.

Looking to the immediate short term and for the long-term future, we are proponents of improved mental health in the workplace, specifically for health care workers.

## Military

Much has been written about the risks and hazards of being in the military, exposure to trauma, and development of mental health issues including posttraumatic stress disorder. Similar predisposing factors are present in those that subsequently develop and are diagnosed with posttraumatic stress disorder.

We recommend our readers to look up Donald Meichenbaum's book titled *Roadmap to Resilience: A Guide for Military, Trauma Victims and Their Families*, for evidence-based insights, action plans, and examples of coping strategies.

The repetitive, unpredictable, and longer lengths of exposure to traumatic events are specific to military, especially active-duty combatants. Likewise, protective factors for those in the armed forces are also similar, including belonging to a community, and how veterans are viewed in societies.

## Military: Moral Injury

Pertinent to this book is the connection between emotion regulation and symptomology severity of the trauma experience. The concept of moral injury is brought up in military mental health literature and is important to understand the unique challenges of being in combat and war. When the individual has thoughts and beliefs, cultural, religious, or otherwise, that conflict with their actions when part of the armed forces, moral injury may develop.

At the time of writing this book, there are several countries where there is active combat. The violence is depicted in new articles and social media, including interviews of soldiers. The ethical dilemma portrayed in their discussion of the events is part of the moral injury theory.

The impact on civilians, day-to-day life, women, children, healthcare workers, and entire communities is being displayed. This mismatch of the individuals' ethical and moral understanding of their world is an additional foundation to the development of symptom severity when exposed to such traumatic events.

## Risk Groups

Factors that increase the risk of being exposed to traumatic stressors, as well as developing an acute and/or posttraumatic stress disorders are included in the following section.

# Risk Group: Cyber Victimization

There is growing research into the development of posttraumatic stress disorder related to cyberbullying and cybervictimization. Even before the pandemic, clinicians were working with schools and workplace settings to identify, treat, and mitigate the effects of virtual bullying.

The cycle of being a victim and also a perpetrator of bullying is similar to the online world, and the mental health impacts on the individual and support system around the person are equally concerning.

The pandemic rapidly shifted education as well as large sectors of employment to a virtual setting, resulting in a need to be even more conscientious of cybervictimization. The ever presence and ability to be online has made it so that the bully, and consequently the victim, have significantly reduced barriers. A traditional bully at school or work is limited to the environment and time to interact.

The individual is often alone, minimal to no witnesses or distractors, and the online bullying can even be done anonymously. Of concern is when younger people are victims, the parents and caregivers may also not be around, resulting potentially in longer times of exposure to the bullying without intervention.

Children and adolescents exposed to such online bullying experience a range of symptoms including avoidance, anxiety, hyperactivity, depression, acute stress, and posttraumatic stress disorder. Older individuals also have increased substance and alcohol use. During our work in acute settings, including emergency rooms, we have seen young children and adolescents requiring emergency room visits, psychiatric intervention, with acute and long-lasting impacts of online bullying.

For more of the interplay between a cyberbully and traditional (real-world) bully patterns, the study by Mateu et al. (2020) is recommended.

Based on our clinical experience, as well as the findings in the study mentioned above, pediatricians, family practice doctors, nurses, mental health clinicians, emergency room doctors and nurses, as well as parents, schoolteachers, and counselors should all have cyberbullying and cybervictimization in mind as a screening question and on their differential diagnosis to uncover potential etiologies of the patient's concerns.

# Risk Group: Displaced Populations

There is an increasing number of people being (forcibly) displaced from their home and/or country. Causes include interpersonal violence, terrorism, war, sex trafficking, or political asylum seeking. Due to the transitory nature and minimal to no roots within the area the individuals and families are displaced to, they often have limited to no access to routine healthcare and certainly minimal to no mental health care. Crisis management mode and emergency care at best is what is available.

These populations are at elevated risk of mood and anxiety disorders, given housing and food insecurity, lack of social support, stable routines, as well as past and present exposure to physical and mental trauma.

Posttraumatic stress disorder is a common illness seen in these individuals, as is a collective sense of community-level trauma. Re-victimization is also unfortunately commonly seen in these populations.

Studies indicate that when ongoing therapy for trauma symptomatology is not available or inconsistent, other forms of partially self-guided therapies are effective.

# Risk Group: Pregnancy

Pregnancy is a time of heightened stress in the mother's life. Studies suggest that intimate partner violence perpetrated against women increases during pregnancy. The stress and anxiety are often shared with the partner of the pregnant person.

See Chapter 7, Family, Children, and Resilience, and Chapter 10, COVID, Disasters, and Loss, for more information on risk factors as well as resilience and protective factors during and after pregnancy.

Pregnancy does not always result in delivery of a viable baby, and therefore, also has associated traumatic experiences.

Pregnancy also does not always occur consensually or in a planned manner. In the context of rape, the trauma of being a victim as well as the burden of carrying the child and all accompanying stressors are intertwined.

Along with anxiety and depression, posttraumatic stress disorder is often associated with pregnancy, during and after delivery of the baby. Baby blues and postpartum depression are losing their stigma in general culture and mothers and families are able to feel comparatively more comfortable speaking about these issues. Treatment including talk therapy as well as medication if clinically warranted are well tolerated, safe, effective, and have positive clinical outcomes.

Adapting to being pregnant, delivering and caring for the newborn are all extremely stressful experience. A large percentage of mothers view the peripartum time as traumatic and anxiogenic.

The experience of having a child brings up many, often times mixed emotions within the parents. Anticipation, fears, worries, desires, and hopes, as well as generational culturally specific fantasies and expectations all become extremely relevant. Genetic testing, if and when available and clinically warranted, decisions surrounding what to do in the event of an undesired testing result are also high stressors.

All the new routines the caregivers must learn and adapt to such as feeding, clothing, bathing, and caring for a healthy infant are overwhelming. Coupled with cultural and medical pressures, decisions to breast feed or formula feed, as well as the ability of the mother to do so, all come with stigma, potential shame, and humiliation. Any semblance of prior routines for the caregivers is eviscerated as sleep schedules are overturned amid the significant demands of the newborn.

Even something as benign as sleep training and the clashing communication of letting the child cry themselves to sleep versus responding every time they wake up in a loving warm manner are all stressful.

Generations ago, women of different ages as well as those in same phases of life would stick with one another, share rituals and stories, and provide support to one another. Now with increased westernization, living in increased isolation, the demand on women to perform, and equitable employment models have changed these networks.

Especially with the pandemic, the whole feeling of being in a tribe, a group of supportive folks that helped with meal prep, childcare, schooling, and even supported breastfeeding has all but vanished.

Women are more and more alone in their endeavor of becoming a mother. Just like in any other relationship, one person cannot fulfill all the roles for someone. When a mother has to rely solely on her prior knowledge and her own emotional bandwidth, the end product can suffer.

Trying to keep a child physically safe, well-nourished, and entertained, as well as care for the tasks of homemaking, all on one's own adds an additional level of feeling inadequate. The increased level of being separate from others feeds the feelings of loneliness, frustration, and anger toward the self and others.

The mother or parent who is spread too thin, whose needs are not met, who is not supported by their community is at risk of attachment trauma. This starts affecting the bonding and attachment between mother and child which can later cause deeper wounding.

When the expectations that used to be fulfilled by the communal collective are now placed on one person or parent, they become unrealistic and near impossible to successfully meet. This is why it is so critical for mothers, parents, and caregivers to early on find a tribe to connect with.

Find a group of folks that may have similar life situations, or babies at the same age, or pregnancies around the same stage. You may connect with people facing similar challenges, such as breast feeding or loss of a child. You can also connect with people with different experience levels, such as older people with older children who can provide guidance and support from different backgrounds and perspectives.

Advise that we received years ago from a pediatrician, which we did not take and thought was absurd and borderline abusive, was to let our child cry himself to sleep at bedtime. The idea was that once we were sure our crying newborn's diaper was clean and he was otherwise fed and not too hot or too cold, we should let him cry to sleep and not go in the room to check on him.

There are different views on sleep training, one being based on attachment-based parenting. Some argue that this style is not conducive of our society today and to a degree we agree. Attachment-based parenting recommends on demand feeding, maximum skin to skin contact with the caregiver and baby and recommends for the baby to be in the same bed with caregivers as long as they desire. Without question, this attachment parenting can cause stress, especially within modern, isolated, nuclear families, and for a mother who needs to perform at work or is unable to breast feed on demand.

It is important for every family to evaluate their needs and demands and work toward what makes sense for them. It's also valuable to remember that babies don't sleep the same way adults do. When a baby turns and when they become more mobile, they startle themselves awake. The sleep patterns of babies aren't the same as adults either. So for some it may be unrealistic to have an eight hour sleep.

For some infants who don't sleep through the night in one episode, the sleep deprivation that develops in the caregiver has its own separate set of stressors, mentally and physically. Now in society, for some families, this is very crucial as it interferes with their parenting functions, which makes sense. Although the baby who may wet themselves, get hungry, or have other physiological needs has no ability to control these concerns. The caretaker has to be available and the one that resolves these issues for them.

During sleep training, the crying out method that is suggested and used by some may interfere with the feelings of trust and safety the infant has. Considering object permanence, when the baby does not see the mother, for the baby, the mother is not there. They have no notion that mom is available, that she still loves him and will return. For the baby, he is all alone in his bed, in the dark, without any way to change his diaper or feed himself. The message they receive is: "they are not coming for me."

Whatever methodology is used for sleep training, never break the trust and bond between the caretaker and the baby. The message should be: "I am here for you," "I will protect you," and "I hear you." The only way a newborn can communicate immediate needs is by crying. When they are hungry or tired or want attention, they call by crying. When they cry and the mother does not respond, this can lead to a learned helplessness, and the baby thinks: "I can cry all I want but no one will hear me," and "what I have to say doesn't matter," or "I am not important."

Duygu specializes in working with new parents with history of childhood trauma and attachment injury. When a traumatized parent has a child, it is common for the parent to experience and relive their childhood trauma. In some cases, this can even lead to re-traumatization. It is important for the parent to seek help in instances like these.

Many times, Duygu worked with parents who had repressed memories of childhood, who did not have access to certain feelings and sensations until their child reached the age at which the trauma or attachment injury occurred. In some severe cases, this led to depression, flashbacks, and even dissociation.

Parents who had toxic relationships with their own parents and whose childhood needs weren't met are at increased risk as well. Those that were mistreated, neglected, or emotionally abused as a child may re-experience their trauma as a parent, and they become anxious and hypervigilant about repeating the trauma with their own children.

Sometimes this increased focus and awareness can lead to overcorrection. For instance, in a parent who comes from a very rigid household with a lot of rules that were not explained well or where punishments were harsh. Experiences as a child of incongruent and unreasonable consequences may result in the adult overcompensating and becoming overly lenient as a parent. They then can have a hard time with boundaries themselves, a hard time saying no.

When we set boundaries with children, we send the message that "I can say no to you, but I will also say no to the world and not let you get harmed." Children need a container that has reliable walls. And this is precisely why kids push these walls. When boundaries are poor, the child will push and push until they find a boundary. Parents that come from harsh discipline will have a hard time putting up these boundaries for their children, that can even pertain to their safety or health like sleep or eating habits.

## Case Example: Boundary Setting

A young mother who came from a religious home, where there were very strict top-down rules, sought therapy when her daughter was two years old. The mother described as a child she was not allowed to play with certain toys, that there was no room for questioning, she had many chores, and harsh, age-inappropriate expectations. She reported always receiving the answer "no" without any explanation. She described a rigid, cold household.

An example she gave was when she remembers having nightmares, that she didn't feel like she had anyone to go to for comfort, that she didn't feel her parents would be receptive or caring.

When this person had her own child, she adopted the model of attachment parenting, where she didn't even put the baby in a stroller. She kept her baby on her body, had the baby sleep in their bed, and breastfed on demand. When the baby turned one and needed more boundaries and exploring more, the mother had a hard time, would get anxious, and was unable to say no to the child.

This led to the child getting restless resulting in long crying spells. This progressed, and by age two, when the child would wake up and demand chocolate milk, the mother would try to say no, although the child knew that if she cried enough, mom would give in.

This pattern repeated, and the kid's teeth began to rot from the sugary chocolate milk snacks. The child started to become even more uneasy, unable to participate in play groups or self-soothe.

Duygu and the mom began working together to explore the mom's unmet childhood needs. They were able to offer the mom's childhood self-love, care, and compassion, while still providing boundaries. They practiced how to say no to the daughter.

With the understanding that we can still be loving, caring parents and still hold ground for our kids, the mother learned to sit patiently with the daughter while she was upset. The mom would say: "I see you are upset; it is not time for chocolate milk."

Mom explored her feelings of being unsettled, and the girl who wanted to be loved and cared for years ago began to heal as this was processed in therapy.

The first night the mother tried this, it took her 87 times to tell her daughter "I love you; I see your pain, it is not time for chocolate milk." The next night it was 57 times, followed by 34 times.

As time passed, she was able to set boundaries and the daughter's separation from mom began developing on a healthy course.

Mom was overcompensating for her rigid upbringing by doing the complete opposite and causing a completely different type of injury. She taught herself how to create secure attachment, to be a compassionate, thoughtful parent, and to respond to the daughter's wants and needs.

She was ultimately able to set boundaries and enforce them in a caring and loving manner.

## Risk Group: Sexual Assault

Sexual assault is defined as the sexual contact with a person that is not consented to. It is illegal, and in literature is categorized as forcible, in the context of substances or being incapacitated, or combined forcible and involvement of substances.

All types of sexual assault are linked to a significant degree of developing posttraumatic stress disorder. If the victim was given substances against their will or knowledge, and combined with forcible sexual assault, this often results in significantly higher rates of developing traumatic stress.

Sexual assault during childhood, as compared to physical assault, develops into different types of pathology. Studies have also looked at the impact of being sexually assaulted by a relative versus a stranger.

Sexual assault by a relative results in more severe symptomatology of posttraumatic stress disorder. The number of assailants during a sexual assault encounter and the frequency of assaults also lead to more severe symptoms.

Studies suggest that sexual assault increases during times of war and natural disaster. Posttraumatic stress disorder developing from sexual assault has been linked to development of subsequent substance use disorders.

Investigations have been done regarding use of substances before, during, or after a sexual assault, and the effect on development of posttraumatic stress disorder symptoms. While the impact of the assault itself is varied based on the study, some suggest that the acute impact is lessened with intoxication, others contradict that. The common theme of the studies is that after the sexual assault, temporal proximity to substance use is connected with a more prolonged chronicity of trauma-related symptoms and a more complicated recovery phase.

## Risk Group: Substance Use

Substance use, as explored in prior sections, during and after the traumatic stressor increases the likelihood of developing mental health consequences. Comorbid substance use disorders in the presence of traumatic stress increase the severity of symptom presentation and acuity of progression of the acute and posttraumatic stress disorder pathology.

Common themes of individuals that exacerbate the symptoms of trauma-related stress include presence of self-blame. If the person is struggling with who they are as a person, that increases risk. Any perception or sense of control over the trauma-related events has a protective factor. Having made decisions before or after the event is also correlated with perception of self-blame and may make the presentation worse.

With substance use and the stigma surrounding it, people are blamed for their use, and deplete their social resources, and often run out of people to reach out to. As it relates to the individual, the person's chosen or found social support network is critical. As described in various sections of this book, isolation, especially in the context of substance use has a deleterious effect and having reliable friends and trusted community and social structures is protective.

There is shame and disappointment and messaging to the substance user of "why can't you just stop?" which gets internalized as blame, victimization, and guilt. This then puts the person at higher risk of accidental overdose, high-risk behaviors, re-traumatization, finding themselves in violent situations as well as harming themselves or others.

Substance use increases the risk of the individual as well as their barrier to healing. It makes it so that there is a lack of empathy toward them due to stigmatization. Mental health issues in general garner less empathy, compared to physical issues such as cancers, and it is even more problematic with substance use. Concepts of "you're not doing anything about it" or "it is your fault" are prevalent in these conditions.

Intoxication and addiction states certainly interfere with the activities of daily living of the person, thereby preventing or prolonging the ability to build resilience and forms of posttraumatic growth. School as well as work, and community-level social support structures, whether they be financial or interpersonal are all negatively affected by ongoing substance use.

Studies suggest that substance use often precedes the development of posttraumatic stress disorder. Research indicates that around 66% of people in substance use treatment have a diagnosis or meet criteria for posttraumatic stress disorder. This may be due to an increase in high-risk behaviors, as well as a decreased ability to think and reason, thereby putting oneself in danger, including a traumatic event.

There are also studies that show that posttraumatic stress disorder is linked with the subsequent development of substance and alcohol use. The events that remind the person of the trauma often lead to the desire to reduce and numb the feelings and thoughts associated with them.

This self-medication hypothesis comes from the thought that the individual uses substances to reduce, numb the feelings of depression, anxiety, hypervigilance, and sleep disturbances, among other trauma-related symptoms.

When treated sequentially or in different settings, the outcomes aren't as optimal as if both the trauma and the substance use are treated simultaneously. The randomized controlled trial by van Dam et al. (2013) discusses this in detail, providing evidence of the benefits of treating them at the same time.

While paying attention to the substance use disorder itself, we remind the reader to always mind their physical health conditions as well. Comorbid acute or chronic medical ailments have a tendency to additionally burden one's mental health and psychiatric issues. Dual diagnosis of mental and physical issues as well as an active substance use all contribute to a significantly higher rates of self-injury and completed suicide.

While it is clinically difficult to untangle the symptoms, causes of and results of the active substance use disorder versus the posttraumatic stress disorder symptoms, studies do show that treating the substance use disorder will decrease the intensity and severity of the trauma-related symptoms. In summary, seeking out and receiving treatment is always better for psychopathology- and substance-related disorders.

## Writing Prompt

Within the framework of the Balan 3-2-1 Method, consider your response to the following:

**If I didn't numb myself, what would I feel?**

3. With intention, set your internal and external environment.
   - **The body**: What mindfulness techniques are you choosing to allow your body to heal?

   _____

   _____

   _____

   - **The setting**: How are you intentionally influencing your setting?

   _____

   _____

   _____

   - **The breath**: Which breathing technique will you use as you prepare for this exercise?

   _____

   _____

   _____

   _____

2. What are your thoughts and feelings in response to the writing prompt above?

   _____

   _____

   _____

   _____

   _____

   _____

   _____

1. What is your one intent or affirmation in context of the writing prompt above?

_____

_____

_____

_____

## Writing Prompt

Knowing our vulnerabilities and what we are prone to is an important step in our self-discovery and healing process. Think of the things you are prone to do. Think of some of the things that you may need to pay attention to. Think of what has and has not worked in the past.

Lastly, think of the resources that you tried to incorporate before and what new resources have been made available to you, through this book and other sources that you would like to try next.

Consider using the space provided below to reflect on the following two-part writing prompt:

1. **What are my vulnerabilities? What are my risk factors?**

_____

_____

_____

_____

_____

_____

_____

_____

2. **What are the resources and strengths I have available to balance, regulate, and counter these risk factors?**

_____

_____

_____

_____

_____

_____

_____

_____

# Chapter 9

# Gaslighting and Other Betrayal Traumas

I secretly think reality exists so we can speculate about it.

*— Slavoj Žižek*

## Introduction

This chapter will review the concept of gaslighting in the clinical, workplace, as well as at the relationship level. Intimate partner violence in the framework of betrayal trauma will be explored along with concepts of violence turned inward and outward. A lengthy case example and clinical discussion is included, as well as practical tools to empower oneself in the setting of these insults and assaults.

## Gaslighting

The term gaslighting comes from the 1938 play by Patrick Hamilton and has since been entered into the common vernacular and popularized by different social movements. The original story is a thriller set in Victorian times about a husband who psychologically manipulates his wife in an attempt to rob her of her inheritance. No spoilers: consider either reading the play or watching any number of the film adaptations that have been made over the years.

The interactions and deliberate behaviors by the husband describe the lengths with which he goes to mentally abuse his spouse with the desired outcome of having her think she is losing her sanity. Lighting is changed, paintings are rearranged by the husband, and when inquired about them, he denied, causing the wife to question her cognitive ability.

Social isolation and lack of interaction with others to corroborate the wife's experiences or even validate her reality is the central theme of the story. The coercion and conspiratorial planning to manipulate the mind of another or group of individuals is therefore what the term gaslighting refers to.

DOI: 10.4324/9781003323815-13

## Betrayal Traumas

Intimate partner violence is the broader umbrella that certainly encompasses gaslighting. During times of stress and uncertainty such as a war, natural disaster, or pandemic, it is known that intimate partner violence increases. As discussed in Chapter 10, COVID, Disasters, and Loss, intimate partner violence has unfortunately significantly increased during the pandemic.

Burdens that increase during disasters and traumatic events include financial instability, loss of employment, loss of community, social isolation, increased substance, and alcohol use. These all are correlated with increased in aggressivity turned inwards as well as outwards. These themes will come up throughout this section.

Findings of studies such as the one by Lyons and Brewer (2021) describe how lockdowns and strict measures during the pandemic were taken advantage of by perpetrators of intimate partner violence. The built-in social isolation and significantly decreased access to appropriate health care systems allowed for fertile ground for mental and physical abuse.

Studies, including the article by Bates (2020), show that aggressivity in context of intimate relationships is similarly perpetrated by men and women equally. When intimate partner violence is present in a relationship, the bidirectionality of aggressivity detailed in research findings is sometimes at odds with the more familiar thesis of male dominated aggressions. Problems with giving up one's own reality and taking on the reality of your aggressor can have irreparable impacts.

While healthcare systems focused solely on the response to the virus, health screening, and mental well-being visits were postponed and neglected. The ability to routinely screen and detect the presence of violence or abuse at home therefore decreased. We have also heard that the feeling of inability to escape during the pandemic created an insurmountable barrier of terror in those experiencing trauma at home.

Gaslighting, as a model for psychological betrayal trauma, can occur at home, as with intimate partner violence, as well as in the workplace. Not surprisingly, institutional betrayal has also increased during the COVID pandemic. The commonality is the trust in a system or trust in the relationship is broken. Effects of retaliation in a work environment are similar to those at home.

Research, including the article by Brewer (2021), describes workplace and institutional betrayal, whistleblower-gaslighting, and the traumatic effects of gaslighting in the workplace. The belief or reliance on an organization's human resources, ethics and standards, and code of conduct when betrayed has significant effects on the individual.

The negative impact deepens when an employee believes that complaints or allegations will be followed up appropriately and confidentially, but either that is not the case, or worse, when the employee faces retaliation. The continued lack of validation, pushing aside, isolation, and managing the employee's every move and decision all exacerbate the effects of the problem.

## Clinical Gaslighting

There are instances of gaslighting specific to clinical interactions between a clinician and their patient and caregivers. The article by Riggs and Bartholomaeus (2018) discusses a specific instance of gaslighting in context of interactions with parents of transgender children. This article goes into the sequelae and harmful consequences of such behaviors.

Clinical gaslighting betrays the doctor–patient relationship and violates the embedded power hierarchy in the interaction. In addition to causing subsequent mistrust in the medical establishment, it has the more specific impact of potentially delaying clinically and medically appropriate care, such as the example in the paper by Riggs, and also inappropriately placing the burden of truth seeking on the vulnerable patient and family. For more information on identity related abuse, see Chapter 8, Culture, Identity, and Society.

Some contextual elements of gaslighting are described above, and we will now get more granular as to the methods the person employing gaslighting will resort to. Predominantly verbal forms include belittling as well as humiliation. Derogatory insults, name calling, including targeted efforts to decrease the individual's self-esteem and self-worth, are also used.

Manipulative verbal gaslighting that has a behavioral component includes blackmail such as emotional or other legal avenues. Verbal aggression, yelling, shouting, and other patterns are often seen. Bullying and other destabilizing interactions can certainly lead to controlling and trapped feelings of the victim.

In a relationship where jealousy is a predominant theme, mechanisms of isolating from friends and family as well as economic deprivation are resorted to. While there are some elements of overlap of intimate partner violence and violence within the family system, the posttraumatic stress disorder symptomatology is quite evident. The aggressor may also resort to monitoring their victim's movements, social media use, the people they interact with, telephone records, and internet browsing history.

Studies indicate that psychological abuse is highly correlated with posttraumatic stress disorder symptomatology, and that more severe symptoms of fear and continued abuse have a greater impact on the victim.

The lengths to which the perpetrator will go to create control over the basic day-to-day freedoms of their victim can be quite severe. The resulting cognitive dissonance further fuels the destabilization of the individual.

Invalidation as well as other manipulative behaviors may result in making it even more difficult for the victim to leave the relationship. Other manipulative and fraudulent mechanisms include bringing in legal as well as administrative systems to believe the perpetrator against the victim through false allegations.

If there are children involved, there may be threats to withhold the children from the other as well as threatening the children directly. This fear of uncertainty of living with the abuse in day-to-day life not only has physical and psychological impact on the individual, it also has serious consequences on the mental health of the children in the house.

Other forms of gaslighting that we have seen clinically include threats of abandoning the victim as well as threatening to hurt or kill themselves to make the other perform or do what they are asking them. This may lead to or include reduction of resources such as access to banking accounts or other forms of economic stability.

## Violence Turned Inward and Outward

There is also a whole other component of sexual aggressivity such as unwanted sexual advances at home and in the workplace. Other sexual forms of gaslighting include lying about being on birth control, coercion relating to getting pregnant or being pregnant. There may be times when the threat of aborting the fetus without discussing with the other is also used. The concept of control and power is certainly one that comes into play during reproductive control and gaslighting.

Lastly, the threat of morbidity and mortality in the context of a weapon such as a firearm is one that has such a power differential that not only reduces the ability to defend oneself but also acts to reduce resilience and even the ability to retaliate.

Several recent reports indicate that firearm ownership has increased in the United States during the COVID pandemic. The presence and access to a firearm directly increases the chances of injury and mortality.

We know clinically and societally that increase in firearm ownership and availability, coupled with times of high stress, results in higher firearm-related violence directed outwards and inwards. Gun violence was at its highest level in 2020. Fatal shootings in the United States increased significantly with an increase of 35% in 2020 compared to 2019.

Unsurprisingly, and even more tragically since the evidence was available to possibly reduce or prevent these issues, we now know that intimate partner violence related fatalities have also increased during the pandemic.

Overall drug related overdoses in the United States in 2021 were up over 15% from 2020 according to the National Center for Health Statistics. Studies report that there were more Americans that died in 2021 of drug overdoses than any other year. Overdose specifically involving fentanyl and other synthetic opioids significantly increased.

Interrelated and tragically concerning is the dramatic rate of increase of completed suicides during the pandemic. Adolescents and young adults comprised the largest group and largest rate of increase where this was observed.

## Case Study: Executive Gaslighting

Throughout this chapter, we have discussed definitions, examples, as well as relevant statistics of recent times. This next section will illustrate gaslighting uncovered during therapy sessions while under the care of one of the authors many years ago.

To ensure privacy and protection of information, all identifiers have been obscured and changed.

The clinical case is of a middle-aged executive, who was in psychotherapy for anxiety and other stressors. During their therapy sessions, they began to encounter issues with their supervisor. These concerns were then explored and worked through.

This executive was already working with their supervisor for four years with superior annual reviews as well as fulfilling all deliverables according to organizational needs. Prior to the onset of the betrayal trauma of gaslighting by the supervisor, the executive had in other contexts described their supervisor as pleasant and generally supportive.

According to the executive, randomly after one meeting, the supervisor began to berate, and in a completely unpredictable and uncharacteristic fashion, began to threaten and say that the executive was on "thin ice" and "short notice" to be terminated. The supervisor told the executive that they would micromanage them out, and it would be "very difficult for both of them," and that the executive had "no place at the organization."

The executive describes feeling taken aback, and upon questioning the superior for specifics as to what occurred, they were yelled at and told that they weren't "performing at their executive level." The executive never had a discussion like this with their supervisor or anyone else at that or any organization.

Over the course of the next several days, the executive reported that there was a failure to support the person as well as consistent noncommunicative and dismissive attitudes by the supervisor. The executive reported the supervisor had several other bursts of anger, pressure of speech at times, and threatening behavior saying that "goals were not being tracked" and "dots were not being connected."

This was in direct contrast with the executive's constant communication with the supervisor's boss and their boss's boss, as well as having documented praise and clear accomplishments of required outcomes. The executive attempted to bring this up with their supervisor, noting that they had emails and texts from the supervisor's boss and boss's boss indicating praise and value to the organization.

In addition to bringing this up in therapy, the executive spoke with the organization's human resources department as well as every other senior executive at their supervisor's level. Human resources stated that it was "unprofessional" of the supervisor and "unacceptable," and that the executive should tell them that, and they also stated that there were no indications or concerns they were aware of regarding the executive themselves.

The colleagues and peers all repeated that there were not only issues with the specific executive, but that the executive's supervisor was in fact under scrutiny by their own boss. Apparently, the supervisor was on a performance improvement plan and being micromanaged by their boss for actually not meeting deliverables in portfolios that did not pertain to this executive.

The executive reported feeling extremely anxious, having disrupted sleep, preoccupied thoughts, feeling scared, betrayed, nervous, hypervigilant while interacting with their supervisor, and cognitively perplexed. These all stemmed from that they were being told one thing that did not match up with not only their reality but anyone else's reality and felt harassed for being threatened to be micromanaged, bullied, and fired.

The supervisor went so far as to disclose to the executive that they "did not care" about the executive's portfolio and that it was "the least of their concern." The supervisor aggressively shouted that they were told to hire the executive by their boss's boss, and that they did not hire them and did not want them. As a reminder, this was after four years of working with this executive and giving them superior annual reviews.

In addition to the direct insults to the individual, the supervisor also said that the executive was known as a "senior expert in their field" and that they had "deep, personal, and meaningful relationships" with people in the organization.

The executive reports feeling this was additionally confusing in that in one breath the supervisor was threatening to fire the person, and in the next breath, they would praise them how wonderful they were but that the supervisor didn't want to work with them. The supervisor even once came to a meeting with a job opening they recommended the executive to apply to, saying how valuable the executive was and would be successful in the other position, which would have constituted a promotion.

This betrayal trauma occurred over the span of several weeks. According to the executive, the supervisor then acted as if none of the damage, harassment, threats, or bullying occurred and continued on meeting with them as if nothing happened.

Six months after this encounter occurred, the executive reported that their supervisor was abruptly leaving the organization. While the executive reported feeling alleviated and somewhat validated in the departure of the supervisor, much of the psychological damage had set deep roots.

Therapy to address the severe stress induced by the superior's outburst and threats lasted for over a year. The executive reported being seriously traumatized, feeling devalued, having to defensively work, and have witnesses when submitting documents or having meetings. While the executive was passionate about the portfolio, the supervisor's manipulative threats kept them questioning their reality, their career, and place in the system.

# Discussion

This is an example of how power differentials in high powered environments with executives earning high salaries under high pressure bring out subclinical psychopathology masked by superficial charm.

The nature of the external appearance and mannerisms that even the executive was describing as previously feeling supported and that the supervisor was generally a nice person made it harder for the executive and folks around them to detect and outwardly identify the insidious effects of what became toxic betrayal trauma in the form of gaslighting.

While there were undoubtedly crumbs to be able to trace and put together the dismissive nature and pattern of failure to support or showcase the work the executive was performing, the supervisor was otherwise falling within the cultural norm of a system that likely harbored similar pathology.

In this case, the executive is impacted by deceptive manipulation, as well as the unpredictability and lack of connection to previous work or feedback, which directly contradicted the information obtained from the boss of the superior.

We would like to draw your attention to the phases of gaslighting as described by Christensen and Evans-Murray (2021). The way this case example unfolded and was written follows the pattern of the phases quite prescriptively. The supervisor was initially seen as collegial and accepting with occasional praise and was even friendly at times.

While there may have been subtle jabs at times that the executive was "only" an expert in their field, this was covered by praise. The phases of gaslighting continued as the supervisor began to devalue and find fault in the executive, which was confusing and frustrating since they did not match the perceived reality of the executive. The trivial accusations became more common, especially during the bouts of threats and yelling.

According to the executive, the supervisor had a pattern of not reading or responding to emails or opening attachments in the past, and that other colleagues had noticed this. This however was swept under the rug and compensated for by frequent reminders and an organizational culture of overlooking a superior's lack of time due to extremely busy schedules.

The experiences of the executive included the supervisor providing vague overgeneralizations without the ability to pinpoint specific needs, as well as lack of clarity or vision for strategy to enhance the portfolio. The supervisor would cancel meetings without notice and not invite the executive to critical meetings where the executive would clearly add value. Of note, these elements follow the phases of gaslighting, especially in the workplace.

The resulting impact on the executive was they felt they needed to try to prove their value and worth to the organization. There was a time where the executive thought of becoming increasingly compliant and agreeing with everything said by the boss as the cycle of manipulation continued.

The executive reported obsessive rumination at times with desire to reverse the course and try to improve the relationship with the gaslighting supervisor. During one of these attempts at repair, the executive reported that the supervisor suggested the executive should find another job, but that they were still willing to work with them if they did not. The direction and support by the supervisor was already minimal and further went down to a non-existent amount.

Through therapy and communicating with human resources, as well as this executive's history of strong and meaningful, personal, and professional relationships, they were able to avoid one of the later stages of gaslighting which is depression.

The executive was able to avoid becoming a willing collaborator with the gaslighter. They were able to transform the feelings of helplessness, defensiveness, volatility, and uncertainty into hope and antifragility as others in the system were increasingly aware of the value the executive provided and the toxic environment the supervisor fostered.

An interesting piece of advice and way to frame the experience of gaslighting is to "not take the medicine" of the gaslighter. Just as one would not take the insulin of someone who has diabetes, one should not take the burden or prescribed solution for someone else's problem.

This executive also had mentors and close friends outside of the organization they were able to consult with, and they also spoke with private legal counsel for their rights and civil liberties relating to the emotional damages that were incurred.

By not creating a self-fulfilling prophecy of dejection and decreased value, in this case example, the executive was able to maintain their productivity and further excel in their career within the organization.

As the person healed, they were able to reflect on the increasingly apparent inferiority and professional jealousy on the part of the supervisor. The common misconception and difference between classic bullying and gaslighters is that the perpetrator of gaslighting is often intimidated themselves. They do not want their victims to do well or succeed, and this feeling of being threatened by status, popularity, power, influence, or values is what we saw elements of in this case example.

## Empowering Yourself at Work

As we described a betrayal trauma that occurred in the workplace and this specific executive involved human resources, there is benefit in diving deeper into aspects specific to work and professional environments.

The human resources department is not on the side of the employee, they are on the side of the organization. Any threat or concern that an employee brings up is only viewed in the context of whether or not it constitutes a threat to the organization or system. Toxicity and gaslighting can be thrown under the rug and reframed as personality clashes at work. When the bottom line and finance dictate strategy and drive behaviors, power hierarchies are easily abused with zero regard to the victim.

Suggestions for empowering yourself at work include asking for things in writing at work. Know the policies and procedures, as well as the code of conduct of the organization or company that you are working in. Consider collecting evidence such as printouts, including emails as well as calls or texts. These are relevant especially if there is manipulation in the perception of reality and gaslighting.

If there is an aggressive or sexualized stressor or psychological concerns, such as the example above, have witnesses at meetings, as well as look into recording meetings. Make sure depending on the state that you are in that you are legally able to record and make sure that if required, you obtain the permission of people in the meetings to be able to record it. The point is that it needs to be clear that the perpetrator will be on the record for their words and actions.

If the organization is large enough to have human resources or other compliance type departments, ensure that they are also made aware of the aggressivity or sexual advances, and consider external legal counsel as well, as these are not only inappropriate, depending on the case, but may also be illegal.

These recommendations for having documentations and having witnesses as well as reporting through the chains of command remove plausible deniability by the gaslighter, company, and human resources department.

While doing all of this, it is also critical that one takes care of their own mental health and relationships. Being mindful of the power dynamics as well as hierarchies is important, as well as the ability to understand what that means to the individual and the choices that they're making. Creating and maintaining relationships allows for the ability to corroborate with others, raise awareness as well as develop resilience.

## Results of Gaslighting

While there are some differences between males and females in terms of response to extreme stressors including gaslighting, in general, people have similar ranges of emotional and physical responses. Studies indicate that males have a higher tendency to externalize their suffering and incorporate self-injurious behavior such as substance and/or alcohol use as part of their coping mechanisms.

As discussed in portions of the case example above, the reality of the victim experiencing anxiety with or without depression is very common. The concern of feeling confused with decreased confidence either at work or in the home setting gradually erodes the ability for the victim to feel whole.

There becomes a time where the victim has a decrease in self-confidence and may even resort to defensive posturing not only in their words and actions but actually in their body posture. Earlier on while this embarrassment and emotional distress is at its most acute phases, there can be a constant feeling to try to seek approval of the perpetrator.

Hypervigilance especially in the workplace is common, although in the home setting in the context of physical or other sexual betrayal traumas, hyperarousal and safety seeking behaviors are unfortunately common.

Clinically, there may be an emotional withdrawing and may go so far as to symptoms of dissociation. There can be loss of dignity, loss of self-worth during a relationship that is toxic with significant traumas, and ultimately damage the ability to self-actualize. Substance and alcohol addictions are all too common comorbidities in these scenarios.

Self-doubt and feeling discredited can lead to replaying the interactions and conversations over and over again. This is exhausting and certainly an avoidable waste of mental and physical energy. Feeling guilt tripped and accompanying symptoms have been described as even feeling similar to the reactions during the grieving process.

Physical symptoms of these types of stressors include psychosomatic issues such as tension headaches, migraines, gastrointestinal issues, as well as sleep disturbances.

What is especially concerning is if there are children or other dependents involved, the exposure of the trauma and its aftereffects are long-lasting. Clinically, if you are responsible for the individual and/or a mandated reporter and this comes up in a session, further exploration is warranted to ensure that minors and those that are unable to care or defend for themselves are not in direct harm's way.

Gaslighting can work as the perpetrator may threaten custody of the child or separating the child from the other parent or guardian, but also may result in the loss of custody of children especially if there is an unsafe environment. Similarly, in the workplace, gaslighting may lead to the loss of one's job or career.

At work, the paranoia that is brought on by activities that were previously not an issue or considered routine in the context of gaslighting becomes a problem. When there is clinical gaslighting as described above, where a clinician might be discrediting or creating an environment where there is a betrayal of the power hierarchy and subject matter expertise, the institution itself suffers moral harm in addition to the direct impact to the victim and their families.

There ends up being a significant waste of energy and time for defensive posturing at home, as well as at the workplace, resulting in decreased energy, wasted resources, as well as decreased productivity.

Additionally, there is an associated increased rate of employee turnover as well as difficulty filling open positions. Decreased satisfaction of end users of the organization leads to reinforcing of negative stereotypes, damaged reputation, and public relations concerns. When these behaviors go unchecked or are not dealt with, we have seen associated decreased in workplace safety, increase in workplace injuries, increase in legal allegations and lawsuits.

## Writing Prompt

Within the framework of the Balan 3-2-1 Method, consider your response to the following:

**What hurt you?**

3. With intention, set your internal and external environment.
   - **The body**: What mindfulness techniques are you choosing to allow your body to heal?

   _____

   _____

   _____

   _____

   - **The setting**: How are you intentionally influencing your setting?

   _____

   _____

   _____

   _____

   - **The breath**: Which breathing technique will you use as you prepare for this exercise?

   _____

   _____

   _____

   _____

2. What are your thoughts and feelings in response to the writing prompt above?

   _____

   _____

   _____

_____
_____
_____
_____
_____
_____
_____
_____

1. What is your one intent or affirmation in context of the writing prompt above?

_____
_____
_____
_____
_____

## Writing Prompt

Within the framework of the Balan 3-2-1 Method, consider your response to the following:

**What gets in the way of forgiveness?**

3. With intention, set your internal and external environment.
   - **The body**: What mindfulness techniques are you choosing to allow your body to heal?

_____
_____
_____

   - **The setting**: How are you intentionally influencing your setting?

_____
_____
_____
_____

– **The breath**: Which breathing technique will you use as you prepare for this exercise?

_____

_____

_____

_____

2. What are your thoughts and feelings in response to the writing prompt above?

_____

_____

_____

_____

_____

_____

_____

_____

_____

1. What is your one intent or affirmation in context of the writing prompt above?

_____

_____

_____

_____

_____

_____

_____

_____

## Chapter 10

# COVID, Disasters, and Loss

Fear is the mind-killer. Fear is the little-death that brings total obliteration. I will face my fear.

*– Frank Herbert*

## Introduction

Research is consistent with the fact that medical illnesses, prolonged suffering, lengthy hospitalizations, and severe acute illnesses are associated with mental health sequelae including depression, anxiety, and acute and posttraumatic stress disorders.

The COVID-19 global pandemic, associated stigma, economic and social implications all add to the acute infection phase and have contributed significantly to an increase in demand for mental health care.

Compared to prior epidemics such as the Severe Acute Respiratory Syndrome (SARS) in 2003, this current pandemic affects us at the height of available communication technologies. We are at a point where even if we try to avoid the news or a post, the "infodemic" is inescapable and ubiquitous.

One does not need to be an expert in trauma-informed care to surmise the negative effects of repetitive morbid information perversely incentivized to generate clicks and revenue.

The issues relating to acute stress, posttraumatic stress, depression, anxiety, psychosocial detriments, increase in substance use, self-injurious behaviors, and completed suicides have been referred to as the "epidemic" within this pandemic.

DOI: 10.4324/9781003323815-14

## Fear

In the beginning phases of the COVID pandemic, at the height of the unknown, fear was commonplace and often dictated decisions. The majority of people undoubtedly met clinical criteria for acute stress disorders, and sadly a subsection of those have gone on to longer-term, posttraumatic stress disorders.

In 1999, Duygu and Yener had just returned home after a night of enjoying the company of friends in Istanbul, Turkey, when around 2 am a devastating earthquake occurred. It was like nothing we ever experienced, at a 7.6 Richter magnitude and lasted over thirty seconds. Thankfully the apartment buildings we lived in were not harmed and we were able to leave the building to spend the next couple of nights outside, camping in our cars, as we endured the subsequent aftershocks.

We recall the injury and death counter that the Turkish news stations displayed on the bottom right corner of the TV screen. All the time. It was horrifying. Watching the counter raise like the odometer on a car was surreal, especially as we heard of the damage caused and our friends and loved ones affected.

When the initial earthquake happened, the shaking and rumbling was so intense, and there was an eerie sound to it that we will never forget.

Then a brief silence, followed by the synchronized wailing of car alarms, barking of street dogs, intense screaming of people in panic, searching for an exit, or calling to their loved ones, and then the ambulance and police sirens. Once the sirens of first responders began, it did not stop. For days and days.

It is interesting how we have not talked about the earthquake in some time, and now as we write this book have memories, essentially flashbacks, of that experience.

The hospitalized and sick and death count on televisions and websites during the COVID pandemic is in and of itself traumatizing, in addition to reopening old wounds of prior traumas.

A significant difference between the traumatic events is that the 1999 earthquake was time limited, lasted thirty plus seconds, while there were many aftershocks, those also subsided quickly. The earthquake was limited to a part of Turkey, and therefore, anyone anywhere else was only affected by the news or vicariously through updates of loved ones.

The COVID pandemic, the virus itself, and responses by global and local authorities continue to progress and evolve, with what appears to be a long-lasting impact on all of our lives. The similarities between something like an earthquake or other natural disaster and COVID are they were both unpredictable and uncontrollable.

At the time of writing this, expectations of another variant of the virus impacting the United States are being discussed, and Europe and parts of Asia are in the throes of another surge in cases and hospitalizations. This virus is ubiquitous with seemingly no end in sight and has affected everyone, everywhere.

For the earthquake and aftershocks, we were able to leave our apartment building and spent time in our cars in the parking lots for fear of potential structural damage to the buildings. We were fortunate to be able to do this, knowing that if we were clear of buildings or trees, the shaking ground would cause little physical damage to us. With the pandemic, the concern of asymptomatic transmission and pre-symptomatic transmission became a part of our lexicon, thereby amplifying the anxiety and global angst.

## Repercussions

Reports suggest that mental health and wellbeing has tremendously suffered during the pandemic, resulting in a significant increase in demand and need for mental health services. According to an article by Dalpati et al. (2022), young adults and students suffered significantly in the context of school closures, limited outdoor activities, and socialization during the pandemic.

Our attention and the information provided to the population in each country throughout the world have been able to be channeled and diverted extremely quickly. This feels like a shift in the speed with which this has been able to occur, given social media and consolidation of messaging around fear.

The authors discuss the effect of increased screen time and social isolation, and its effects on increasing stress, resulting in a demonstrable increase in anxiety disorders, mood disorders including depression, posttraumatic stress disorders, and even psychotic disorders.

The uncertainties about the academic year, examination schedule, and switching to virtual and screen-based learning are also discussed. Student's concerns about graduating, internships, and trainee placements were put on hold with significant uncertainty as to how and when things would resume, if ever.

Mental health and behavioral conditions exacerbated or caused by the COVID pandemic and associated lockdowns, quarantines, social distancing measures, stringent hygiene practices, financial pressures, and school and workplace closures include the following:

■ Absenteeism flourished.
  – Absenteeism is defined as a pattern of staying away from work or school, regardless of reason. There has unfortunately been a significant increase in absenteeism.
■ Alcohol use increased:
  – Relapse of unhealthy drinking behaviors increased.
  – Increase in alcohol related physical illnesses, acute and chronic have increased.
  – Reports indicate that one out of three adults were drinking during the workday during the pandemic.
  – Alcohol related risky behaviors increased.
■ Anxiety disorders increased, including:
  – Phobic anxieties:
    • Germ phobia, resulting in increased hand washing, mask wearing, and social distancing
    • Public transportation anxieties
    • Claustrophobia
    • Agoraphobia
  – Anxiety of being away from work and society.
  – Anxiety of having to go back to work and prior routines.
  – Anxiety of being perceived as not following rules.
  – Anxiety of not understanding the rules or recommendations.
  – Obsessive compulsive disorders flourished:
    • Fear of contamination increased.
    • Increased hand washing was recommended.
    • Continued symptom checking was observed.
    • Compulsive testing for the disease, regardless of risk and exposure.
  – The study by Sanchez-Gomez et al. (2021) discusses the pandemic as a collective, mass traumatic event. The authors discuss the continuous hyperarousal throughout the pandemic resulting fear, anxiety, and ultimately posttraumatic stress disorder. The study refers to headline stress disorder in context of media reports and associated stress and anxiety it produced. It also discusses the interconnectivity between states of hyperarousal, intrusions, avoidance, fear of COVID specifically, and one's mental health in general.
■ Behavioral addictions increased, including:
  – Internet addictions including social media consumption have increased.
  – Gaming addictions such as video games and gambling resulting in loss of productivity as well as financial repercussions.
  – Constantly checking media, news, internet, and social media:
    • Repeated exposure to traumatic photos and headlines.
    • Fear based, sensationalized messaging disguised as information to sell views and articles.
    • Information not consistent with governmental recommendations, confusion, distrust, cynicism, and polarizing energy.

- ▪ Bereavement, existential as well as secondary and realized loss has increased:
  - – Related to grief and loss discussed throughout this section, symptoms of bereavement increased.
- ▪ Burnout increased:
  - – Globally, we are witnessing a significant increase in signs and symptoms of burnout that impacts relationships personally and professionally.
  - – Leading to exhaustion.
  - – Increased feelings of depersonalization.
  - – Resulting in increased risk for other psychiatric issues including depression, suicidality, anxiety, and other traumatic stress disorders.
  - – Highest impacted groups include medical caregivers and educators.
  - – The United States Bureau of Labor Statistics report that in 2021 close to 47 million people left their jobs voluntarily!
- ▪ Child abuse and neglect increased:
  - – Significant increase of physical abuse of children has been reported, compared to pre-pandemic, and is associated with increase in intimate partner violence described in this section.
  - – The World Health Organization and UNICEF sounded the alarm in July 2022 reporting that global vaccination coverage decreased, with over 25 million babies not receiving life-saving immunizations against illnesses such as diphtheria, measles, tetanus, and pertussis.
    - • This concerning information, described as a red alert in their communications, suggests that this was due to service chain disruptions, as well as containment measures during the pandemic that limited supply to an already vulnerable set or populations around the world.
    - • The predicted morbidity and mortality that will follow as a result is tragic.
- ▪ COVID-related distress blossomed:
  - – Defined loosely as the fear of ongoing symptoms, fear of being infected, infecting someone else, as well as traumatic stress related to being ill.
- ▪ Depression increased:
  - – Studies show direct correlation between timing from lockdown in response to the virus and statistically significant increase in depression scores of individuals affected.
  - – Most of us are not skilled or trained to appropriately assess risk of threats. People have difficulty reading scientific data or evidence in an unbiased way. Our view on the world is colored by the narrative we hold true at the time of perceiving the stimulus. Depression alters and skews the lens with which we receive information. A person who is depressed or otherwise unable to function in their activities of daily living and has been indoctrinated in self-hate, blame, shame, and anxiety is unable to remember their own why and succumbs to the narrative being fed to them.
- ▪ Existential crises manifested during the advent of the pandemic include:
  - – Catastrophizing
  - – Magical thinking
  - – Resulting in large life changes made based on fear, with an irrational mind, such as moving and deciding on relationship changes
  - – Realization that one never had full control of life and circumstances surrounding life anyway

- – Increased insight into governmental, local, and national responses, as well as priorities
- – Realization that the average person has minimal to no real understanding of risk calculations
■ Fatigue increased in the following domains:
  - – Caregiver fatigue
  - – Compassion fatigue
  - – Fatigue from real and imagined impacts of the virus
■ Fear of the following issues increased:
  - – Getting sick
  - – Dying, also termed death anxiety, took full force of the globe
  - – Dying alone
  - – Getting a loved one sick
  - – Caring for loved one
  - – The illness and death of a loved one
■ Grief and all its stages increased:
  - – Denial
  - – Anger
  - – Bargaining
  - – Sadness
  - – Acceptance
  - – Losses: irreplaceable losses such as loss of life, loved ones, as well as replaceable losses such as jobs, material things, and routines
■ Guilt skyrocketed:
  - – Pre-symptomatic spread, associated anxiety and guilt of the unknown and unknowable all contributed to increasing guilt.
  - – Fear of asymptomatic spread, similarly causing fear and terror, increased guilt.
  - – Rumination, thinking about over and over again if possibly exposed someone without knowing, then feeling guilty when hearing of someone becoming ill, became a common pattern.
■ Helplessness increased:
  - – Feeling of loss of control.
  - – Loss of confidence in systems and organizations. See Chapter 8 on Culture, Identity, and Society for a discussion on occupational hazards.
■ Hopelessness increased:
  - – Inability to control situations.
  - – Inability to calculate true risks of behavioral choices made for self and family.
■ Hormonal impact became apparent:
  - – Changes in fertility, birthrates have been noted.
    Impact on menstrual cycle due to the virus itself, compensatory measures, and general immune and hormonal system dysregulation.
■ Intimate Partner Violence flourished:
  - – Previously termed Domestic Violence, we have witnessed a significant increase in violence among partners.
  - – Studies indicate a 50%–70% increase in intimate partner fatalities since 2020, the first year of the pandemic.

■ Isolation increased:
  – Loneliness increased, as a feature of social distancing and a side effect of its sequalae.
  – Exacerbation of mental and other physical ailments.
  – COVID pods and bubbles created in attempt to emulate normalcy early on, resulting in frustration, loss of friendships, and increased frustration, isolation, anger, cynicism.
■ Life expectancy has been seriously impacted:
  – According to studies, including the one by Schwandt et al. (2022), life expectancy decreased during the years 2020 and 2021 of the pandemic compared to pre-pandemic levels.
■ Psychosomatic complaints manifested:
  – There has been a significant increase in primary care visits that are directly linked with anxiety and concerns as a consequence of the pandemic.
  – As discussed earlier in the book, there are reports that upwards of 90% of primary care doctor visits are related to stress and other mental health concerns.
■ Physical routine changes leading to mental health issues:
  – Less walking, more sitting/sedentary activities.
  – Less access to daylight during lockdowns.
  – Technology use increase resulting in:
    • Back and neck pains.
    • Sedentary lifestyle bringing on or exacerbating medical conditions due to inactivity, such as heart disease and blood sugar imbalances and diabetes.
    • Addictive behaviors, resulting in anxiety, attention difficulties, depression, bullying and being a victim of bullying, all the way to self-injury and suicide. As of the writing of this book, there are lawsuits against one of the major social media companies alleging usage of the app resulted in mental health harms of the children using them.
■ Nutritional intake changes were observed:
  – We have seen a significant impact on the consumption of food and unhealthy choices being made, resulting in weight gain in adults as well as the pediatric population. As a country that has already suffered with a weight problem pre-pandemic, we now see this problem become significantly worse, with consequences on immediate and future physical and mental health that we currently cannot even imagine.
  – Eating disorders have exacerbated.
  – Poor dietary choices due to availability as well as sedentary lifestyle brought on by lockdowns, quarantining, and general fear have increased.
  – Unhealthy choices in general, as it relates to beverage consumption, unbalanced meals, poorer quality of foods chosen, all contribute to a nutritional portrait that has suffered.
■ Peripartum issues including postpartum depression worsened:
  – The research article by Shuman et al. (2022) discusses the peripartum issues in conjunction with the pandemic. Per the article, one out of three participants were positive for postpartum depression (higher than pre-pandemic prevalence), those who fed their infants formula as well as those whose infants required admission to the neonatal intensive care unit were at significantly greater odds of screening positive for postpartum depression.
■ Concern about themselves as well as their babies contracting the virus was also a significant predictive factor. The authors discuss additional impacts such as the need for social distancing as well as the significant change in hospital admission visitor policies in place during the pandemic, as well as parenting and breastfeeding classes being switched to online.

■ They discuss the impact of decreased social support structures in place for pregnant and postpartum patients as a risk for issues with breastfeeding leading to formula feeding.

 – We have several friends who delivered during the early months of the pandemic, and they describe the sense of isolation due to visitor rules, the dampening effect of such a joyous occasion, and how much more medicalized and unceremonious the birthing experience was. Because so much was unknown at the onset of the pandemic, the mothers tell us how extremely anxious they were, viewing every contact as a potential hazard to themselves and their baby. Although understandable, the masking requirement and diminished social connections to in-person Lamaze or parent education classes had an effect of making them feel less special and cared for. The financial impact, even though they were routine deliveries, was a topic of discussion, given the uncertainty of the economy.

 – The review by Campos-Garzón et al. (2021) discusses the gestation period and vulnerabilities during pregnancy. From a physiological perspective, and how the response to the pandemic psychologically may have impact on the pregnant person and then to the unborn child.

■ Presenteeism increased:

 Presenteeism is defined as the loss of productivity when a student or employee is not functioning at their fullest, while preset at their job or school.

 – While this is associated with burnout, it is certainly impacted by loss of hope, structure, feelings of helplessness, exhaustion, as well as existential angst.

 – Similar to absenteeism, this also results in decreased productivity, decreased value add, spiraling of morale, and a negative health impact to the organization and the individual.

■ Posttraumatic stress disorder diagnoses have increased:

 – Individual trauma has increased.

 – Collective trauma has also increased.

■ Reckless behaviors increased:

 – Dangerous sexual behaviors have gone up in prevalence.

 – Increased substance and alcohol use has been documented.

 – Increase in other risk-taking behaviors has been observed.

■ Shame increased:

 – Shame is a defense response. It makes it so that we make ourselves submissive and smaller, as well as more obedient. In situations of stress, violence, and oppression, when we internalize shame, it ends up being a genius mechanism of staying alive.

 – When we don't have shame, we might go against the oppressor and resist victimhood.

 – The internalization of "I am at fault," "I am not good," or "there is nothing that I can do" resembles helplessness, although is protective during the traumatic scenarios described earlier. Making oneself small, not catching the attention of anyone, not causing resistance is protective, as it could create increased conflict and even be more dangerous.

 – Shame is also a mechanism of control as it makes people doubt themselves. Shame makes people not use their defenses or draw from their strengths. Shame makes people weaker and erases their ego and identity. It takes away nuances of identity when you are ashamed of who you are. A person with shame doesn't express themselves as they would have, and they certainly don't go against anything considered a limit. There is minimal to no exploration externally in shame.

 – Similarly, our thoughts are controlled when we are shamed and feel ashamed. We don't explore different ideas or ideologies when you feel like you are inferior. It is more of a

numbing when you don't have the feeling of credibility and that you are a being that can create thoughts and ideas.
- Shame certainly increased during the pandemic and associated responses, resulting in difficulty in believing in oneself, and the mass absorption of the thoughts of others that have been downloaded onto the public.

■ Self-injury rates have increased:
- There has been an alarmingly high increase in the incidence of self-injury and suicide attempts.
- The rate with which these self-injurious behaviors have increased has also correlated with an unfortunate dramatically increased number of completed suicides. Losses that could have been prevented.

■ Sleep disorders have proliferated:
- The negative impacts on sleep schedule, falling asleep, staying asleep, early awakening have all been documented.
- Decrease in restorative sleep has resulted in tiredness during the daytime, further exacerbating absenteeism, presenteeism, and decreased productivity.

■ Substance use has risen at an unprecedented rate:
- There has been an increase in reported relapses.
- There are reports of an increase of up to 40% of cannabis sales compared to pre-pandemic volume.
- There is also an increase in emergency room visits relating to substance use, especially opioid use, and unintentional overdoses.

■ Violence turned outwards has also increased:
- Globally, and certainly in the United States, there has been an increase in aggressivity and violent behaviors.

# Writing Prompt

Consider your current exposure to media, social media, and news sources.

Have you made a link between exposure to media or social media and impact on your mental health upon consuming such media?

Consider using the space provided below to reflect on the following two-part prompt:

1. **Take time to identify your media-related triggers.**

_____

_____

_____

_____

_____

_____

_____

2. **What are your plans to limit your exposure to potentially triggering sources?**

_____

_____

_____

_____

_____

_____

_____

## Long Term

According to the study by Magnúsdóttir et al. (2022), a large group of participants were studied, and they reviewed the prevalence of adverse mental health symptoms in individuals with COVID-19 up to sixteen months after diagnosis. The study suggests an association with long term mental health concerns including sleep disturbances and depression. This is also the first study to look at disease severity as a modifier of long-term mental health.

The longer-term health consequences, specifically death anxiety as well as posttraumatic stress disorder, were documented in the research article by Zhang et al. (2021). This cross-sectional study followed participants over several months and concluded that even after the pandemic related lockdowns were lifted, people continued to be affected. Of note, death anxiety was shown to be a predictor to subsequently developing posttraumatic stress disorder. The article highlighted higher risk groups such as the elderly as well as healthcare workers as those having been more significantly impacted. This information can and should be incorporated in risk profiling of individuals to identify/diagnose early on and provide education and treatment planning as appropriate to potentially mitigate progression or worsening of symptoms.

Long-term, long-haul, chronic-COVID have all been used to refer to the persistence of mental and physical symptoms and aftereffects of the illness itself as well as its impact on the psyche of the individual. The timeframe of the risk window during, after, and how long after the acute infection phase of COVID these develop is still unclear. It is clear, though, that those infected are at significantly higher risk and are recommended to be screened and mindful about going to their primary care provider as well as mental health clinicians.

The research article by Chan et al. (2021) is the first to examine and discuss individual and family resilience in the context of stressors relating to the pandemic. The authors discuss differences between cultures ranging from individualistic to family-oriented and associated protective factors of having strong individual resilience and that of a community-based support structure. For more information, see Chapter 8, Culture, Identity, and Society, and Chapter 7, Family, Children, and Resilience.

Those with any type of predisposition to have an addiction, depression, anxiety, psychosis have been at a disadvantage with this high amount of stress for the past several years. The level of isolation and unpredictability that COVID and the responses to it has caused amplified those at risk. The stress diathesis model of the blossoming of pathology under the appropriate conditions has shown to be the case during the pandemic.

Mental illness continues to increase as a result of reduction in human contact, as well as coping mechanisms like closure of organizations, gyms, community centers, schools, employment areas, and other social activities like sports.

Anything we tended toward was amplified. Pre-pandemic, in the before times, we had an idea of what life was like. Life wasn't always great, and it was challenging and difficult at times. There was a lot that was wrong in the world, but we had a template and thought we knew how things worked. With COVID, the whole world shut down and everything we knew up until then wasn't valid anymore.

Even though there was always disappointment, the unpredictability and not being able to count on anything in life all of a sudden shattered our perception. The template of what we thought the world was, our place in it, and our connection with it were all destroyed. This continues into the third year of the pandemic and will affect all of our psychologies for many years to come.

For example, we live very far from our families. In the before times, we felt the world was small. We had the feeling of freedom and independence where we felt that we could get to our home country, if our aging parents wanted us or needed us to come home. The pandemic shattered this, too.

All of a sudden, we were unable to travel, and when there was a need to, we couldn't. Our belief system of living on the other side of the world and that we are mobile beings that could travel around shifted. The idea of travel became doubt ridden, morbid, and very dangerous. This affected many people in the same way. All of our resources and strengths were not reliable anymore. Where everything that we felt like we had gathered or any coping mechanism we had established became invalid, canceled, and no longer was compatible in the new normal.

The inequities of access to care, ability to socially distance, ability to maintain employment or school in safe environments, access to vaccines, and general physical and mental health care are all exacerbating the impact of the pandemic itself. Social determinants of health such as housing insecurity, and food insecurity have become a focal point to ensure an appropriate ability to heal.

The damage of school closing has been most impactful on children already with history of ACEs, keeping them away from others, having restorative experiences, and being able to access playgrounds and heal. How these mental health effects of the pandemic exacerbate an already polarized and exhausted public remains to be seen.

Regarding personality types and the long-term effects, we look at the concepts of introversion and extroversion. In some ways, the pandemic affected extroverts tremendously. The person who thrives on social interactions all of a sudden was cut from their lifeline. For introverts, what might have looked as if they got the time to do the things they wanted, especially during lockdowns, their introversion deepened. Isolating activities like reading or painting are healthy with a balance. In day-to-day living, introverts are for the most part forced to interact with others. When that was taken away, it may have caused more damage in the sense that social skills were not developed or even regressed.

We are also witnessing the regression in children, where developmentally appropriate navigation and social interactions were obliterated. Children who were unable to socialize, unable to defend themselves, learn from peers, voice their opinions, take turns, and learn from adults other than their immediate caregivers lost many of their social skills. This will continue to be an issue long term, similar to the consequences of school closing and the decline in reading, writing, and mathematics aptitude scores.

For some, COVID created an environment where people engaged in activities that they previously could not. Introverts were able to lose themselves in a solitary world. Many people veered toward substance use. These similarly address the idea of managing the concept of loss of certainty and loss of hope.

In the before times, there was always some element of our lives that we felt we had in our control. The unpredictability of the disease, the way it spread and affected the whole world, brought on a sense of hopelessness, the feeling of having no control. Even the idea of immigrating to another place or entertaining the thought of having a different life was crushed. Before the pandemic, there was always another option, for many people. The pandemic is global and so unclear that everything else that we thought we could control zoomed out of focus.

The article by Brewin et al. (2020) discusses the need to incorporate mental health care into planning for pandemics, including short- and long-term strategies to identify early, and treat as appropriate to reduce psychosocial and financial burdens. As with any treatment, appropriate identification, diagnosis, and treatment modalities are critical.

## Writing Prompt

Within the framework of the Balan 3-2-1 Method, consider your response to the following:

**Are you an introvert or an extrovert? How did the pandemic affect your style and coping mechanisms?**

3. With intention, set your internal and external environment.
   - **The body**: What mindfulness techniques are you choosing to allow your body to heal?

   _____

   _____

   _____

   - **The setting**: How are you intentionally influencing your setting?

   _____

   _____

   _____

   - **The breath**: Which breathing technique will you use as you prepare for this exercise?

   _____

   _____

   _____

2. What are your thoughts and feelings in response to the writing prompt above?

   _____

   _____

   _____

_____

_____

_____

_____

1. What is your one intent or affirmation in context of the writing prompt above?

_____

_____

_____

_____

_____

_____

_____

# Grief

Grief is the natural reaction to loss. It is typically adaptive and provides the foundation to process emotions and thoughts. Symptoms of grief include sadness, feelings of denial or disbelief, anxiety, and sleep disturbances.

Grief in the context of COVID and the pandemic is multifaceted, and as of the writing of this workbook, is continuing to unfold.

In addition to the loss of millions of lives worldwide, we have all been affected by the pandemic and many of us tragically have experienced loss. The loss of lives and health has been paramount, and we have also experienced the loss of stability, past routines, jobs, mobility, roles, and statuses.

Types of loss during the pandemic resulting in grieving reactions include:

■ Loss of Life:
  – Millions of individuals lost their lives directly and indirectly due to the virus, associated lockdowns, inability to access healthcare, food, shelter, and other critical resources.
  – During more intense waves of the pandemic, family members were not allowed to be in proximity to their deceased loved ones due to fear of contagion. This has undoubtedly complicated the grieving process with unresolved emotions.
■ Deferred and delayed physical and mental health:
  – The article by Pinto et al. (2020) discusses self-inflicted harm, suicide, and the survivors of suicide in the context of COVID-19, as well as the consequences of the effects of the pandemic on mental health. The article discusses recommendations around identification of symptoms and risk factors, social structures such as social media and community factors for the support of the individual. The article notes that suicide increased during the 1918 influenza pandemic in the United States, as well as in 2003 during the SARS epidemic in Hong Kong.
  – Medical care, especially non-urgent or emergent procedures and surgeries were deferred.

- – Routine medical appointments and immunizations were pushed off or not done at all resulting in missed diagnoses and worsening medical health conditions.
- – The article by Kuehn (August 2022) discusses the impact of the disruptions in access to HIV testing during the pandemic, resulting in a significant decrease in the diagnosis of HIV. Coupling this with the known increase in risky sexual behaviors, one can only imagine the public health crises that will unfold just from this.
- ■ Occupation specific stressors:
  - – Caregivers and clinicians experienced as much if not more levels of mental health effects during the pandemic. Increased workload, fear of getting infected as well as going home and infecting family, as well as dealing firsthand with the devastation the virus caused.
  - – At the time of writing of this book, healthcare systems in the United States were experiencing significant issues with clinician burnout, absenteeism, turnover, and an inability to recruit and hire staff.
  - – Most clinicians have not been trained to address acute trauma or severe crises such as a pandemic or a war. This poses several serious issues relating to competency of care, as well as the lack of providers able to or willing to do this work.
- ■ Sense of stability:
  - – Constant fear and anxiety generated by mainstream media, social media, and the fear of the virus itself exacerbated an already strained mental health crisis pre-pandemic to a crisis of unmet demand, skyrocketing need, deferred, and delayed care.
  - – Caregivers have also been affected themselves, coping with their own personal anxieties and loss as well as having to take care of patients. We anticipate the impact described in this book will long surpass the pandemic phase of the crisis.
- ■ Loss of hope:
  - – Brought on by increase clinical mood disorders, anxieties, and substance use.
  - – Shattered illusions of officials in politics and the scientific world to be able to care for the population.
  - – Of ever returning to pre-pandemic life.
  - – Of anyone other than family and very close loved ones caring for the children.
  - – In institutions such as healthcare to ensure healthy lives.
- ■ Loss of ability to plan for future:
  - – Disrupted plans, canceled flights, closed hotels, shut down establishments, worsening spikes in infections, new regulations, and ever-changing biosecurity requirements all added to the instability and difficulty in planning.
- ■ Loss of certainty:
  - – Rapidly shifting messaging on how to maintain health and safety.
  - – Changes in ability to maintain employment, in context of supply chain uncertainty, closures.
  - – Decreased consistency of availability of resources.
- ■ Financial insecurity:
  - – Loss of income streams.
  - – Increase in prices due to shortages and increased demand.
  - – Inflation and decreased spending capability.
- ■ Loss of employment:
  - – Either due to closing of businesses or not adhering to various mandates.
- ■ Loss of housing:
  - – Folks were displaced either due to the virus itself or the need for the housing for other purposes.

- Landlords took advantage of decreased attention to legal matters, resulting in evictions and other disruptions.
  - Increased prices of rent and home costs and repairs resulting in inability to keep up with payments or necessary maintenance.
- Food insecurity:
  - In addition to the disrupted finances, the impact of the pandemic on the supply chain, decreased availability of options and distribution all impacted the most vulnerable.
  - Food pantries and available social safety-net resources were significantly limited, and when re-opened, were disproportionately impacted by the burden of the virus.
- Loss of roles, transitions, and daily routines:
  - The act of getting up, going to work or school, and returning home was lost. The transitions between activities, such as driving or getting on the subway, then arriving at a place, the rituals of morning, afternoon, or evenings either ended or were severely colored by extreme fear and uncertainty.
- Disruption of leisure activities and extracurricular activities:
  - Lead to disturbances in physical and mental health.
  - Lead to increase in substance use and addictions.
  - Lead to decreased ability to socialize and give and receive support from community networks.
- Limitations to travel:
  - During lockdowns, travel was significantly restricted and monitored.
  - Visitation to health care agencies was limited to mitigate exposure, resulting in decreased ability to visit or aid in care of loved ones.
  - Leisure travel significantly reduced, and new regulations and mandates were imposed.
- Loss of certain civil liberties:
  - Additional mandates, requirements, regulations in the context of medical safety exacerbated fear and anxieties, created increased financial burden, and continue to be confusing, inconsistent, and routinely changing in contradictory ways.
- Decrease in trust in institutions:
  - Throughout the pandemic, as people were locked down and socially distancing, they watched as the narrative shifted, suggestions changed, and inconsistencies were plenty.
  - Institutions thought of as having the public's best interest to protect were shown to be unable to do so, and their promises were unable to be kept.
- Shift in childcare:
  - As the desire to limit exposure and pervasive fear resulted in significant decrease in childcare options, families were forced to adjust schedules and availabilities.
  - This then resulted in a decreased ability to focus at work or school, decreased productivity, as well as rising interpersonal tensions in the household.
- Friendships, communities, and support networks were split apart.
- Postponing of religious gatherings and ceremonies.
  - The value of communing in person and sharing the spiritual experience was severed early on with attempts to shift services online with minimal success.
- School systems:
  - As discussed in other parts of this book, the complete devastation of school systems had disastrous consequences on the student, resulting in years of delayed academic skills.

## Writing Prompt

Within the framework of the Balan 3-2-1 Method, consider your response to the following:

**What can you control?**

3. With intention, set your internal and external environment.
   - **The body:** What mindfulness techniques are you choosing to allow your body to heal?

   _____

   _____

   _____

   _____

   - **The setting:** How are you intentionally influencing your setting?

   _____

   _____

   _____

   - **The breath:** Which breathing technique will you use as you prepare for this exercise?

   _____

   _____

   _____

   _____

2. What are your thoughts and feelings in response to the writing prompt above?

   _____

   _____

   _____

   _____

   _____

   _____

   _____

   _____

1. What is your one intent or affirmation in context of the writing prompt above?

_____

_____

_____

_____

_____

## Writing Prompt

Consider using the space below to reflect on the following three-part prompt on connections:

1. **Who do you want to be connected with?**

_____

_____

_____

_____

_____

_____

_____

_____

2. **How can you show them you are connected?**

_____

_____

_____

_____

_____

_____

_____

3. **What kind of gestures of love, connection, or care can you send to those around you to show them that you are thinking of them?**

_____

_____

_____

_____

_____

_____

_____

_____

# RESOURCES FOR OUR FUTURE

**5**

# Chapter 11

# Safety Planning

And I asked myself about the present: how wide it was, how deep it was, how much was mine to keep.

*– Kurt Vonnegut*

## Introduction

A safety plan is essentially an exercise that facilitates communication between the clinician and the client regarding the most fundamental aspect of care. Without the foundation of current physical safety and perception of mental safety, therapy, deeper introspection, or even basic regulation of affect will not succeed.

The safety plan should be easy to follow and encourage dialogue where the clinician listens and engages the client empathically, all of which aid in the healing journey. By definition, the safety plan is to ensure the person continues to maintain a sense of bodily and psychological safety, with the plan to reduce potential future harm through the strategies described below.

Different clinical settings and different symptom clusters benefit from variations on the theme of safety planning. While there are few true psychiatric emergencies, the most alarming are dangerousness to self and dangerousness to others. There are many underlying causes for aggressivity turned inwards or outwards from severe affective disorders, psychotic disorders, severe anxiety disorders, substance use, intoxication states as well as any number of the causes of encephalopathies.

Safety planning is inherent to all modalities of care, typically through establishing relationships and understanding the concerns, issues, and treatment preferences the client has. There are times, however, when a written document must be created, memorialized, and referred to with the client, family/support network as clinically appropriate, and treating team.

When structuring your safety plan and implementing it in treatment planning, we recommend including sections in the plan on warning signs and triggers, coping strategies, family, social and professional contacts, and specific mechanisms to maintain the client's physical and psychological safety.

DOI: 10.4324/9781003323815-16

We encourage the safety plan be written down, together, or at minimum reviewed when the client completes it. There are many levels of value in having the client fill out the form in their own handwriting. See Chapter 3, Value of Treatment, for more information on the benefits of expressive writing.

Once the client completes the safety plan, we recommend making a copy of it and putting a copy in their medical record and giving the original to the client to keep with them. This exercise acts to reinforce the point that this is a tool to be referred to, is serious enough to go into the medical record, and dynamically updated as needed.

During subsequent visits and with other members of the care team as needed, the safety plan can be referenced. Involving the client, the discussion can be tailored to determine what has been working, what they were able to accomplish, and what did not work. This allows for the client and the treatment team to coordinate efforts to update the plan further for the medical record as well as for the client's benefit.

## Section 1: Warning Signs

"Warning signs" is the title of the first section we recommend to include in a safety plan. Think of these as external triggers as well as internal cues that the person may be exposed to, feeling or perceiving. The questions and flow of the safety plan must be within the context of safety and be stigma and judgment free. It should be easy to read and easy to follow, especially since the person will be reviewing this under a stressful time. The primary purpose of this section is to ensure the client comprehends when and why their safety plan can and should be used.

This section should list emotional, physical, behavioral, or external cues that the client can use to indicate that they are heading toward a state of unrest. Consider queuing any number of the following questions as per clinical appropriateness of the person's needs:

- When will the safety plan be used?
- Write a list of emotions that can be identified and that are associated with an increase in feelings of fear, panic, anger, and loss of control.
- Write a list of behaviors that have been observed that, in the past, may have been done in context of a trigger resulting in decreased safety.
- Write a list of thoughts that come to mind when there is an increase in feelings of sadness, anxiety, or terror.
- Describe what goes on, the experiences in your body, which part of the body.
  - For example, in the head as a headache, neck as a pain, stomach as feeling need to go to the bathroom, hands or feet as tingling or warmth.
- What are your warning signs for specific emotions?
  For example, if anger is a component of the warning sign, what happens? For example, heart rate increases, feel tense in head and jaw, tingling in fingers and around mouth, breathing rate increases, or notice breathing slows down to even holding breath.
  - Similarly complete for other intense emotions as part of warning signs, like for sadness, anxiety, or fear.
- If numbing is a component of the sensations and experiences felt, describe the feeling of numbness in context of a warning sign that may bring it on.
  - Is it in association with an interaction, a specific relationship, what happens, what is concerning, worrisome about the numbness itself?

■ What are behavioral or experiential things that have been happening around the same time of an escalation that may lead to unsafe patterns of behavior, such as self-injury, using substances to address the feelings and thoughts brought up?
  – Each one of the examples below can and are associated with real, separate medical issues that should be worked up medically as appropriate. Only until the medical concern is ruled out, should they be part of the psychological cluster.
  – Even then, they should be brought up and documented with the primary care provider and team and allow for them to decide if further medical investigation is required. It is not only possible, but unfortunately common for people dealing with psychological issues who may also have medical comorbidities. There is a propensity for decreased immunity, resulting in worsening of medical health as well.
  – Also, there sadly is a level of tolerance that sometimes is breached sooner in some clinicians than others to dismiss someone with a history of posttraumatic stress disorder as having psychosomatic problems that are "all in their head."
  – If you are a clinician and notice this in yourself, discuss with your own consultation group or therapist to ensure you are providing the best possible care for your clients.
  – If you are a client and have experienced this or are currently feeling as if you are working up hill to "convince" your provider you need more help or tests, and know your own body and are feeling stigmatized, ignored, or worse, laughed away as being a nuisance, change your provider and consider putting in formal complaints. This sort of behavior is not only not acceptable but also extremely harmful.

■ Having mentioned all that, if you are in a relationship with a medical provider and clinical team you trust, have a proven track record of being empathically listened to and have been provided care when clinically indicated, consider the following as items to generate ideas that may remind you of something you are working on for yourself or with your clinician:
  – For example, is sleep change or sleep disturbances a concern?
    • Have you been having an increase in taking naps?
    • Is there an association with new onset of the presence or absence of dreaming?
    • Is there a change in intensity of dreams?
    • Is new onset of nightmares potentially a warning sign?
  – Are there bodily sensations associated? See "Triggers" section for further exploration.
    • Have there an been increased number of calls to the physical medicine doctor for things that happen around the time of intense emotions such as:
      ■ Headaches and migraines
      ■ Chest pains
      ■ Breathing pattern changes
      ■ Stomach cramps, diarrhea, and constipation
      ■ Difficulty falling asleep
      ■ Twitching or numbness or tingling in the fingers or toes
  – Are patterns of aggressive outbursts or angry ways you talk or think in an encounter with a friend, colleague, family member a hint toward a warning sign?
  – Within your pattern of relationships:
    • Is there a noticeable trend toward pushing away people that are regularly part of your day-to-day routine?
    • Conversely, is there a pattern of getting closer, increased romantic partners, outwardly sexualized behaviors outside of the day-to-day patterns?
  – Association with substance use?

- Is there a change in pattern or choice of substance during times of intense stress, as a potential warning sign?

## Case Example: Self-Medicating

A clinical case example of a client Yener cared for with a history of trauma hinged on a subtle change in choice of the client's alcoholic beverage. This person would routinely enjoy beer, traditionally known to have a lower alcohol content, and a warning sign was a switch to harder drinks, liquors with higher alcohol by volume content, such as gin or vodka.

During several sessions, this was disclosed and almost discovered by the client himself as a mechanism to drink more, faster numb the psychic pain, and with the clear liquors, feel as if he did not smell of alcohol as much.

When this was incorporated into the safety plan and the client's partner was brought in to discuss coping mechanisms as well as safety strategies, it was evident that the partner was well aware of this pattern.

Interestingly, the client thought they were getting away with something, when the shame and feelings of guilt of self-medicating were only increasing the torment of panic, terror, and shame the client already had.

By simply uncovering this and talking about it non-judgmentally, in fact curiously with the intention to heal, was what allowed the person to be significantly more mindful, decrease their alcohol intake in general, and improved communication with the partner.

## Writing Prompt

Consider using the space provided to reflect on the following:

**What are your warning signs?**

_____

_____

_____

_____

_____

_____

_____

_____

_____

_____

_____

_____

# Triggers

The section "triggers" can be its own or can be incorporated into the "warning signs" section. We think it is important to have the conversation and label these triggers. Attach them with a bodily sensation, smell, or sound, and then consider writing them in the safety plan, if applicable for the individual. Chapter 5, Language of Mind and Body, has an in-depth discussion of feelings, sensations, and exercises to assist in identifying and labeling them as well as their impact on oneself.

Similar to how we discussed about not ignoring medical symptoms as they are a mechanism for the body telling us if something is not functioning properly to spend more time and energy on that part and/or get medical attention, triggers are also typically adaptive and protective.

The concept of triggers has developed a negative almost weaponized connotation, and in the popular vernacular, an even shaming and belittling quality. The word has become shorthand for anything that is even slightly bothersome or to shut someone down entirely. In schools and workplaces, it can be used maliciously even to target someone, make allegations, and indefensibly trap the other.

Triggers are perceptions.

If we accept that perceptions are reality, and someone is accusing someone or a behavior or any other associated aspect of them as triggering, there is no recourse for the accused. While this can be productive if there is a discussion of what can be done differently to ensure the triggering is discontinued, flat out blaming someone without an ability to change is concerning.

It is important to step back and realize the heart of any relationship, be it at work or school or with a therapist relies on communication and conveying of information and ideas from one brain to another. Obviously, we are not talking about something illegal, unethical, immoral or against the accepted rules of conduct and principles of behavior of the workplace/school where the issue is occurring.

For the purposes of triggers in safety planning, they should be thought out and described in a way that can be simple to define, practical in nature as to either correct, avoid or minimize, and actionable to ensure continued safety.

We have included a sample set of triggers our clients have taught us over the years. Consider reading these for either insights into one's own triggers and adopt as appropriate, or write in whatever unique trigger that is of current concern.

Some possible triggers are:

■ **People:** Is there a specific person or set of people?
  - Being with people in general, for example, in a crowd, busy street, in a long line with people behind you, in a movie theater, on a plane.
  - Being with specific people with specific issues. For example, Duygu had a client that could not bear being around other people who talked about their own trauma histories. Therefore, group trauma therapy settings were paradoxically unhelpful and prevented this person from advancing in their healing.
  - Conversely, is being alone a trigger?
■ **Places:** Is there a physical location or an archetype of places such as hospitals, public transportation, or airports?
  - The act of being in a car, sense of being trapped, either alone if driving oneself or being driven by someone else.
■ **Specific things:** Are there items that remind you of an event or series of events?

- Things that could be encountered randomly that may be triggering include a TV show or a movie.
- Currently ubiquitous and unfortunately increasing is the fear of the illness itself. Consider the bombardment of media and messaging, advertising, and discussions surrounding the pandemic, along with all the associated mandates and health and hygiene recommendations.
- As we are concluding this book, a new virus dubbed Monkey Pox has arisen, triggering harrowing memories of HIV and exacerbating the death anxiety of the current pandemic.

■ **Sights**: This may include seeing an individual thing or a set of events, such as triggering things on the news or on social media, such as explosions, car crashes, fights, conflicts, or images of war.
  - Similar to the nuances in the specifics above, is there a time within the day, daylight, early morning, evening, or late night that are associated with triggers?

■ **Smells**: Are there associated smells, such as perfume, alcohol on breath, distinct smell of one's home?

■ Certain times of the year, anniversaries, and holidays.
  - Apart from the societal pressures surrounding holidays, forced artificial cheer, manufactured, insistent consumerism and obligatory family gatherings and rituals, for folks with traumatic histories, these times are often exponentially more devastating.

■ **Bodily sensations**: Frequently people with anxiety disorders, such as obsessive-compulsive disorder, specific phobias, generalized anxiety, or posttraumatic stress disorder, will often also experience their anxiety somewhere in their body.
  - Headaches, neck pains, muscle strains, stomach aches, feeling the need to use the restroom, chest tightness, and tingling in arms or fingers.
  - These are real sensations that can be part of a physical disease, and as mentioned before, should be evaluated by a medical practitioner to ensure appropriate medical follow-up. They do, however, get conditioned with the feeling of powerlessness, feeling stuck, remind the person of a traumatic event or time, and are common triggers.
  - These internal sensations are a focus throughout our book. One's stomach might grumble for many reasons, most commonly when hungry. It also may be something very serious. But most commonly, it is thankfully benign. For people who do not have anxiety, these paragraphs may appear superfluous and over-exaggerating.
  - People with anxiety, however, are acutely aware of their bodily sensations, and they exhaust themselves trying to self-diagnose and worry about the worst scenario. These triggers should be written down, and we encourage the individual to spend time with their medical provider and mental health clinician to explore them.

When the warning signs and triggers are written in the own words of the client, we have found improved adherence and appreciation of the safety planning exercise.

To recap, this section that includes warning signs and triggers is meant to act as a guideline for the client during a crisis and to have pre-identified aspects of their own experience. If the safety plan is being shared, for example, with a family member or a guardian, we find that self-described warning signs are significantly more helpful for the outside observer, clinician, or patient advocate. The process of completing the safety plan inherently improves rapport and alliance building.

# Writing Prompt

Consider using the space provided to reflect on the following:

**What are your triggers?**

_____

_____

_____

_____

_____

_____

_____

_____

_____

_____

_____

_____

# Section 2: Coping Strategies

This section of the safety plan is all about trying to improve the sense of control of the client and likewise decrease the sense of loss of control. Coping strategies are recommended as a means to reduce the effect of posttraumatic stress disorder symptoms such as flashbacks or dissociation. They are also meant to ensure continued physical and mental safety, decrease self-injurious thoughts and behaviors such as cutting or engaging in risky behaviors, or using substances.

- Engage the client by asking what coping and self-soothing skills they use that they have found helpful during a crisis situation.
- Discuss strategies the person can use to decrease self-harming behaviors.
- Consider asking the person what does the term "safety" itself mean to them. Where and when and how does the person feel safe? This can be the framework to then list their coping strategies.
- Occupying one's time and mind may work for some, such as:
  - Writing exercises in this workbook
  - Reading
  - Watching television
  - Listening to music, podcasts, or an audiobook
  - Playing an instrument
  - Looking at art online or at a museum

- Occupying one's senses may also work. Consider things such as:
  - A favorite food that has positive associations, that is supportive and calming (e.g., cheesecake for Yener).
  - A specific smell: smells of home cooking, a soothing candle.
- Physical coping strategies such as:
  - Does the person meditate?
  - Do they exercise at home or at a gym?
  - Do they use deep breathing exercises? Chapter 4, Balan 3-2-1 Method, explores therapeutic breathing techniques which we encourage the reader to consider.
  - Are walks in nature calming? How about a walk around the block? What may work wonders for one may be a calamitous trigger for another.
  - Does the person find a warm shower or a steam bath comforting?
- Is there a specific "other" that allows the person to feel safe and reduces arousal and fear states, such as:
  - **A good friend**: write their name and information – explore what it is about this person. When and where and how being with them is important, is it by phone, video chat, or in person?
    **A family member**: same as above
  - **A pet**: if not immediately available, are there substitutes such as a stuffed animal, photo, or video clip of this pet that can be used instead for this purpose?
- Self-talk coping strategies include rehearsed phrases like those on meditation apps. Things such as "I am centered, and balanced." Find whatever works. Some may sound silly or cheesy, some may sound absurdly uncharacteristic, although when you find one that works for you or you make your own up, it will have the power to revolutionize your experience.
  - These can be a wish for yourself, such as "I will have control over my headaches" or affirmations of current attributes.
  - Consider the following empowering, calming, self-talk phrases:
    - "This will also come to an end."
    - "I am at peace with myself."

Discussing coping strategies gives the person a sense of control over their current sensations, symptoms, and behaviors during a crisis. It also serves to give hope, as they learn and realize that others have gone through similar issues and have successfully been able to cope with similar things they have been dealing with.

## Writing Prompt

Consider using the space provided to reflect on the following:

**What are your coping strategies?**

_____

_____

_____

_____

_____

_____

_____

_____

_____

_____

_____

_____

## Section 3: Family, Social, and Professional Contacts

This section is used to brainstorm and document names and contact numbers for the client's main social support network. This may include family members, friends, neighbors, therapists, doctors, and clergy/spiritual advisors.

Considerations for people to include on this list should include those that can actively do something of value. Think of a trustworthy person, if the contact can keep the person safe, calm them, decrease their anxiety, and get them to safety, such as an emergency room, if needed.

For trauma-specific support systems, consider also including associations or shelters that are available in the area, or easily accessible by phone/internet. For example, an intimate partner violence shelter or an alcoholics anonymous group. See the section we have included toward the end of the book that lists websites and contact information of resources.

It is also recommended to list them in order of priority, for example, call this person first, this professional agency next.

## Writing Prompt

Consider using the space provided to reflect on the following:

**Who are members of your family, your friends, and your professional contacts?**

_____

_____

_____

_____

_____

_____

_____

_____

_____

_____

_____

_____

## Section 4: Keeping Me Safe

In this section, the person is asked to think of a couple of ways that they could use to stay safe before the onset of and during a crisis.

This section can be sub-divided into a category such as "Keeping the environment safe."

- Depending on the clinical circumstances, the level of seriousness and dangerousness of the scenarios should be prioritized.
- If there are mechanisms of high lethality such as firearms around, an item in this section could include a family member removing the firearm or locking the medications that may be used in an overdose attempt.

The person can brainstorm practical ideas such as:

- Leave the triggering area.
  - Specify where they would go, how they would get there, who would they contact to let them know their plan. Also think about what they would bring with them, such as their keys, wallet, and phone.
- Go for a walk.
  - This safety behavior can be linked to the coping strategies listed above.
- Go to a friend's house.
  - This can be linked to a contact listed above.
  - Consider having the person talk this through with the friend they identify before there is a crisis and also think of alternatives if that friend is not available at the moment.
- Go somewhere safe and healing.
  - If there is an emergency, calling 911 and/or going to the nearest emergency department.
  - If there is intimate partner violence or abuse, going to the specific professional agency and connecting with a social worker or peer advocate at one of those places. Think this through and document who will be called and how they will get there.

In addition to the practical and obvious benefits of a safety plan, this section allows for the client to practice these steps before a crisis. The client and therapist can talk through imaginary and real barriers in order to rehearse what they would do in case of a triggering event or an emergency.

This way the client will have thought about these issues and can either look at the written safety plan or remember what they thought of during the development of their plan.

## Writing Prompt

Consider using the space provided to reflect on the following:

**What behaviors can you use to keep yourself safe?**

_____

_____

_____

_____

_____

_____

_____

_____

_____

_____

_____

_____

# Section 5: Signature Section

The act of signing and dating something adds a certain gravitas to a document. We recommend including a signature section where the client signs and dates the plan. This exercise is separate from and is not intended to be a "safety contract." The client isn't contracting to anything and isn't promising anything. They are brainstorming ideas and practicing behaviors in a safe environment before an actual crisis occurs.

The safety plan acts to engage the person, provide guidelines and structure they developed, and add hope as they are moving forward with their healing. The therapist can be attuned with the level of energy and participation the person has while crafting the safety plan. If you are reading this workbook alone, without working with someone, we encourage you to introspect as to your own barriers and choices you are making when choosing a coping strategy or who you would contact first or second.

Sometimes, a safety plan would benefit from being developed with a family member or advocate. While this may add some complexity, we have also experienced it to be deeply rewarding for all parties involved. As in the clinical case example above of the person drinking progressively stronger drinks, the involved members present there to support the person and ensure their safety and health may not have had a structured conversation such as this.

Once the safety plan is created and in its final stage, it may also provide to ease concerns of the involved family member, knowing their loved one has a plan and is working toward their health.

In terms of practical next steps, think about role-playing the actions that can be taken. Think about where the person will keep the safety plan, how they will find it during a crisis. For example, a photo of it can be taken and kept on their cell phone.

Lastly, consider role-playing what will be said and asked of the contact person when they are called. These steps are empowering and serve to decrease anxiety and states of arousal, to ensure the person has their best opportunity to stay well.

# Writing Prompt

Consider using the template below to reflect on each of the writing prompts to draft your entire safety plan.

This can be done with a clinician or on your own. Consider sharing with your clinician if you are working with one.

# Safety Plan

**My Warning Signs:**

_____

_____

_____

_____

_____

_____

_____

_____

_____

_____

**My Triggers:**

_____

_____

_____

_____

_____

_____

_____

_____

_____

_____

_____

**My Coping Strategies:**

_____

_____

_____

_____

_____

_____

_____

_____

_____

_____

**Family, Social, and Professional Contacts: (Include names and contact phone numbers)**

_____

_____

_____

_____

_____

_____

_____

_____

_____

_____

_____

**Keeping Me Safe:**

_____

_____

_____

_____

_____

_____

_____

_____

_____

_____

_____

**Signature**                                    **Date**

_____          _____

## Chapter 12

# Long Haul to a New Normal, Our Path Forward

Yesterday is but today's memory, and tomorrow is today's dream.

*– Khalil Gibran*

## Our Path So Far

Just as we congratulated you, the reader, for taking the first step on your journey of healing, we again congratulate you for taking step after step to discover and learn.

Throughout this book, we have explored many subjects within the umbrella of trauma and related stressors. We defined trauma, along with the medical diagnostic criteria and its impact on day-to-day life. Various available therapeutic modalities as well as pharmacological options were discussed.

We gave statistics for pre-pandemic mental health needs and the current rapid growth in demand in the setting of a dramatic mismatch of supply.

We discussed the personal, financial, physical, and most importantly, mental health benefits and return on investment of caring for yourself. The specific modality we focused on has been expressive writing, as a complement to other treatment modalities, and we have provided many writing prompts and creative explorations for an interactive experience.

We formally introduced the Balan 3-2-1 Method and have explained the value of setting the conscious stage for self-care, while learning to be in tune with your breathing and allowing for self-compassion. We connected culture with the language of mind and body and discussed the medical aspects of the brain as an organ.

How our impulses and chemical signals are translated to our behaviors and feelings was discussed, as we dove deeper into the pathology of trauma, explained the real-world consequences, as well as the hope and real change that treatment is able to provide.

DOI: 10.4324/9781003323815-17

Themes of resilience and gratitude have been the golden threads that wove throughout the book. We discussed familial risk as well as protective factors. We explored adverse childhood experiences and their impact on later life.

As a person reading this, either for yourself, or as a clinician as a tool to further help your clients, we all can benefit from increased empathy. The context of actual physical brain changes in the context of trauma and how that affects how different people can perceive the exact same stimuli completely differently is eye-opening. We discussed the interpersonal value of this knowledge in relationships, as well as financial return on investment in the workplace.

The concept of culture and identity was discussed in the setting of trauma and factors that increased the prevalence of trauma related stress. Gaslighting and betrayal traumas were discussed with a sobering case example within corporate culture.

As this book is being completed, the world is in the third year of the COVID pandemic, a new set of medical health emergencies including Monkey Pox is arising, and there continues to be wars with thinly veiled nuclear threats. It is timelier than ever to ensure that the topics we covered are heeded, especially the mental health impact of these stressors on society, collectively as well as on the individual level. The themes of loss and grief in a broader context, as well as specific to these disasters, were expanded on in great detail.

Safety planning for physical and mental health safety was the final preceding chapter, as it provides a tool for setting the stage of hope, security, and looking forward.

This brings us to the present chapter, where we explore our long haul to a new normal.

## Equitable Access

The best way to reduce potential harmful effects of traumatic stress such as those described throughout this book is by preventing them altogether. We have discussed the range of ages, identities, roles, cultures, occupations, and types of traumas and how to manage and care for those impacted.

We first and foremost continue to emphasize the need for equitable access to mental health and substance use treatment for all. Improving access to physical health care will also allow for the screening of symptoms and ensure the individual or family is directed to appropriate professional resources. This will then allow for early detection of potential concerns, and through early intervention, mitigate worsening symptoms and pathology.

## Reducing Harmful Effects

Throughout our careers, we have continued to work toward improving the awareness of mental health issues. In an effort to spell out the things that need to occur to prevent and/or reduce the harmful effects of trauma related stressors, we include the following list of things we must continue to strive for.

We must:

■ Improve awareness of trauma
  - Educate how to recognize when it occurs and when it becomes an issue.
  - Realize that it is not normal or OK to silently suffer.
  - Inform that there is help available.

- – Improve identification of bullying and harassment.
- – Improve identification of microaggressions as easily as macroaggressions.
- ■ Create a culture that empowers a witness of gaslighting or other betrayal traumas to be able to intervene, speak up, and seek help to remedy and reduce the offense.
- ■ Create spaces that are psychologically and physically safe.
- ■ Encourage disclosure and discussion.
- ■ Improve healthy communication by:
  - – Improving trauma informed education of health care providers, law enforcement, first responders, schoolteachers, and administrators, as well as human resources at corporations.
  - – Reducing isolation.
- ■ Decrease stigma of reporting trauma, including intimate partner violence and other related stressors, regardless of the victim's gender, race, culture, ethnicity, creed, or religion. All must be empowered in an environment where the stigma does not exist, and the victim is listened to compassionately and care and safety is able to be provided.
- ■ Improve training, which will:
  - – Result in improved screening at doctor's visits including adult family medicine, obstetrics and gynecology, maternal child medicine, pediatricians, mental health clinicians, as well as in emergency departments.
  - – Increase awareness of, improve education around and eliminate oppressive dynamics in relationships, as well as in schools and workplace environments.
  - – Increase mindfulness of victim blaming and preventing it from occurring.
  - – Reduce secondary microaggressions of invalidating the victim's experiences.
  - – Prevent the victim from becoming a gaslighter themselves.
- ■ Recognize that intimate partner violence and other trauma related stressors are very common, and they are unfortunately increasing rapidly in the context of the pandemic.
- ■ Increase sensitivity to marginalized groups and the experiences and risks of those underrepresented and underserved.
- ■ Increase awareness of privilege and minimize and eliminate dominating discussions and reinforcing gender or race or ethnicity-based stereotypes.
- ■ Improve education around language and communication to acknowledge biases, to reduce and eliminate stereotypical phrases, and/or gender specific patterns of communication and tropes.
- ■ Know warning signs such as those that occur after large-scale disasters including wars, earthquakes, pandemics, floods, and prepare resources accordingly.
- ■ Expand on available resources, including:
  - – Legal systems
  - – National helplines
  - – Social safety net organizations
  - – School based support
  - – Shelters
  - – Police
  - – Healthcare settings
  - – Workplace education for identification and mitigation strategies
- ■ Increase availability and perhaps overlap of these types of services to prevent such closures that occurred during the pandemic.
- ■ Continue to work toward improving on evidence-based therapeutics and improving on measurable clinical outcomes for the clinical pathology of trauma related stress.

## Writing Prompt

Consider using the space below to reflect on the following prompt:

**What are some measures you have seen implemented or you have put in place yourself that has resulted in reducing the harmful effects of traumatic stressors?**

_____

_____

_____

_____

_____

_____

_____

_____

_____

_____

_____

_____

## Going Forward

The change we need for posttraumatic growth comes from within. The empowering tools we have provided in this book will allow for continued development of your personal strengths.

As you identify your own strengths, what can you do to reinforce them? We have outlined ways to prepare for foreseeable traumatic stressors, and in doing so, set a framework for antifragility. Identifying weakness and areas of opportunities in ourselves is critical to apply and test the various coping skills we covered.

We encourage you to continue to learn to process emotions, accept the patterns and habits you have needed, and integrate yourself as you learn to self-soothe.

We discussed skills for resilience of the self as well as the family structure. Continue to work toward appreciating that continual, active, intentional time and energy is required for relationships to do well.

Incorporate humor in your self-talk, as well as interactions with others. Now of course this isn't degrading or at the expense of someone, certainly not belittling or talk that takes away. Humor as a mature defense mechanism has huge implications in finding meaning and fostering relationships. It allows us to put things in perspective and accept mistakes and failures while maintaining hope.

You chose to read this far in this book for a reason, and we want to reiterate that it is never too late to start or pick up where you left off of self-care. Going forward, as your mindfulness skills are increasing, make them a routine. Think of how you can remind yourself to incorporate mindfulness every day.

## Writing Prompt

Consider using the space below to reflect on the following prompt:

**How will you incorporate mindfulness in your daily routine?**

_____

_____

_____

_____

_____

_____

_____

_____

_____

_____

_____

_____

We covered very specific strategies in this workbook, including various breathing techniques in Chapter 4, Balan 3-2-1 Method. Implement the coping skills you learned. Be focused and intentional on changes in your eating and sleeping habits. Work toward appreciating the impact of inflammatory foods and stressors and the resulting effect it has on your ability to feel your best.

Within the framework of mindfulness of the body and the connection to our mind and spirit, consider changes in your physical habits and behaviors. Incorporate exercise in your daily routine. Work toward identifying and then decreasing self-harming activities such as gambling or risky sexual encounters.

If you drink alcohol or use other substances, consider working with your health care provider to address these habits and work toward changing them to improve your health.

Identify your support systems. Think of members of your community, those that are around you during spiritual or religious gatherings. Identify your family, including your chosen family. In Chapter 7, Family, Children, and Resilience, we discussed strengths derived from relationships. Learn to speak the language of "we," recognizing that we cannot do much alone.

Work toward identifying your triggers that lead to avoidant behaviors. Consider reducing them as well as isolating yourself. Identify your friends and be intentional about managing your relationships with them.

If you have children or are involved in school-related activities, identify members of that community, as well as other extracurricular activities such as sports, ballet, piano, that are around you and can be of support.

Similar to personal relationships, work on changes in relationships at work. Be intentional and calculated when managing those interactions as well.

# Writing Prompt

Within the framework of the Balan 3-2-1 Method, consider your response to the following:

**What can you genuinely forgive?**

3. With intention, set your internal and external environment.
   - **The body**: What mindfulness techniques are you choosing to allow your body to heal?

   _____

   _____

   _____

   _____

   - **The setting**: How are you intentionally influencing your setting?

   _____

   _____

   _____

   - **The breath**: Which breathing technique will you use as you prepare for this exercise?

   _____

   _____

   _____

   _____

2. What are your thoughts and feelings in response to the writing prompt above?

   _____

   _____

   _____

   _____

   _____

   _____

1. What is your one intent or affirmation in context of the writing prompt above?

   _____

   _____

   _____

   _____

Seek mental health services and physical health care if needed. These are other types of relationships that you can manage purposely.

Work toward a script in your mind as to when and how you can mobilize these support networks, when needed.

We have provided a framework for developing a safety plan and psychological resources throughout this workbook. Highlight the ones that work for you. We also have a section of external resources, helplines, and websites in the next chapter. Familiarize yourself with the ones that may be applicable to you or your loved ones. Have these skills and resources in an easy to find area to use when necessary.

To be able to mindfully prepare for the future, we also discussed physical things you can keep in a safe spot, including important documents as well as food items. This act of preparing provides security and often serves to reduce anxiety.

Make an inventory of all the things that you have already overcome and adapted to until now. This is a key mental model to hold, especially when stressed. You made it to this point in your life, career, and relationships, and you are now working to better yourself. Be proud and take a moment to acknowledge this and congratulate yourself.

As you learn to understand your body, with data inputs you are receiving, depending on the angle you are coming from, and the way you perceive the data, your interpretations will change. It is up to us to do this meaningful work, this mental work to figure these things out. Continue to strive to be able to discern who and which data sources to trust, as well as how we know who and what to trust.

Assimilate the writing prompts and structure learned using the Balan 3-2-1 Method into your daily practice. You are working on learning to tell your story, to yourself, and if you choose, to others. Use phrasing and perceptions that shift to those that emphasize overcoming, adapting, and hope.

Increase your positive language and thinking. Work toward self-compassion, forgiveness, and gratitude. We have given many examples as well as prompts to get you to these places, and now you can work on them at your own pace.

Finally, embrace hope. Develop concrete, future-oriented plans. Model and reinforce these proactive plans to your friends, family, and children. Focus on the positive and expect good things to happen to you and your loved ones.

Create a sense of purpose for yourself and your family and recognize the shared values with those you love and trust. Continue on your quest to learn to listen to yourself and to others. As we continue to learn about ourselves and know who we are, what we believe, what our morals and values are, and the boundaries we hold true, we will be empowered to re-write our own narratives.

> Let everything happen to you: Beauty and terror. Just keep going. No feeling is final.
>
> *– Rainer Maria Rilke*

## Writing Prompt

Within the framework of the Balan 3-2-1 Method, consider your response to the following:

**How do you dream your future?**

3. With intention, set your internal and external environment.
   – **The body**: What mindfulness techniques are you choosing to allow your body to heal?

   _____

   _____

   _____

   – **The setting**: How are you intentionally influencing your setting?

   _____

   _____

   _____

   – **The breath**: Which breathing technique will you use as you prepare for this exercise?

   _____

   _____

   _____

   _____

2. What are your thoughts and feelings in response to the writing prompt above?

   _____

   _____

   _____

   _____

   _____

   _____

   _____

   _____

1. What is your one intent or affirmation in context of the writing prompt above?

   _____

   _____

   _____

   _____

   _____

# Appendix

## Websites and Phone Numbers

If you or someone you know is having a psychiatric emergency, including suicidal thoughts:

In the United States, dial 911, and or go to the nearest emergency room.

## Websites

### United States

1-800-CHILDREN
> A parenting helpline for local resources and support such as housing, food, employment, childcare, health, education, safety and legal.
> – kcsl.findhelp.com

Anxiety and Depression Association of America
> – adaa.org/understanding-anxiety/posttraumatic-stress-disorder-ptsd/resources

American Psychological Association
> – APA.org/topics/trauma

American Psychiatric Association
> – Psychiatry.org

Federal Emergency Management Agency (FEMA)
> – Fema.gov

International Association for Suicide Prevention
> – iasp.info

National Alliance on Mental Illness
> – NAMI.org

National Center for PTSD
> – ptsd.va.gov

National Child Traumatic Stress Network (NCTSN)
- Nctsnet.org

Psych Central
- Psychcentral.com

Psychology Today
- Psychologytoday.com

RAINN: Rape, Abuse & Incest National Network
- Rainn.org

Substance Abuse and Mental Health Services Administration
- Samhsa.gov

Trauma Survivors Network
- Traumasurvivorsnetwork.org

## Canada

Canadian Mental Health Association
- cmha.ca

## United Kingdom

PTSD UK
- ptsduk.org

## Australia

Phoenix Australia
- phoenixaustralia.org

# National Helplines and Hotlines
## United States

1-800-CHILDREN; (800) 244-5373
National Alliance on Mental Illness: (800) 950- 6264; (800) 950-NAMI
National Child Abuse Hotline: (800) 422-4453; (800) 4-A-CHILD
National Domestic Violence Hotline: (800) 799-7233; (800) 799-SAFE
National Parent Helpline: (855) 427-2736; (855) 4-A-PARENT

National Sexual Assault Hotline: (800) 656-4673; (800) 656-HOPE
National Suicide Prevention Lifeline:

- 988
- (800) 273-8255; (800) 273-TALK

Trans Lifeline: (877) 565-8860
Trevor Lifeline: (866) 488-7386

## Canada

Canadian Mental Health Association: (833) 456-4566

Please use the space below to write your own resources and contact information you find useful for your situation, and country.

_____

_____

_____

_____

_____

_____

_____

_____

_____

_____

_____

_____

# Bibliography

Abraham, A., Jithesh, A., Doraiswamy, S., Al-Khawaga, N., Mamtani, R., Cheema, R. Telemental health use in the COVID-19 pandemic: A scoping review and evidence gap mapping. *Frontiers in Psychiatry*. 2021; 12: 748069.

Ahern, K. Institutional betrayal and gaslighting. *The Journal of Perinatal & Neonatal Nursing*. 2018; 32(1): 59–65.

Ahlers, C.G., Lawson, V., Lee, J., March, C., Schultz, J., Anderson, K., Neeley, M., Fleming, A.E., Drolet, B.C. A virtual wellness and learning communities program for medical students during the COVID-19 pandemic. *Southern Medical Journal*. 2021; 114(12): 807–811.

American Psychiatric Association. *Diagnostic and Statistical Manual of Mental Disorders*. Text Revision DSM-5-TR, 5th ed. Washington, DC: American Psychiatric Association, 2022.

Angelou, M., Basquiat, J., Boyers, S.J. *Life Doesn't Frighten Me (25th Anniversary Edition)*. New York: Harry N. Abrams, 2018.

Aspesi, D., Pinna, G. Could a blood test for PTSD and depression be on the horizon? *Expert Review of Proteomics*. 2018; 15: 983–1006.

Ayyala, R.S., Coley, B.D. Promoting gender equity and inclusion through allyship. *Pediatric Radiology*. 2022 Jun; 52(7): 1202–1206. doi: 10.1007/s00247-022-05345-3.

Balan, Y., Murrell, K., Lentz, C. *Big Book of Emergency Department Psychiatry: A Guide to Patient Centered Operational Improvement*. Boca Raton, FL: CRC Press, 2018.

Baldwin, D. Primitive mechanisms of trauma response: An evolutionary perspective on trauma related disorders. *Neuroscience Biobehavioral Reviews*. 2013; 37: 1549–1566.

Ballenger, J.C., Davidson, J.R., Lecrubier, Y., Nutt, D.J., Marshall, R.D. Nemeroff, C.B., Shalev, A.Y., Yehuda, R. Consensus statement on posttraumatic stress disorder from the international consensus group on depression and anxiety. *Journal of Clinical Psychiatry* 2000; 61(Suppl. 5): 60–66.

Başoğlu, M., Salcioğlu, E., Livanou, M., Kalender, D., Acar, G. Single-session behavioral treatment of earthquake-related posttraumatic stress disorder: A randomized waiting list controlled trial. *Journal of Traumatic Stress*. 2005; 18(1): 1–11.

Bates, E.A. "Walking on eggshells": A qualitative examination of men's experiences of intimate partner violence. *Psychology of Men & Masculinities*. 2020; 21(1): 13–24.

Baxter, S., Sanderson, K., Venn, A.J., Blizzard, C.L., Palmer, A.J. The relationship between return on investment and quality of methodology in workplace health promotion programs. *American Journal of Health Promotion*. 2014; 28: 347–363.

Belleville, G., Dubé-Frenette, M., & Rousseau, A. Sleep disturbances and nightmares in victims of sexual abuse with post-traumatic stress disorder: An analysis of abuse-related characteristics. *European Journal of Psychotraumatology*. 2019; 10(1): 1581019.

Bird, C.M., Webb, E.K., Schramm, A.T., Torres, L., Larson, C., deRoon-Cassini, T.A. Racial discrimination is associated with acute posttraumatic stress symptoms and predicts future posttraumatic stress disorder symptom severity in trauma-exposed black adults in the United States. *Journal of Traumatic Stress*. 2021; 34(5): 995–1004.

Black, M.C., Basile, K.C., Breiding, M.J., Smith, S.G., Walters, M.L., Merrick, M.T. et al. The National Intimate Partner and Sexual Violence Survey (NISVS): 2010 summary report. Atlanta, GA: National Center for Injury Prevention and Control, Centers for Disease Control and Prevention, 2011.

Blanchard, E., et al. Emergency room vital signs and PTSD in a treatment seeking sample of motor vehicle accident survivors. *Journal of Traumatic Stress.* 2002; 15(3): 199–204.

Bozzatello, P., Rocca, P., Baldassarri, L., Bosia, M., Bellino, S. The role of trauma in early onset borderline personality disorder: A biopsychosocial perspective. *Frontiers in Psychiatry.* 2021 Sep 23; 12: 721361. doi: 10.3389/fpsyt.2021.721361.

Brach, T. *Radical Acceptance: Embracing Your Life with the Heart of a Buddha.* New York: Bantam, 2004.

Brailovskaia, J., Margraf, J. Relationship between sense of control, psychological burden, sources of information and adherence to anti-COVID-19 rules. *Journal of Affective Disorders Reports.* 2022; 8: 100317.

Breet, E., Seedat, S., Kagee, A. Posttraumatic stress disorder and depression in men and women who perpetrate intimate partner violence. *Journal of Interpersonal Violence,* 2019; 34(10): 2181–2198.

Brewer, K.C. Institutional betrayal in nursing: A concept analysis. *Nursing Ethics.* 2021; 28(6): 1081–1089.

Brewin, C.R., DePierro, J., Pirard, P., et al. Why we need to integrate mental health into pandemic planning. *Perspectives in Public Health.* 2020; 140(6): 309–310.

Brown, B. *Daring Greatly: How the Courage to Be Vulnerable Transforms the Way We Live, Love, Parent, and Lead.* New York: Avery, 2013.

Campos-Garzón, C., Riquelme-Gallego, B., de la Torre-Luque, A., Caparrós-González, R.A., Soundy, A. Psychological impact of the COVID-19 pandemic on pregnant women: A scoping review. *Behavioral Sciences.* 2021; 11(12): 181. doi: 10.3390/bs11120181.

Carter, R.T., Reynolds, A.L. Race related stress, racial identity status attitudes, and emotional reactions of Black Americans. *Cultural Diversity and Ethnic Minority Psychology.* 2011; 17(2): 156–162.

Chan, A.C.Y., Piehler, T.F., Ho, G.W.K. Resilience and mental health during the COVID-19 pandemic: Findings from Minnesota and Hong Kong. *Journal of Affective Disorders,* 2021; 295: 771–780.

Chard, K.M. An evaluation of cognitive processing therapy for the treatment of posttraumatic stress disorder related to childhood sexual abuse. *Journal of Consulting and Clinical Psychology.* 2005; 73(5): 965–971.

Christensen, M., Evans-Murray, A. Gaslighting in nursing academia: A new or established covert form of bullying? *Nursing Forum.* 2021; 56: 640–647.

Cloitre, M., Petkova, E., Su, Z., Weiss, B. Patient characteristics as a moderator of post-traumatic stress disorder treatment outcome: Combining symptom burden and strengths. *British Journal of Psychiatry Open.* 2016; 2: 101–106.

Contractor, A.A., Banducci, A.N., Jin, L., Keegan, F.S., Weiss, N.H. Effects of processing positive memories on posttrauma mental health: A preliminary study in a non-clinical student sample. *Journal of Behavior Therapy and Experimental Psychiatry.* 2020; 66: 101516.

Cronholm, P.F., Forke, C.M., Wade, R., Bair-Merritt, M.H., Davis, M., Harkins-Schwartz, M. et al. Adverse childhood experiences: Expanding the concept of adversity. *American Journal of Preventive Medicine.* 2015; 49(3): 354–361.

Cross, J. *Writing Ourselves Whole: Using the Power of Your Own Creativity to Recover and Heal from Sexual Trauma.* Coral Gables, FL: Mango Publishing Group, 2017.

Dalpati, N., Jena, S., Jain, S., Sarangi, P.P. Yoga and meditation, an essential tool to alleviate stress and enhance immunity to emerging infections: A perspective on the effect of COVID-19 pandemic on students. *Brain, Behavior, & Immunity - Health.* 2022; 20: 100420.

Das, A., Singh, P., Bruckner, T.A. State lockdown policies, mental health symptoms, and using substances. *Addictive Behaviors.* 2022; 124: 107084.

Davis, L.L., Suris, A., Lambert, M.T., Heimberg, C., Petty, F. Post-traumatic stress disorder and serotonin: New directions for research and treatment. *Journal of Psychiatry & Neuroscience.* 1997; 22(5): 318–326.

Dawson, R.L., Calear, A.L., McCallum, S.M., McKenna, S., Nixon, R.D.V., O'Kearney, R. Exposure-based writing therapies for subthreshold and clinical posttraumatic stress disorder: A systematic review and meta-analysis. *Journal of Trauma Stress.* 2021; 34(1): 81–91.

de Roos, C., van der Oord, S., Zijlstra, B., Lucassen, S., Perrin, S., Emmelkamp, P., de Jongh, A. Comparison of eye movement desensitization and reprocessing therapy, cognitive behavioral writing therapy, and wait-list in pediatric posttraumatic stress disorder following single-incident trauma: A multicenter randomized clinical trial. *Journal of Child Psychology and Psychiatry.* 2017; 58(11): 1219–1228.

Dehelean, L., Papava, I., Musat, M.I., Bondrescu, M., Bratosin, F. et al. Coping strategies and stress related disorders in patients with COVID-19. *Brain Science.* 2021; 11(10): 1287.

DeLucia, J.A., Bitter, C., Fitzgerald, J., Greenberg, M., Dalwari, P., Buchanan, P. Prevalence of post-traumatic stress disorder in emergency physicians in the United States. *Western Journal of Emergency Medicine.* 2019; 20(5): 740–746.

Dickerson, S.S., Kemeny, M.E. Acute stressors and cortisol responses: A theoretical integration and synthesis of laboratory research. *Psychological Bulletin.* 2004; 130(3): 355–391.

Emerson, D., Hopper, E. *Overcoming Trauma through Yoga: Reclaiming your Body.* Berkeley, CA: North Atlantic, 2012.

Emmons, R.A., Crumpler, C.A. Gratitude as a human strength: Appraising the evidence. *Journal of Social and Clinical Psychology.* 2000. 19(1), 56–69.

Ennis, N., Shorer, S., Shoval-Zuckerman, Y., et al. Treating posttraumatic stress disorder across cultures: A systematic review of cultural adaptations of trauma focused cognitive behavioral therapies. *Journal of Clinical Psychology.* 2020; 76(4): 587–611.

Fear, N.T., Jones, M., Murphy, D., Hull, L. et al. What are the consequences of deployment to Iraq and Afghanistan on the mental health of the UK armed forces? A cohort study. *The Lancet.* 2010; 375(9728): 1783–1797.

Felitti, V.J., Anda, R.F., Nordenberg, D., Williamson, D.F., Spitz, A.M., Edwards, V. et al. Relationship of childhood abuse and household dysfunction to many of the leading causes of death in adults: The Adverse Childhood Experiences (ACE) study. *American Journal of Preventative Medicine.* 1998; 14(4): 245–258.

Finley, E.P., Garcia, H.A., Ketchun, N.S., McGeary, D.D., McGeary, C.A., et al. Utilization of evidence-based psychotherapies in veterans affairs posttraumatic stress disorder outpatient clinics. *Psychological Services.* 2015; 12: 73–83.

Fiorillo, A., Gorwood, P. The consequences of the COVID-19 pandemic on mental health and implications for clinical practice. *European Psychiatry.* 2020; 63(1): e32.

Fisher, J. *Transforming the Living Legacy of Trauma: A Workbook for Survivors and Therapists.* Eau Claire, WI: PESI Publishing, 2021.

Foa, E.B., Hembree, E., Rothbaum, B.O. *Prolonged Exposure Therapy for PTSD: Emotional Processing of Traumatic Experiences Therapist Guide.* New York: Oxford University Press, 2007.

Foa, E.B., Keane, T.M., Friedman, M.J., Cohen, J.A., *Effective Treatments for PTSD: Practice Guidelines from the International Society for Traumatic Stress Studies.* New York: Guilford Press, 2008.

Foa, E.B., Rothbaum, B.O., Furr, J.M. Augmenting exposure therapy with other CBT procedures. *Psychiatric Annals.* 2003; 33: 47–53.

Fogel, A. *The Psychophysiology of Self-Awareness: Rediscovering the Lost Art of Body Sense,* 1st ed. New York: W.W. Norton, 2009.

Frankl, V.E. *The Will to Meaning: Foundations and Applications of Logotherapy.* New York: World Publishing Co., 1969.

Franklin, C.L., Raines, A.M., Cuccurullo, L.J., et al. Twenty-Seven ways to meet PTSD: Using the PTSD-checklist for DSM-5 to examine PTSD core criteria. *Psychiatry Research.* 2018; 261: 504–507.

Gamber, A.M., Lane-Loney, S., Levine, M.P. Effects and linguistic analysis of written traumatic emotional disclosure in an eating-disordered population. *The Permanente Journal.* 2013; 17(1): 16–20.

Gawlytta, R., Kesselmeier, M., Scherag, A., Niemeyer, H., Böttche, M., Knaevelsrud, C., Rosendahl, J. Internet-based cognitive-behavioural writing therapy for reducing post-traumatic stress after severe sepsis in patients and their spouses (REPAIR): Results of a randomised-controlled trial. *BMJ Open.* 2022; 12(3). e050305.

Ghafoerkhan, R.S., van Heemstra, H.E., Scholte, W.F., van der Kolk, J.R.J., ter Heide, J.J.F., de la Rie, S.M., Verhaak, L.M., Snippe, E., Boelen, P.A. Feasibility and predictors of change of narrative exposure therapy for displaced populations: A repeated measures design. *Pilot and Feasibility Studies.* 2020 May 21; 6: 69. doi: 10.1186/s40814-020-00613-1.

Gilbert-Eliot, T. *Trauma Recovery Journal: Reflective Prompts and Evidence-Based Practices to Help you Recover, Heal, and Thrive.* Emeryville, CA: Rockridge Press, 2021.

Glaus, J., Pointet Perizzolo, V., Moser, D.A., Vital, M., Rusconi Serpa, S., Urben, S., Plessen, K.J., Schechter, D.S. Associations between maternal post-traumatic stress disorder and traumatic events with child psychopathology: Results from a prospective longitudinal study. *Frontiers in Psychiatry*. 2021 Aug 30; 12: 718108. doi: 10.3389/fpsyt.2021.718108.

Goleman, D. *Emotional Intelligence*. New York: Random House, 2006.

Gong, A.T., Kamboj, S.K., Curran, H.V. Post-traumatic stress disorder in victims of sexual assault with pre-assault substance consumption: A systematic review. *Frontiers in Psychiatry*. 2019 Mar 13; 10: 92. doi: 10.3389/fpsyt.2019.00092.

Gordon, N.S., Forberow, N.L., Maida, C.A. *Children & Disasters*. London: Routledge, 1999.

Greeson, J.M., Zarrin, H., Smoski, M.J. Brantley, J.G., Lynch, T.R., Webber, D.M. et al. Mindfulness medication targets transdiagnostic symptoms implicated in stress-related disorders: Understanding relationships between changes in mindfulness, sleep quality, and physical symptoms. *Evidence-Based Complementary and Alternative Medicine*. 2018; 2018: 1–10.

Guérin-Marion, C., Sezlik, S, Bureau, J.F. Developmental and attachment-based perspectives on dissociation: Beyond the effects of maltreatment. *European Journal of Psychotraumatology*. 2020; 11(1): 1802908.

Gundogan, S. The relationship of COVID-19 student stress with school burnout, depression and subjective well-being: Adaptation of the COVID-19 student stress scale into Turkish. *Asia-Pacific Education Researcher*. 2022: 1–12. doi: 10.1007/s40299-021-00641-2.

Gutner, C.A., Gallagher, M.W., Baker, A.S., Sloan, D.M., Resnick, P.A. Time course of treatment drop-out in cognitive-behavioral therapies for posttraumatic stress disorder. *Psychological Trauma: Theory, Research, Practice, and Policy*. 2016; 8(1): 115–121.

Hankerson, S.H., Moise, N., Wilson, D., Waller, B.Y., Arnold, K.T. et al. The intergenerational impact of structural racism and cumulative trauma on depression. *American Journal of Psychiatry*. 2022, 179: 434–440.

Hembree, E.A., Foa, E.B., Dorfan, N.M., Street, G.P., Kowalski, J., Tu, X. Do patients drop out prematurely from exposure therapy for PTSD? *Journal of Trauma Stress* 2003; 16: 555–562.

Herman, J. *Trauma and Recovery: The Aftermath of Violence- from Domestic Abuse to Political Terror*. New York: Basic Books, 1992.

Hoge, C.W., Grossman, S.H., Aucherlonie, J.L, et al. PTSD treatment for soldiers after combat deployment: Low utilization of mental health care and reasons for dropout. *Psychiatric Services* 2014; 65: 997–1004.

Horsch, A., Tolsa, J.F., Gilbert, L., du Chêne, L.J., Müller-Nix, C., Bickle Graz, M. Improving maternal mental health following preterm birth using an expressive writing intervention: A randomized controlled trial. *Child Psychiatry Human Development*. 2016; 47(5): 780–791.

Huang, L., Yao, Q., Gu, X. et al. 1-year outcomes in hospital survivors with COVID-19: As longitudinal cohort study. *The Lancet*. 2021; 398: 747–758.

Idsoe, T., Vaillancourt, T., Dyregrov, A., Hagen, K.A., Ogden, T., Nærde, A. Bullying victimization and trauma. *Frontiers in Psychiatry*. 2021 Aug; 40(6): 901–911. doi: 10.1007/s10802-012-9620-0.

Jeličić, L., Sovilj, M., Bogavac, I., Drobnjak, A., Gouni, O., Kazmierczak, M., Subotić, M. The Impact of maternal anxiety on early child development during the COVID-19 pandemic. *Frontiers in Psychology*. 2021; 12: 792053. doi: 10.3389/fpsyg.2021.792053.

Johnson, V.E., Nadal, K.L., Sissoko, D.R.G., King, R. "It's not in your head": Gaslighting, 'splaining, victim blaming, and other harmful reactions to microaggressions. *Perspectives on Psychological Science*. 2021; 16(5): 1024–1036.

Joseph, N., Benedick, A., Flanagan, G., Breslin, M., Vallier, H. Risk factors for posttraumatic stress disorder in acute trauma patients. *Journal of Orthopaedic Trauma*. 2021; 35(6): e209–e215.

Kalaitzaki, A.E., Tsouvelas, G., Tamiolaki, A., Konstantakopoulos, G. Post-traumatic stress symptoms during the first and second COVID-19 lockdown in Greece: Rates, risk, and protective factors. *International Journal of Mental Health Nursing* 2021. doi: 10.1111/inm.12945.

Keating, L., Muller, R.T. LGBTQ+ based discrimination is associated with PTSD symptoms, dissociation, emotion dysregulation, and attachment insecurity among LGBTQ+ adults who have experienced Trauma. *Journal of Trauma and Dissociation*. 2020; 21(1): 124–141.

Klimovich-Mickael, A., Kubick, N., Milanesi, E., Dobre, M., Lazarczyk, M., Wijas, B., Sacharczuk, M., Mickael, M. Trends of anger and physical aggression in Russian women during COVID-19 lockdown. *Frontiers Global Womens Health*. 2021; 2: 698151.

Knaevelsrud, C., Böttche, M. Schreibtherapie nach traumatischen Belastungen: Therapieansätze und Wirkmechanismen [Writing therapy after traumatic events: therapeutic approaches and mechanisms of change]. *Psychother Psychosom Med Psychology*. 2013; 63(9–10): 391–397.

Kuehn, B.M. Reduced HIV testing and diagnoses during COVID-19 pandemic. *JAMA*. 2022; 328(6): 519.

Kuester, A., Niemeyer, H., Knaevelsrud, C. Internet-based interventions for post traumatic stress: A meta-analysis of randomized controlled trials. *Clinical Psychology Review*. 2016; 43: 1–16.

Laborde-Cárdenas, C., Tornero-Aguilera, J.F. The impact of the COVID-19 pandemic on mental disorders: A critical review. *International Journal of Environmental Research Public Health*. 2021; 18(19): 10041.

Larsen, S.E., Stirman, S.W., Smith, B.N., Resnick, P.A. Symptom exacerbations in trauma-focused treatments: Associations with treatment outcome and non-completion. *Behaviour Research and Therapy*. 2016; 77: 68–77.

Lee, D., Yu, E., Kim, N.H. Resilience as a mediator in the relationship between posttraumatic stress and posttraumatic growth among adult accident or crime victims: The moderated mediating effect of childhood trauma. *European Journal of Psychotraumatology*. 2020 Jan 9; 11(1): 1704563. doi: 10.1080/20008198.2019.1704563.

Lee, D.J., Marx, B.P., Thompson-Hollands, J., Gallagher, M.W., Resick, P.A., Sloan, D.M. The temporal sequence of change in PTSD symptoms and hypothesized mediators in cognitive processing therapy and written exposure therapy for PTSD. *Behavior Research and Therapy*. 2021; 144: 103918.

Lee-Won, R.J., Jang, I., Kim, H., Park, S. The relationship between future anxiety due to COVID-19 and vigilance: The role of message fatigue and autonomy satisfaction. *International Journal of Environmental Research and Public Health*. 2022; 19(3): 1062.

Levine, P.A. *Waking the Tiger: Healing Trauma: The Innate Capacity to Transform Overwhelming Experiences*. Berkeley, CA: North Atlantic Books, 1997.

Levine, P.A. *In an Unspoken Voice: How the Body Releases Trauma and Restores Goodness*. Berkeley, CA: North Atlantic Books, 2010.

Lewis, C., Roberts, N.P., Simon, N., et al. Internet-delivered cognitive behavioural therapy for posttraumatic stress disorder: Systematic review and meta-analysis. *Acta Psychiatrica Scandinavica*. 2019; 140: 508–521.

Lichtenthal, W.G., Cruess, D.G. Effects of directed written disclosure on grief and distress symptoms among bereaved individuals. *Death Studies*. 2010; 34(6): 475–499.

Lindert, J., Jakubauskiene, M., Bilsen, J. The COVID-19 disaster and mental health-assessing, responding, and recovering. *European Journal of Public Health*. 2021; 31(Supplement_4): iv31–iv35.

Litz, B.T., Stein, N., Delaney, E., Lebowitz, L., et al. Moral injury and moral repair in war veterans: A preliminary model and intervention strategy. *Clinical Psychology Review*. 2009; 29(8): 695–706.

Lyons, M., Brewer, G. Experiences of intimate partner violence during lockdown and the COVID-19 pandemic. *Journal of Family Violence*. 2021; 37(6): 969–977. doi: 10.1007/s10896-021-00260-x.

Magnúsdóttir I, Lovik A, Unnarsdóttir AB, McCartney D, Ask H, Kõiv K, Christoffersen LAN, Johnson SU, Hauksdóttir A, Fawns-Ritchie C, Helenius D, González-Hijón J, Lu L, Ebrahimi OV, Hoffart A, Porteous DJ, Fang F, Jakobsdóttir J, Lehto K, Andreassen OA, Pedersen OBV, Aspelund T, Valdimarsdóttir UA; COVIDMENT Collaboration. Acute COVID-19 severity and mental health morbidity trajectories in patient populations of six nations: an observational study. Lancet Public Health. 2022 May; 7(5): e406-e416. doi: 10.1016/S2468-2667(22)00042-1.

Maiberger, B. *EMDR Essentials: A Guide for Clients and Therapists*. New York: W.W. Norton & Co., 2009.

Mao, W., & Agyapong, V.I.O. The role of social determinants in mental health and resilience after disasters: Implications for public health policy and practice. *Frontiers in Public Health*. 2021. May 19; 9: 658528. doi: 10.3389/fpubh.2021.658528.

Mate, G. *When the Body Says No: Understanding the Stress-Disease Connection*. New York: Random House, 2011.

Mateu, A., Pascual-Sánchez, A., Martinez-Herves, M., Hickey, N., Nicholls, D., Kramer, T. Cyberbullying and post-traumatic stress symptoms in UK adolescents. *Archives of Disease in Childhood*. 2020; 105(10): 951–956.

Mavranezouli, I., Megnin-Viggars, O., Grey, N., Bhutani, G., Leach, J., Daly, C., Dias, S., Welton, N.J., Katona, C., El-Leithy, S., Greenberg, N., Stockton, S., Pilling, S. Cost-effectiveness of psychological treatments for post-traumatic stress disorder in adults. *PLoS One*. 2020; 15(4): e0232245.

McCullough, M.E., Emmons, R.A., Tsang, J.-A. The grateful disposition: A conceptual and empirical topography. *Journal of Personality and Social Psychology*. 2002; 82(1): 112–127.

McLean, C.P., Foa, E.B., Prolonged exposure therapy for post-traumatic stress disorder: A review of evidence and dissemination. *Expert Review of Neurotherapeutics*. 2011; 11: 1151–1163.

Meichenbaum, D. *Roadmap to Resilience: A Guide for Military, Trauma Victims and Their Families*. Florida: Institute Press, 2012.

Mekawi, Y., Watson-Singleton, N.N., Kuzyk, E., Dixon, H.D., Carter, S., Bradley-Davino, B., Fani, N., Michopoulos, V., Powers, A. Racial discrimination and posttraumatic stress: Examining emotion dysregulation as a mediator in an African American community sample. *European Journal of Psychotraumatology*. 2020; 11(1): 1824398.

Meshberg-Cohen, S., Svikis, D., McMahon, T.J. Expressive writing as a therapeutic process for drug-dependent women. *Subst Abuse*. 2014; 35(1): 80–88. doi: 10.1080/08897077.2013.805181.

Miller, A. *The Drama of the Gifted Child: The Search for the True Self*. New York: Basic Books, 1997.

Mills, K.L., Barrett, E.L., Merz, S., Rosenfeld, J., Ewer, P.L., Sannibale, C., Baker, A.L., Hopwood, S., Back, S.E., Brady, K.T., Teesson, M. Integrated exposure-based therapy for co-occurring post traumatic stress disorder (PTSD) and substance dependence: Predictors of change in PTSD symptom severity. *Journal of Clinical Medicine*. 2016; 5(11): 101.

Mills, K.L., Teeson, M., Ross, J., Darke, S. The impact of post-traumatic stress disorder on treatment outcomes for heroin dependence. *Addiction*. 2007; 102: 447–454.

Mitchell, J.M., Bogenschutz, M., Lilienstein, A. et al. MDMA-assisted therapy for severe PTSD: A random-ized, double-blind, placebo-controlled phase 3 study. *Nature Medicine*. 2021; 27; 1025–1033.

Moncrieff, J., Cooper, R.E., Stockmann, T. et al. The serotonin theory of depression: A systematic umbrella review of the evidence. *Molecular Psychiatry*. 2022. doi: 10.1038/s41380-022-01661-0.

Mueller, P.A., Oppenheimer, D.M. The pen is mightier than the keyboard: Advantages of longhand over laptop note taking. *Psychological Science*. 2014; 25: 1159–1168.

Muscatelli, S., Spurr, H., O'Hara, N.N. et al. Prevalence of depression and posttraumatic stress disorder after acute orthopedic trauma: A systemic review and meta-analysis. *Journal of Orthopedic Trauma*. 2017; 31: 47–55.

Nagarajan, R., Krishnamoorthy, Y., Basavarachar, V., Dakshinamoorthy, R. Prevalence of post-traumatic stress disorder among survivors of severe COVID-19 infections: A systematic review and meta-analysis. *Journal of Affective Disorders*. 2022; 299: 52–59.

Olff, M., Primasari, I., Qing, Y., Coimbra, B.M., Hovnanyan, A., Grace, E., Williamson, R.E., Hoeboer, C.M., Consortium, T.G. Mental health responses to COVID-19 around the world. *European Journal of Psychotraumatology*. 2021; 12(1): 1929754.

Park, H.Y., Park, W.B., Lee, S.H., et al. Posttraumatic stress disorder and depression of survivors 12 months after the outbreak of Middle East respiratory syndrome in South Korea. *BMC Public Health*. 2020; 20: 605.

Payne, P., Levine P.A., Crane-Godreau, M.A. Somatic experiencing: using interoception and proprioception as core elements of trauma therapy. *Frontiers in Psychology*. 2015; 4(6): 93.

Pennebaker, J.W. Expressive writing in psychological science. *Perspectives on Psychological Science*. 2018; 13(2): 226–229.

Pennebaker, J.W., Beall, S.K. Confronting a traumatic event: Toward an understanding of inhibition and disease. *Journal of Abnormal Psychology*. 1986; 95(3): 274–281.

Pennebaker, J.W., Chung, C.K. Expressive writing, emotional upheavals, and health. In: H. Friedman and R. Silver (Eds.), *Foundations of Health Psychology* (pp.263–284). Oxford: Oxford University Press, 2007.

Pennebaker, J.W., Evans, J.F. *Expressive Writing: Words that Heal*. Enumclaw, WA: Idyll Arbor, 2014.

Pinna, G. Endocannabinoids and precision medicine for mood disorders and suicide. *Frontiers in Psychiatry.* 2021 May 20; 12: 658433. doi: 10.3389/fpsyt.2021.658433.

Pinto, S., Soares, J., Silva, A., Curral, R., Coelho, R. COVID-19 suicide survivors-a hidden grieving population. *Frontiers in Psychiatry.* 2020; 11: 626807.

Qian, J., Zhou, X., Sun, X., Wu, M., Sun, S., Yu, X. Effects of expressive writing intervention for women's PTSD, depression, anxiety and stress related to pregnancy: A meta-analysis of randomized controlled trials. *Psychiatry Research.* 2020; 288: 112933.

Qiu, D., Li, Y., Li, L., He, J., Ouyang, F., Xiao, S. Prevalence of post-traumatic stress symptoms among people influenced by coronavirus disease 2019 outbreak: A meta-analysis. *European Psychiatry.* 2021 Apr 12; 64(1): e30. doi: 10.1192/j.eurpsy.2021.24.

Rajkumar, R. COVID-19 and mental health: A review of the existing literature. *Asian Journal of Psychiatry.* 2020; 52: 102066.

Read, J.P., Brown, P.J., Kahler, C.W. Substance use and posttraumatic stress disorders: Symptom interplay and effects on outcome. *Addictive Behaviors.* 2004; 29; 1665–1672.

Resick, P.A., Monson, C.M., Gutner, C.A., Maslej, M.M. Psychosocial treatments for adults with PTSD. In: M.J. Friedman, T.M. Keane, and P.A. Resick (Eds.) Handbook of PTSD: Science and Practice (pp. 419–436). New York: Guilford Press, 2014.

Riggs, D.W., Bartholomaeus, C. Gaslighting in the context of clinical interactions with parents of transgender children. *Sexual & Relationship Therapy.* 2018; 33(4): 382–394.

Robjant, L., Fazel, M. The emerging evidence for narrative exposure therapy: A review. *Clinical Psychology Review,* 2010; 30(8): 1030–1039.

Rothbaum, B.O., Schwartz, A.C. Exposure therapy for posttraumatic stress disorder. *American Journal of Psychotherapy.* 2002; 56: 59–73.

Rothenberg, W.A., Hussong, A.M., Langley, H.A., Egerton, G.A., Halberstadt, A.G., Coffman, J.L., Costanzo, P.R. Grateful parents raising grateful children: Niche selection and the socialization of child gratitude. *Applied Developmental Science.* 2017; 21(2): 106–120.

Rothschild, B. *The Body Remembers: The Psychophysiology of Trauma and Trauma Treatment.* New York: W.W. Norton & Co., 2000.

Rubin, C.L., Chomitz, V.R., Woo, C., Li, G., Koch-Weser, S., Levine, P. Arts, culture, and creativity as a strategy for countering the negative social impacts of immigration stress and gentrification. *Health Promotion Practice.* 2021; 22(1_suppl): 131S–140S.

Ruini, C., Mortara, C.C. Writing technique across psychotherapies-from traditional expressive writing to new positive psychology interventions: A narrative review. *Journal of Contemporary Psychotherapy.* 2022; 52(1): 23–34.

Sanchez-Gomez, M., Giorgi, G., Finstad, G.L., Urbini, F., Foti, G., et al. COVID-19 pandemic as a traumatic event and its associations with fear and mental health: A cognitive-activation approach. *International Journal of Environmental Research and Public Health,* 2021 Jul 12; 18(14): 7422. doi: 10.3390/ijerph18147422.

Sanderson, W., Arunagiri, V., Funk, A., Ginsburg, K., Krychiw, J., Limowski, A., et al. The nature and treatment of pandemic-related psychological distress. *Journal of Contemporary Psychotherapy.* 2020; 50: 251–263.

Schiraldi, G. *The Adverse Childhood Experiences Recovery Workbook: Heal the Hidden Wounds from Childhood Affecting Your Adult Mental and Physical Health.* Oakland, CA: New Harbinger Publications. 2021.

Schnyder, U., Bryant, R.A., Ehlers, A., Foa, E.B., Hasan, A., Mwiti, G., Kristensen, C.H., Neuner, F., Oe, M., Yule, W. Culture sensitive psychotraumatology. *European Journal of Psychotraumatology.* 2016; 7: 31179.

Schwartz, A. *The Complex PTSD Workbook: A Mind-Body Approach to Regaining Emotional Control & Becoming Whole.* Berkeley: Althea Press, 2016.

Schwandt, H., Currie, J., von Wachter, T., et al. *Changes in the Relationship between Income and Life Expectancy Before and during the COVID-19 Pandemic,* California, 2015–2021. JAMA. 2022, doi: 10.1001/jama.2022.10953.

Seligman, M.E. *Helplessness: On Depression, Development, and Death.* San Francisco: W. H. Freeman, 1992.

Shuman, C.J., Morgan, M.E., Chiangong, J., Pareddy, N., Veliz, P., Peahl, A.F., Dalton, V.K. "Mourning the experience of what should have been": Experiences of peripartum women during the COVID-19 pandemic. *Maternal and Child Health Journal.* 2022 Jan; 26(1): 102–109. doi: 10.1007/s10995-021-03344-8

Sloan, D.M., Marx, B.P., Bovin, M.J., Feinstein, B.A., Gallagher, M.W. Written exposure as an intervention for PTSD: A randomized clinical trial with motor vehicle accident survivors. *Behaviour Research and Therapy.* 2012; 50(10): 627–635.

Sloan, D.M., Marx, B.P., Epstein, E.M., Lexington, J.M. Does altering the writing instructions influence outcome associated with written disclosure? *Behaviour Research and Therapy.* 2007; 38(2): 155–168.

Sloan, D.M., Marx, B.P., Greenberg, E.M. A test of written emotional disclosure as an intervention for posttraumatic stress disorder. *Behaviour Research and Therapy.* 2011; 49(4): 299–304.

Sloan, D.M., Marx, B.P., Lee, D.J., Resick, P.A. A brief exposure-based treatment vs cognitive processing therapy for posttraumatic stress disorder: A randomized noninferiority clinical trial. *JAMA Psychiatry.* 2018; 75(3): 233–239.

Sloan, D.M., Marx, B.P., Resick, P.A. Brief treatment for PTSD: A non-inferiority trial. *Contemporary Clinical Trials.* 2016; 48: 76–82.

Smyth, J.M., Hockemeyer, J.R., Tulloch, H. Expressive writing and post-traumatic stress disorder: Effects on trauma symptoms, mood states, and cortisol reactivity. *British Journal of Health Psychology.* 2008; 13(Pt 1): 85–93.

Spies, J.P., Cwik, J.C., Willmund, G.D., Knaevelsrud, C., Schumacher, S., Niemeyer, H., Engel, S., Küster, A., Muschalla, B., Köhler, K., Weiss, D., Rau, H. Associations between difficulties in emotion regulation and post-traumatic stress disorder in deployed service members of the German Armed Forces. *Frontiers in Psychiatry.* 2020 Sep 15; 11: 576553. doi: 10.3389/fpsyt.2020.576553.

Stein, N.R., Dickstein, B.D., Schuster, J., Litz, B.T., Resick, P.A. Trajectories of response to treatment for posttraumatic stress disorder. *Behavior Therapy.* 2012; 43(4): 790–800.

Stuckey, H.L., Nobel, J. The connection between art, healing, and public health: A review of current literature. *American Journal of Public Health.* 2010; 100(2): 254–273.

Sun, Z., Yu, C., Zhou, Y., Liu, Z. Psychological interventions for healthcare providers with PTSD in life-threatening pandemic: Systematic review and meta-analysis. *Frontiers in Psychiatry.* 2021 Jul 29; 12: 697783. doi: 10.3389/fpsyt.2021.697783.

Sykes, D.L., Holdsorth, L., Jawad, N., Gunasekera, P., Morice, A.H., Crooks, M.H. Post Covid-19 symptoms burden: What is long-COVID and how should we manage it? *Lung.* 2021; 199: 113–119.

Tan, C. *Search Inside Yourself: The Unexpected Path to Achieving Success, Happiness (and World Peace).* New York: HarperOne, 2012.

Tausch, A., Souza, R.O., Viciana, C.M., Cayetano, C., Barbosa, J., Hennis, A.J. Strengthening mental health responses to COVID-19 in the Americas: A health policy analysis and recommendations. *Lancet Regional Health Americas.* 2022; 5: 100118.

Thompson-Hollands, J., Marx, B.P., Sloan, D.M. Brief novel therapies for PTSD: Written exposure therapy. *Current Treatment Options Psychiatry.* 2019; 6(2): 99–106.

Toso, K., de Cock, P., Leavey, G. Maternal exposure to violence and offspring neurodevelopment: A systematic review. *Paediatric and Perinatal Epidemiology.* 2020; 34(2): 190–203.

Trautmann, S., Goodwin, L., Hofler, M., Jacobi, F., Strehle, J., et al. Prevalence and severity of mental disorders in military personnel: A standardized comparison with civilians. *Epidemiology and Psychiatric Sciences.* 2017; 26(02): 199–208.

Usher, K., Durkin, J., Bhullar, N. The COVID-19 pandemic and mental health impacts. *International Journal of Mental Health Nursing.* 2020; 29(3): 315–318.

van Dam, D., Ehring, T., Vedel, E., Emmelkamp, P.M. Trauma-focused treatment for posttraumatic stress disorder combined with CBT for severe substance use disorder: A randomized controlled trial. *BMC Psychiatry.* 2013; 19(13): 172.

van der Kolk, B.A. *The Body Keeps the Score: Brain, Mind, and Body in the Healing of Trauma.* New York: Viking, 2014.

van der Kolk, B.A., Fisler, R. Dissociation and the fragmentary nature of traumatic memories: Overview and exploratory study. *Journal of Traumatic Stress.* 1995; 8: 505–525.

van Emmerik, A.A., Reijntjes, A., Kamphuis, J.H. Writing therapy for posttraumatic stress: A meta-analysis. *Psychother Psychosom*. 2013; 82(2): 82–88.

van Minnen, A., Foa, E.B. The effect of imaginal exposure length on outcome of treatment for PTSD. *Journal of Traumatic Stress*. 2006; 19: 427–438.

Voith, L.A., Russell, K., Lee, H., Anderson, R.E. Adverse childhood experiences, trauma symptoms, mindfulness, and intimate partner violence: Therapeutic implications for marginalized men. *Family Process*. 2020; 59(4): 1588–1607.

Vranceanu, A.M., Bachoura, A., Weeining, A., et al. Psychological factors predict disability and pain intensity after skeletal trauma. *Journal of Bone and Joint Surgery American*. 2014; 96: e20.

Walsh, F. The concept of family resilience: Crisis and challenge. *Family Process*. 1996; 35(3): 261–281.

Weathers, F.W., Blake, D.D., Schnurr, P.P., Kaloupek, D.G., Marx, B.P., Keane, T.M. The Life Events Checklist for DSM-5 (LEC-5). Instrument available from the National Center for PTSD, 2013a. www.ptsd.va.gov.

Weathers, F.W., Litz, B.T., Keane, T.M., Palmieri, P.A., Marx, B.P., Schnurr, P.P. *The PTSD Checklist for DSM-5 (PCL-5)*. Boston, MA: National Center for PTSD, 2013b.

Wile, J.E., West, J.C., Farifteh, D.F., Herrell, R.K., Rae, D.S., Hoge, C.W. Use of evidence-based treatment for posttraumatic stress disorder in army behavioral healthcare. *Psychiatry*. 2013; 76(4): 336–348.

Williams, D.R. Stress and the mental health of populations of color: Advancing our understanding of race-related stressors. *Journal of Health and Social Behavior*. 2018; 59(4): 466–485.

Zahn, R., Garrido, G., Moll, J., Grafman, J. Individual differences in posterior cortical volume correlate with proneness to pride and gratitude. *Social Cognitive and Affective Neuroscience*. 2014; 9(11): 1676–1683.

Zatzick, D., Jurkovich, G.J., Rivara, F.P., et al. A national study of posttraumatic stress disorder, depression, and work functional outcomes after hospitalization for traumatic injury. *Annals of Surgery*. 2008; 248: 429–437.

Zhang, M., Yang, Z., Zhong, J., Zhang, Y., et al. Thalamocortical mechanisms for nostalgia-induced analgesia. *Journal of Neuroscience*. 2022. doi: 10.1523/JNEUROSCI.2123-21.2022.

Zhang, Q., Zheng, R., Fu, Y., Mu, Q., Li, J. Mental health consequences during alerting situations and recovering to a new normal of coronavirus epidemic in 2019: A cross-sectional study based on the affected population. *BMC Public Health*. 2021 Aug 3; 21(1): 1499. doi: 10.1186/s12889-021-11550-w.

Zhen, R., Zhang, J., Pang, H., Ruan, L., Liu, X., Zhou, X. Full and partial posttraumatic stress disorders in adults exposed to super typhoon Lekima: A cross-sectional investigation. *BMC Psychiatry*. 2021 Oct 18; 21(1): 512. doi: 10.1186/s12888-021-03528-0.

Zurbriggen, E.L., Gobin, R.L., Kaehler, L.A. Trauma, attachment, and intimate relationships. *Journal of Trauma and Dissociation*. 2012; 13(2): 127–133.

# Index

absenteeism 35, 134, 149, 176, 180
abuse
    childhood sexual 106
    emotional 107
    physical 105
    sexual 105
acceptance 11, 74, 129, 141
accidental overdoses 3, 158
activities of daily living 9, 158, 177
acute physical trauma 97–98
acute stress disorder 8
addiction 158
adjustment disorder 8
adrenal glands 93
adrenaline 93
adverse childhood experiences (ACEs) 103, 105
    care and management 112–113
    emotional abuse 107
    impact on the individual and society 106
    isolation and stigma 110–111
    issues at school and work 111–112
    neglect 110
adversity 114, 122, 141
advocates 109, 141, 148, 198, 202, 203
affective disorders 3, 193
affirmation 44, 48, 56
aftershocks 174, 175
aggressivity 3, 133, 162, 163, 167, 193
alcohol use 176
alliance building 198
alternate nostril breathing 52
American Psychiatric Association (APA) 7
American Psychological Association (APA) report 34
Americans with Disabilities Act (ADA) 33
amygdala 91
    function 91–92
    impact of trauma 92
analogy, sea 41–42
anchoring 132
anger 70, 71
angst 3, 133, 175, 180
anhedonia 9, 10, 132
ANS *see* autonomic nervous system (ANS)
antidepressants 21–22

antifragility 167, 210
antipsychotic medications 22–23
anxiety 13, 14, 31
anxiety disorders 28, 175–176
anxiogenic stimulus 22
appreciation 27, 37, 68, 82, 129, 132, 198
arousal 94, 203
    emotional 132
arousal state 9, 81
assignments 15, 23
asthma 12
Ativan 22
attachment theory 104
attachment trauma 14, 155
attention 15, 17, 27, 42, 58, 59
autonomic nervous system (ANS) 94
    parasympathetic nervous system 96
    sympathetic nervous system 96
avoidance 98, 116, 133
awareness 6, 17, 32

baby blues 154
balance 84, 183
Balan, Duygu xxiii, xxvii, 15
Balan family crest 127–129
Balan 3-2-1 Method 5, 43, 58, 207
    body 44–45
    breath 49
    setting 45–48
Balan: 3-2-One 56–57
Balan: 3-Two-1 55–56
Balan, Nadir xxvii
Balan, Yener xxiv, xxv
barrier 23, 83, 113
behavioral addictions 176
behavioral conditions, mental health and 176
behaviors, reckless 180
benzodiazepines 22
bereavement 177
betrayal traumas 162
bias, narrative 4
*Big Book of Emergency Department Psychiatry* (Balan) 150
biopsychosocial factors, trauma 11–12
biosecurity 4, 186

blame 15, 158
blood pressure 18, 20, 29, 73
blood sugar 83, 96, 179
blood vessels 96
bodily sensations 13, 19, 29, 30, 81, 198
body, mind and 70–71
bond 38, 107, 113, 145
borderline personality disorder 12, 97
boundaries 10, 13, 104, 106
boundary setting 156–157
box breathing 54
breast feeding 1 51, 145
breathing, diaphragmatic 49
breathing technique 1 49
breathing technique 2 50
breathing technique 3 51
breathing technique 4 52
breathing technique 5 52–53
breathing technique 6 53
breathing technique 7 54
breathing techniques 15
bullying 11, 148, 150, 167, 179
burnout, stress and 150

California 105, 122, 129, 143
cannabis 81, 181
caregiver 148, 154, 155
caregiver fatigue 178
caregiving, post trauma 134
case example 107, 110, 114, 146, 156, 196
catastrophizing 12, 177
CBT *see* Cognitive Behavioral Therapy (CBT)
centering and mindfulness 81
Centers for Disease Control and Prevention (CDC) 105
ceremonies 140, 187
child abuse and neglect 177
childhood sexual abuse 106
chronic illnesses 106
chronic medical conditions 10, 106
civil liberties 167, 187
clinical gaslighting 162–163
coercion 161, 163
Cognitive Behavioral Therapy (CBT) 4, 15
Cognitive Behavioral Writing Therapy 15–16
cognitive dissonance 163
cognitive processing 18
Cognitive Processing Therapy (CPT) 15
cognitive restructuring 31
collective trauma 180
community 40
comorbid 10
comorbid substance use disorders 157–158
compassion 15, 30, 38
compassion fatigue 178
compromise 122
conflict 146, 152
connectedness 82
connecting 68

consciousness 47, 91
continued consequences 12
contracts 146–147
coping mechanisms 16, 116, 119, 168, 183, 196
coping strategies 199–200
cortisol 29, 93
Couples Therapy 115
COVID pandemic 134, 174, 195
CPT *see* Cognitive Processing Therapy (CPT)
creative prompt, family crest 124–125
crisis 37, 40, 202, 203
culturally sensitive approach 139–140
culture 139
    language and 65–67
custody 168
cyber bullying 139
cyber victimization, risk group 153
cynicism 83, 176, 179

death 8, 22, 84, 114
death anxiety 182, 198
deep breathing 15, 49, 50, 52, 53
defense mechanisms 15
delayed care 186
depersonalization 177
depression 177
depressive disorder, major 28
desensitization 16, 150
diabetes 106, 167, 179
Diagnostic and Statistical Manual of Mental Disorders
        (DSM) 7
    criteria for adjustment disorder 8
diaphragmatic breathing 49, 50
diazepam 22
disappointment 14, 84, 158, 183
discrimination, racial 148–149
disgust 75
disinhibited social engagement disorder 7
displaced populations, risk group 153–154
disposition 10, 113, 122
dissociation 9, 156, 168, 199
distress, emotional 104
diversity 143
divorce 105, 110, 116
domestic violence 3
drop out 23, 35, 41, 140
dysphoric mood 31
dysregulation 107, 148, 178

economic burden of posttraumatic stress disorder 28
education 11
effexor 22
egocentric 110, 111
embarrassment 168
EMDR *see* Eye Movement Desensitization and
        Reprocessing (EMDR)
emergency department 10, 140, 150
emotional abuse 105, 107

emotional arousal 132
emotional damage 167
emotional distress 104
emotional expression 31, 114, 141
emotional intelligence 112
emotional lability 9
emotional palette 73
emotional withdrawing 168
emotions 71
employment 11
empowering 20, 56, 84
    at work 167–168
encoding 97
engagement 112, 129
environment 11
    healing 40–41
equal 54
equitable access 208
erection 20, 96
ethnicity 11, 68, 148
evidence-based therapeutics 209
evidence-based treatment modalities 27
excitement 14
executive gaslighting 164–165
exercise, mindfulness 81–82
exhaustion 107, 177
existential angst 3, 180
existential crises 177–178
explicit memory 93
exposure 8, 9, 114, 137
    prolonged 17
expressive writing 32
    benefits of 35
    spending energy working on 31
expressive writing therapy 16, 28–30
    financial benefits 33–35
    mental and emotional benefits 30–32
    personal benefits to 32
    personal reasons benefits 32–33
    physical and physiological benefits 29–30
extroversion 183
Eye Movement Desensitization and Reprocessing
    (EMDR) 16, 35

fail to keep 35
family 103
family contacts 201
family creat
    Balan 127–129
    creative prompt 124–125
family dynamics, protective factors 121–122
family system, protective factors in 113–114
fatherhood 145, 146
fatigue
    caregiver 178
    compassion 178
fear 174–175
feedback loop 70, 82

feelings 71
fertility 178
fight-or-flight mode 4, 49
finger tapping 81
fire 150, 165
firearms 3, 105, 164, 202
firefighters 9, 11
flashbacks 9
flooding 9, 35, 81, 115
fluoxetine 22
Food and Drug Administration (FDA) 16
food insecurity 4, 105, 113, 129, 153, 183, 187
forgiveness 17, 170, 213
Frankl, Viktor 16
freezing 15
future oriented 122, 213

gambling 10, 176, 211
gaslighting 161, 162
    clinical 162–163
    contextual elements of 163
    executive 164–165
    forms of 163
    manipulative verbal 163
    results of 168–169
gastrointestinal tract 96
Gatto, James Taylor 32
gender 11
genetic factors 11
German 34
Gibran, Khalil 207
gratitude 82–85
grief 185–187
grounding 41, 46
group therapy 16, 33, 111
gun violence 105, 164

harassment 165, 209
harmful effects, reducing 208–209
headache 132, 168, 194, 198
headline stress disorder 176
healing environment 40–41
heal preparation 37
healthcare providers 149–151
heart disease 12, 106, 112, 179
heart rate 10, 96, 117, 194
helplessness 107, 115, 132
Herbert, Frank 173
Herman, Judith xv
hippocampus
    formation of new memories 93
    impact of trauma 93
    making long-term memories 93
    spatial memory 93
HIV 106, 186, 198
holistic 4
homeless xxv
homework 6

hopelessness 12, 178, 184
housing insecurity 183
HPA axis *see* hypothalamic pituitary adrenal (HPA) axis
human resources 105, 150, 162, 165, 167
humming breath 53, 54
humor 5, 41, 84, 127, 210
hyperarousal 168, 176
hyper-reactivity 10
    prolonged 10
hypervigilance 9, 29, 97, 158, 168
hypothalamic pituitary adrenal (HPA) axis 92
hypothalamus 92

identity 37
    self-identity 12
    trauma 140–141
Imagery Rehearsal Training (IRT) 16
Imaginal Exposure Therapy 16
immune system 4, 106
individual therapy 150
inflammation 18, 83
inflammatory response 29, 30
infodemic 173
informed consent 18, 19
insight 31
insomnia 10
intelligence, emotional 112
intensive care unit 98, 150, 179
intergenerational 11
intergenerational transmission 149
intergenerational trauma 139
interpersonal violence 153
interpreting 72–73
intimate partner violence (IPV) 131, 162, 178
intoxication 158
introspection 42, 193
introversion 183
intrusive thoughts 9
invalidate 141, 151
IPV *see* intimate partner violence (IPV)
irritability 132, 150
IRT *see* Imagery Rehearsal Training (IRT)
isolation and stigma, ACEs 110–111
isolation 12, 40, 106
Istanbul 65, 127, 174

jealousy 14, 163, 167
judgment 21, 73, 122, 133, 143, 151, 194
Jung, Carl xxix

Kaiser Permanente 105
"keeping the environment safe" 202
Kerouac, Jack 43

labeling 72, 197
language
    and culture 65–67

*versus* learning 65
lawsuit 152, 169, 179
learning, language *versus* 65
Le Guin, Ursula 58
LGBTQ+ community, trauma 148
lifestyle 29, 134, 142, 143, 179
life-threatening traumatic event 9
limbic system 89
lion's breath 51
lockdown 5, 162, 176, 177, 185, 187
locus of control 59, 119
logotherapy 16
long-haul 182
long-term memory 93
lorazepam 22
love 46, 56, 57

magical thinking 114, 177
major depressive disorder 28
maladaptive interpretation 73
maladaptive thinking patterns 15
manipulative verbal gaslighting 163
man-made traumatic events 8
materialism 83
MDMA-assisted therapy 16–17
medical consequences 98
medication
    management 4
    side effects of 20
Meichenbaum, Donald 152
memory
    explicit 93
    long-term 93
    spatial 93
menstrual cycle 178
mental health
    and behavioral conditions 176
    deferred and delayed 185–186
mental illness 183
mental model 69
messaging 68–69
metabolism 18
microaggression 148, 209
Middle East 144
migraine 168, 195
military 152
    moral injury 152
mind and body 70–71
mindful breathing 52
mindfulness 112
    centering and 81
    exercise 81–82
    meditation 17
    programs 34
minimize 45, 84, 137, 197, 209
miscarriage 140
mistrust 10, 12, 162

Monkey Pox 198, 208
mood stabilizers 22–23
moral harm 169
moral injury 152
Morrison, Toni 27, 71
motherhood 145, 146
motor vehicle accident 98

narrative 3, 42
    bias 4
Narrative Exposure Therapy 17
narrative psychology 5
National Alliance on Mental Illness (NAMI) 215
National Child Abuse Hotline 216
National Domestic Violence Hotline 216
National Suicide Prevention Lifeline 217
natural disasters 8, 129, 131, 157, 175
negative self-talk 12
neglect 105
    adverse childhood experiences (ACEs) 110
    child abuse and 177
neighborhood 11, 105, 140
neonatal intensive care unit 179
nervous system 9, 15, 17
    autonomic 94
    parasympathetic 96
    sympathetic 96
neurodevelopmental disabilities 137
neuroplasticity 42
neurotransmitters 104
new normal 3, 69, 133, 183, 208
New York City 145
nightmare 9, 10, 16, 132, 156
night terror 132
non-pharmacological therapies, trauma 15–18
numbness 12, 194, 195
nutritional intake changes 179

obsessive compulsive disorder 176, 198
occupational hazard 149, 178
occupation specific hazards, healthcare providers
    149–151
opioid 3, 164, 181
Orwell, George 89
overdose, accidental 3, 158
overwhelm 12, 19, 35, 56
oxytocin 82

PACT approach *see* Psychobiological Approach to
    Couples Therapy (PACT) approach
pain 12, 14, 34, 41
pandemic 134
panic disorder 28
paradigm shift 14
paranoia 168
parasympathetic nervous system 96

parenting style, protective factors 118–119
paroxetine 22
paternity 145
patience 82
patient advocate 198
patient satisfaction 35, 98, 151
Paxil 22
penile erection 96
Pennebaker, James 31
perceptual distortion 9
peripartum 131, 154, 179
personal protective equipment 150
pharmacological options, trauma 18, 21–23
physical abuse 105
physical activity 17
physical health, deferred and delayed 185–186
physical trauma, acute 97–98
pituitary gland 92
placebo effect 21
PMP *see* Positive Memory Processing (PMP)
polarization 3, 4
Positive Memory Processing (PMP) 17
positive psychology 17
postpartum depression 154, 179
post trauma
    caregiving 134
    goals 135
posttraumatic growth 37
posttraumatic stress disorder 8–10, 28, 153, 180
    economic burden of 28
    prevalence of 150
    psychological diagnosis of 12
    risk of developing 11–12
power hierarchy 162, 169
pre-COVID 28
prefrontal cortex 94
    function 94
    impact of trauma 94
pregnancy, risk group 154–156
prescriber 18–21
presenteeism 35, 180
prevalence 28
prevention 105, 112
prior risk factors, trauma 10
productivity 34, 35, 169, 176, 180
professional contacts 201
prolonged exposure 17
prolonged grief 7
prolonged hyper-reactivity 10
propaganda 68
prosocial 82
protective factors
    culture and community 129
    family dynamics 121–122
    in family system 113–114
    parenting style 118–119
Prozac 22

Psychobiological Approach to Couples Therapy (PACT) approach 115
psychosomatic 132
psychosomatic complaints 179
psychotic disorder 175, 193

quarantine 176

racial discrimination 148–149
racism 4, 11, 40, 140, 149
rape 106, 154
rapport 70, 198
reactions 9, 10, 13, 16, 133, 150, 151
reactive attachment disorder 7
Rea, Rashani 65
reckless behavior 9, 180
recurrent thought 9
re-experiencing 9
reframing 15, 31, 59
regressing 14
regulation 10, 187, 193
relationships 5, 6, 7, 10, 103, 104, 108
    social interactions and 10
relaxation techniques 17
religion 65, 68, 209
remission 13
repercussions 175–181
resilience 4, 10, 12, 13, 31, 37, 113, 114
resistance 38, 180
resolution 83
Rest and Digest 96
return on investment 5, 27, 34, 35, 207, 208
Rilke, Rainer Maria 213
risk, biopsychosocial determinants and 11–12
risk factors, prior 10
risk group 152
    cyber victimization 153
    displaced populations 153–154
    pregnancy 154–156
    sexual assault 157
    substance use 157–159
ritual 140, 154, 187
*Roadmap to Resilience: A Guide for Military, Trauma Victims and Their Families* 152
roles 144
Rumi 103
rumination 166–178

sadness 14, 46, 70, 71, 84, 115
safety planning 193–194, 204–206
    coping strategies 199–201
    family, social, and professional contacts 201–202
    keeping me safe 202–203
    signature section 203–204
    warning signs 194–196
SARS *see* Severe Acute Respiratory Syndrome (SARS)
school-based interventions 112

schools 133
screen time 175
SE *see* Somatic Experiencing (SE)
sea analogy 41–42
Selective Serotonin Reuptake Inhibitors (SSRIs) 21–22
self-acceptance 14
self-actualization 168
self-blame 158
self-care 9
self-confidence 168
self-disclosure 111
self-doubt 168
self-esteem 13, 163
self-identity 12
self-injury 3, 28, 133, 158, 179
    rates 181
self-knowledge 42
self-mastery 33, 42
self-medicate 129, 196
self-talk, negative 12
sensations, bodily 13, 19, 29, 30, 81, 198
sense of control 6, 19, 29, 31, 122, 158, 199
sense of stability 106
serotonin 97
Serotonin and Norepinephrine Reuptake Inhibitor (SNRI) 22
sertraline 22
Severe Acute Respiratory Syndrome (SARS) 173
sex trafficking 153
sexual abuse 105, 106, 110, 113
    childhood 106
sexual assault, risk group 157
sexual function 20, 73
sexually transmitted infection 106
shame 70, 110, 148, 154, 180–181
side effect 19–20, 22, 33, 179
signature section 203
sleep disorders 181
sleep disturbances 10
sleep hygiene 29, 109
sleep quality 16, 34
Sloan, Denise 28, 31
social contacts 201
social determinants of health 183
social interactions and relationships 10
social isolation and lack of interaction 161
social media 68, 69, 111, 133, 145, 152, 163
social skill 183
socioeconomic status 11–12, 106, 129
Somatic Experiencing (SE) 17–18
soul 46, 101
spatial memory 93
SSRIs *see* Selective Serotonin Reuptake Inhibitors (SSRIs)
stabilizers, mood 22–23
startle response 9
stigma 7, 14, 34, 110–111, 145, 194

stimulant 3
story 40, 41, 116, 161, 213
stress
    and burnout 150
    traumatic 132–133
stress diathesis model 182
stress disorder
    acute 8
    posttraumatic 8–10
stressors 131
    occupation specific 186
stress reaction 37, 131, 132, 149–151
stress-related disorders 7, 8
stress tolerance 10
subject matter expertise 169
substance use disorders 3
    comorbid 157–158
substance use, risk group 157–159
suffering 10, 12, 27, 37, 111, 168, 173
suicide 3, 5, 28, 105, 106, 181, 185
support network 38
suppression 12
surgeon 150
sympathetic nervous system 96
synthesizing 79

talk therapy 22, 30, 31, 38, 46, 154
Tan, Chade-Meng 34
temperament 10, 113
temperamental vulnerabilities 10
temporal lobes 106
tension headache 168
terrorism 140, 153
thalamus
    function 91
    impact of trauma 91
therapeutic yoga 18
therapy
    cognitive behavioral writing 15
    non-pharmacological 15–18
thumb sucking 132
tragedy 129
transition 4, 38, 109, 187
trauma
    acute physical 97–98
    antidepressants 21–22
    awareness of 208–209
    betrayal 162
    biopsychosocial determinants and risk 11–12
    biopsychosocial factors 11–12
    as diagnosis 7–8
    identity 140–141
    LGBTQ+ community 148
    non-pharmacological therapies 15–18
    pharmacological options 18–19, 21–23
    prior risk factors 10
    treatment 13–15

trauma, impact of
    amygdala 92
    hippocampus 94
    thalamus 91
trauma-related disorders 8
traumatic events
    life-threatening 9
    man-made 8
traumatic stress 132–133
treatment plan 13, 27, 42, 56, 103, 105, 182, 193
treatment, trauma 13–15
triggers 197–198
trust 40, 42, 70, 213
Turkey 65, 127, 129, 174, 175
Turkish 144, 174
turnover 34, 134, 149, 169
TV 21, 81, 145, 174, 198

uncertainty 4, 127, 162, 163, 166, 180, 186
UNICEF 177
United States 16, 21, 28, 65, 112, 113, 140, 149

validation 162
valium 22
venlafaxine 22
ventilator 150
verbal gaslighting, manipulative 163
Veteran 9, 98, 152
victim 97, 98, 105, 153, 163
violence
    domestic 3
    gun 105, 164
    interpersonal 153
    intimate partner 162
violence turned inward 163–164
violence turned outward 163–164
volatility 105
Vonnegut, Kurt 193
vulnerability 10, 148

war 4, 8, 40, 140, 152, 153, 198
warmth 84, 104, 119, 194
warning signs, safety planning 194–196
WET *see* Written Exposure Therapy (WET)
witness 3, 4, 10, 150, 167
work, empowering at 167–168
workplace injury 169
workplace safety 169
World Health Organization 177
Writing Prompt 12–13, 23, 35–36, 39, 45, 48, 50–55,
    60–62, 66–67, 71–77, 79–81, 85–87, 98,
    108–109, 117–118, 130, 135–137, 141–148,
    151–152, 159–160, 169–171, 181–182,
    184–185, 188–190, 196, 199–204, 210–214
    family 122–123

writing therapy 32
    expressive 28 (*see also* expressive writing therapy)
Written Exposure Therapy (WET) 18

yoga, therapeutic 18
youth

post trauma 131–132
traumatic stress 132–133
Zappa, Frank 139
zip code 11
Žižek, Slavoj 161
Zoloft 22